MO YAN SPEAKS

MO YAN SPEAKS

Lectures and Speeches by the Nobel Laureate from China

MO YAN

translated and edited by Shiyan Xu

Foreword by Jonathan Stalling

CAMBRIA
PRESS

Amherst, New York

Requests for permission should be directed to
permissions@cambriapress.com, or mailed to:
Cambria Press
100 Corporate Parkway, Suite 128
Amherst, New York 14226, USA

Front cover photo of Mo Yan by Bengt Nyman, https://commons.wikimedia.org/
wiki/File:Mo_Yan_7_2012.jpg, with modifications made to color and background.

Library of Congress Cataloging-in-Publication Data

Names: Mo, Yan, 1955- author. | Xu, Shiyan, 1976- editor.

Title: Mo Yan speaks : lectures and speeches by the Nobel laureate from China /
Mo Yan; edited by Shiyan Xu.

Description: Amherst, New York : Cambria Press, [2021] | Includes index.

Identifiers: LCCN 2019031684| ISBN 9781604979893 (hardcover) |
ISBN 9781621964889 (epub) | ISBN 9781621966203 (paperback)

Subjects: LCSH: Mo, Yan, 1955- | Literature.

Classification: LCC PL2886.O1684 A2 2021 |
DDC 895.13/52--dc23
LC record available at https://lccn.loc.gov/2019031684

*The publication of this book
has been made possible
with the assistance of the
Chinese Fund for the
Humanities and Social Sciences.*

TABLE OF CONTENTS

ACKNOWLEDGMENTS

Special thanks to Mo Yan, who generously authorized our translation of his speeches. The translation project was funded by a generous grant from the Chinese Fund for the Humanities and Social Sciences in 2017. Heartfelt thanks go to my collaborator on this project, Jonathan Stalling. He offered valuable ideas on the translation of the speeches and the publication of the book, and his significant work with *Chinese Literature Today* and the Chinese Literature Translation Archive plays an important role in introducing Chinese literature and culture to the world. My deepest thanks also go to Jesse Field and Ella Schwalb, who translated most of the speeches and worked with me throughout the entire process of the translation. I learned a lot from our discussions about how to ensure fidelity to the original texts while delivering them in beautiful and fluent English, how to achieve the best combination of domestication and foreignization techniques, and how to clarify background information that is often strange to Anglophone readers. I also am very grateful to the renowned translators Howard Goldblatt and Sylvia Li-chun Lin. Two speeches translated by Sylvia and published in *World Literature Today* are included in this book, and the introduction and the prefaces to the book's sections quote extensively from Mo Yan's Nobel Lecture and "The Story of My Life," translated by Howard Goldblatt. Special thanks go to the team at Cambria Press, especially director Toni Tan and editor David Armstrong, without whose support from the very beginning to the end the publication of the book would be impossible. I also wish to express my appreciation to Allison Van Deventer, who edited the initial draft of the manuscript. I am deeply grateful to my colleagues at the School of Foreign Languages and Cultures of Nanjing Normal University, especially to Prof. Lin Minjie for her support and Prof. Zhang Jie for his encouragement.

Mo Yan Speaks

Peasant Realism

On Mo Yan's Public Voice

Jonathan Stalling

Most English readers became familiar with the Chinese novelist Mo Yan after he was awarded the 2012 Nobel Prize for Literature. This was the first time a Chinese novelist had attracted such widespread national attention in the United States; and as the editor of the new literary journal and book series *Chinese Literature Today*, I was tremendously optimistic that contemporary Chinese literature was about to go mainstream. I happened to be in Boulder, Colorado, with Mo Yan's English translator, Howard Goldblatt, the day the news broke. He was on the phone all day answering queries from mainstream journalists, providing quotes, and scheduling future interviews. I, as were many others, was contacted by the *Wall Street Journal* and other news outlets, so I know I was not alone in thinking that Chinese literature was about to have its moment. Yet in the weeks and months that followed the "Mobel," the Western media did not seem interested in discussing Mo Yan's writing but was instead only interested in the author's politics, or lack of politics.

The most famous row had to do with an infamous interview a few days before the Nobel Prize ceremony when Mo Yan answered questions from reporters and ostensibly stated that Chinese censorship was both natural and "as necessary as security checks at airports."[1] After this statement, Salman Rushdie described him as a "patsy of the regime."[2] Nobel laureate Herta Müller called Mo Yan's winning of the prize "a slap in the face for all those working for democracy and human rights."[3] Years later Lucas Klein showed that the term "censorship" in Western reporters' questions was translated to Mo Yan not as *shencha* (审查) but *jiancha* (检查), which Klein points out is closer to "check" than to "censor," hence related to "security checks at embassies and airports."[4] While such questions from the Western press are to be expected, it soon became clear that the "Mobel" moment was not yet to be.

Part of the problem around Mo Yan's Western reception arose from the fact that English speakers did not have access to his public record. In the months that followed the announcement, much was made of the small tidbits of information making their way imperfectly into the Western media through a handful of poorly translated comments. While Mo Yan famously said in his Nobel acceptance speech that "for a writer, the best way to speak is by writing" (对一个作家来说，最好的说话方式是写作), he has also spoken publicly on many other related topics. When English speakers heard that his name meant "don't speak," and that there was little to no accessible record of his public comments on any given topic, those who were against Mo Yan receiving the prize saw this perceived silence as Mo Yan's complicity with the status quo. Others saw this lack as the dilemma of an author who has been silenced by others. The publication of this volume of his speeches, however, reveals that the author has spoken at great length on many topics over several decades, thus setting the record straight.

Though each of Mo Yan's speeches cover several topics at a time, Xu Shiyan has organized them into sections based on topics like his writing style, literary influences, biographical information, and, finally, values. He also speaks on many other topics such as class divisions, world literature, translation, the anxieties of Western influence in China, the homogenization of globalization, the pitfalls of narrowly defined nationalistic literary definitions, and many others. As we follow Mo Yan on his journey across China, Europe, and North America, this enigmatic author becomes less mysterious and more impressive as his real interests come more clearly into view. Those who are predisposed to read Mo Yan for his literary appeal will no doubt hear a generous, perceptive, witty intellect committed to producing quality literary fiction at the crossroads of local and global influences. Those who are more interested in tracing the relationship between the author's politics and aesthetics will also find more to work with. All readers, regardless of disposition, will discover new connections between the oral folk traditions Mo Yan was exposed to in his youth and those influences from classical vernacular Chinese prose works and translated fiction from Japan, North and South America, and Europe.

I found valuable the distinctions he makes between his own "peasant" upbringing and its influence on his writing and writers he describes as writing in the popular "grassroots literary movements." He argues that "class," while a valuable way to analyze social divisions and power relations, was a less useful concept when crudely mobilized by Maoist "revolutionary realism." He criticizes those whom he sees continuing to exploit such purely ideological connections today. I find these moments in Mo Yan's speeches particularly interesting because they point to subtle complexities that not only differentiate him from other Chinese writers past and present but also reveal something deeper about how morality relates to aesthetics in his fiction. Mo Yan's work in the exquisite translations of Howard Goldblatt offers an opportunity for English speakers to see the relationship of aesthetics and morality in a world where morality is not wholly conflated with politics. In Mo Yan's fictional world of Gaomi County in Shandong, nature and state power are largely exogenous factors in the lives of those who populate his stories. The dimensional instability of Mo Yan's fictional worlds is thus partly grounded in cultural technologies developed by and for "peasants" to help them navigate such powerful external forces. When the Nobel committee described Mo Yan's fiction as an example of "hallucinatory realism," they perhaps inadvertently suggested that the "peasant" worldviews inhabiting Mo Yan's novels were both unreal and possibly pathological in nature. Read in relation to Mo Yan's discussion of his background and aesthetic experimentation, these "magical" moments in his fiction can be seen as far more than hallucinations.[5]

While the word "peasant" seems at first glance to be a pejorative term in English, Mo Yan repeatedly uses it in an honorific sense, one wholly distinct from the inverted class striation of Marxist ideology. Mo Yan argues that literature's Chinese roots "are in the lower classes —storytellers performing in tearooms and taverns," noting that "tales were passed on orally, told to audiences full of cart pushers and broth peddlers."[6] He contrasts this with so-called grassroot literature which he argues "is currently so popular and in vogue,"[7] which "is in fact just a revival of the ashes of 'revolutionary realism,' a resurgence of the creative ideology that governed Chinese literary circles and dominated the thinking of countless writers for decades."[8]

He goes on to explain that from his "peasant perspective," "good novels never provide solutions, or at least never provide them outright. Nor do good novelists fixate on any single societal issue. Instead, they focus on the people in our society—on humanity's difficult struggle to break free from the desires that cling to us so stubbornly." Read in light of his focus on individual liberation (in this case a notion, influenced by Buddhism, that suffering is caused by an individual's clinging to illusory desires), Mo Yan's speeches push against the desire to read his work as political allegory and point to morality at the granular level of individual human lives and relationships. We can read such public statements to see a deeper relationship between his self-positioned peasantness and the formal experimentalism I would like to recast as his distinct "peasant realism."

It is important, however, that when we hear Mo Yan talking about "peasants" in these speeches, we do not think of the people he describes as somehow equivalent to those in feudalistic Europe. Rather, the characters in Mo Yan's works exist at the tail end of a very different history, one with its own distinct cosmologies and scales of moral agency. When we read Mo Yan's speeches, just as when we read his fiction, we are given an opportunity to take in distinct perspectives and sensibilities other than those cast as universal liberal democratic values. To be uninterested in or unmoved by the existence of such perspectives or, worse yet, incapable of imagining a world so different from our own, underlines the critical importance of reading world literature. How can we expect to understand or forge better US-China relationships if we can only recognize the aspects of Chinese literature that reflect Western values?

We need Mo Yan's work, both his fiction and his ideas about the world expressed in these speeches, if only because they provide an opportunity for empathic reading, even if, or perhaps precisely because, Western readers may find the darkness presented in his fictional world so vexing. One cannot turn on the lights to encounter the darkness of another's night, but we must suspend the clarity of one's own moral framework long enough to explore the obscurity of another's. Mo Yan describes his own "peasant" upbringing as one filled with such unknowns, and discusses how the oral traditions of his childhood navigated its opaqueness, not by casting it into doubt, or banishing it with the light of reason, but through interacting with opacity through enthralling mythos:

> Back then, come evening, the whole village went dark, and I mean one big patch of darkness, black as lacquer, so dark that if you stretched out your hand, you wouldn't even see your fingers. To pass the long nights, old people told the children tales of ghosts and monsters. In these tales, it seemed that all plants and animals could become people, or had the power to control people's thoughts. The old people gave no hint that the stories weren't true. Anyhow, we kids certainly believed them. The stories got us scared, but

they also made us excited. The more we listened, the more scared
we got. And the more we had to listen![9]

Understood as an extension of this oral tradition, we can see how the
"magical" or "hallucinatory" elements in Mo Yan's fiction spring from
the epistemic aesthetics of his own lived experiences, ones still largely
governed by opaque forces, where the moral imaginary of limited human
agency is recast into a variety of folk cultural traditions, tropes, and
techniques. Here English readers encounter fictional Gaomi County
not as visual landscapes but through the gateways of our lesser-devel-
oped sensorium—through its textures, temperatures, tastes, odors, and
fragrances, each of which reveals how exhilaratingly and unbearably
vulnerable we are. When we enter Mo Yan's work thus exposed, eyes
closed, fingers outstretched, we can begin to feel something of the
folk technologies for navigating highly circumscribed realms of human
agency where morality must be understood as the space where characters discover how to be accountable to one another despite, or perhaps
because, the world is not accountable to them.

Reframing Mo Yan's work as "peasant realism" not only helps us
situate the dimensional instability of his work, but it also goes a long
way to understand the nature of Mo Yan's social commentary and satire.
At several points in his speeches and lectures, Mo Yan presents the scale
of human agency in terms of an existential pathos, writing that "the
universe is so large, and humanity is so small, time and space extend
forever, but human life is so short."[10] I would argue that many of Mo Yan's
works take such a view as a given, which leads one to think about the
function of social commentary in an undemocratic life world where the
human drama unfolds beneath the stars' machinations. For many Western
readers, social commentary and satire derive their moral status vis-à-vis
political action in the context of multiparty electoral politics. Fixating on
darkness without imagining this in terms of activating political agency
to effect change might be construed as exploitation, but reading cross-
culturally offers an opportunity to suspend such judgments, at least long

enough to imagine the moral force of such commentary from within the context of a different experience of the world than one's own.

The peasant realism of *Sandalwood Death,* for example, draws upon the folk technologies of operatic drama to allegorize the experience of geopolitical and state power. He does this not to condemn a tyrannical Qing dynasty or the colonial brutality of Western colonialism, for the characters within the drama find themselves only capable of playing roles dealt to them by the stars. The narrative unfolds from the perspectives of those being tortured and executed, those carrying out the violence, and those who gather to take in the public spectacle. Mo Yan explains that the "characters in the drama live less in a realistic world than in a dramatic world. At certain points, even they themselves cannot say what is drama and what is real."[11] Yet the more Mo Yan speaks about his experience in writing this novel, the more I come to feel neither he nor the reader can find a more stable vantage point. In a speech given at Lu Xun's old residence, he admits "though the writing appears to be about long, buttoned robes, braids, and bound feet, it's in fact about the modern mentality."[12] He goes on to say that "the conclusion I came to startled me. I think, in some sense, or under certain particular circumstances, the great majority of us would all take on the role of executioner and that too of the numb onlooker. There is a Zhao Jia hidden in the depths of each and every one of our souls." He continues, "this kind of novel cannot be separated from its nationality or folk essence. Many critics say I don't have any ideology, and frequently I admit it myself that I don't have any. But actually I do have ideology, though it is at times excessively extreme, and at other times shallow. But extreme or shallow, it is still ideology."[13]

The ambivalent reception of Mo Yan in the West largely comes down to not understanding what this "ideology" is. I would argue that it is difficult to discern because it exists largely as an aesthetic approach to history and agency, one we can, given his public statements, cast in terms of a "peasant realism" charged with moral pathos precisely because it has not or cannot translate morality into politics. *Sandalwood Death* does not offer redemption via political resistance but suggests that one may exist morally. In most of Mo Yan's fiction, humans must learn how to become better to one another within the context of exogenous power.

It is my hope that reading Mo Yan's public-speaking record will show that Mo Yan's "peasant realism" offers a coherent framework within which to view his take on modern Chinese aesthetics—one that is neither beholden to the political instrumentalism of Marxist realism nor that of Western liberal democratic values, but instead is something else altogether. As someone interested in comparative cultural poetics, I have long explored the relationship between epistemology and aesthetics, especially as these are mediated through translation and read across different cultural horizons of expectation. I always assumed that the point of such work was to build the cultural and cognitive scaffolding needed to counter the homogenizing effects of reading from our own habitual frames of reference. Only when we attend to the lensing effects of reading across cultures can we hope to dwell in their proximity. And only when we share proximity with difference can we develop our own moral resilience.

The Mobel moment in the Western media in many ways prefigured controversies today around free speech on American college campuses where some views are thought to be so dangerous that they must be "de-platformed." The logic of these debates in the United States suggests that American censorship is first and foremost an expression of morality with the understanding that some thoughts and ideas are not only morally repugnant but dangerous and that a college, for instance, should not host a speaker with ties to racist politics because to do so validates immoral and dangerous ideas. While this debate has been wrongly cast in terms of censorship to shift blame onto vulnerable student populations, it would seem that the criticism of Mo Yan's Nobel Prize might be productively read as a desire to de-platform an international writer whose ideology did not conform to the role of a "prodemocratic dissident."

Western readers need to grapple with whether we believe the value of reading world literature is really finding and promoting shared political values. Throughout most of human history, and even for the majority of people alive today, the moral dimensions of being human must be worked out within single-party political structures. Is it not reasonable, therefore, to suggest that there should be a space to think through their aesthetic and moral dimensions not in comparison to our own but on their own terms as much as possible? Susan Sontag may have summarized this prospect best when she wrote in her St. Jerome Lecture on Literary Translation, noting that "literary translation ... is preeminently an ethical task, and one that mirrors and duplicates the role of literature itself, which is to extend our sympathies; to educate the heart and mind; to create inwardness; to secure and deepen the awareness (with all its consequences) that other people, people different from us, really do exist."[14]

Notes

1. Associated Press in Stockholm, "Censorship is a must, says China's Nobel winner," *The Guardian*, December 6, 2012, https://www.theguardian.com/world/2012/dec/07/mo-yan-censorship-nobel.
2. David Daley, "Rushdie: Mo Yan is a 'patsy of the regime,'" *Salon*, December 7, 2012, https://www.salon.com/2012/12/07/rushdie_mo_yan_is_a_patsy_of_the_regime/.
3. Husna Haq, "Herta Muller calls Mo Yan's Nobel win 'a catastrophe,'" *The Christian Science Monitor*, November 27, 2012, https://www.csmonitor.com/Books/chapter-and-verse/2012/1127/Herta-Muller-calls-Mo-Yan-s-Nobel-win-a-catastrophe.
4. Lucas Klein, "A Dissonance of Discourses: Literary Theory, Ideology, and Translation in Mo Yan and Chinese Literary Studies," *Comparative Literature Studies* 53, no. 1 (2016): 170–197.
5. See Jonathan Stalling "Mo Yan and the Technicians of Culture," *World Literature Today*, October 29, 2012, https://www.worldliteraturetoday.org/mo-yan-and-technicians-culture.
6. See chapter 2, "Fiction and Society."
7. Ibid.
8. Ibid.
9. See chapter 15, "Fear and Hope."
10. See chapter 14, "The Mysterious Cow of My Home."
11. Ibid.
12. See chapter 3, "The Tradition of Chinese Fiction."
13. Ibid.
14. Susan Sontag, "The World as India: The St. Jerome Lecture on Literary Translation," http://www.susansontag.com/prize/onTranslation.shtml.

The Nobel Laureate From China

Shiyan Xu

Mo Yan, whose name literally means "don't speak," was born Guan Moye in Northeast Gaomi Township on February 17, 1956. The son of peasants, Mo Yan had a childhood that was marked by extreme poverty and constant hunger. He dropped out of school when he was only eleven years old, but he had remarkable storytelling skills, especially when it came to repeating stories he heard from the storytellers in the marketplace. In vivid detail, he would regale his audience, which included his mother, his older sisters, his aunts, and his maternal grandmother, sometimes changing the ending to please them. As much as she enjoyed his storytelling, Mo Yan's mother worried about his future: "What will you be like when you grow up, son? Will you wind up prattling for a living one day?"[1] Especially at that time in China, talkative children could bring trouble to themselves and to their families, and his mother often cautioned him not to talk so much.

Despite her persistent warnings, his natural desire to be talkative never went away, and "that is what makes my pen name—Mo Yan, or 'don't speak'—an ironic expression of self-mockery."[2]

In February 1976, the year the Cultural Revolution ended, Mo Yan was recruited into the army and for the first time left his hometown, which he both loved and hated. With the ideological emancipation and literary fervor of the 1980s, he began creating storylines in his head while he was on duty and hiding out in the toolshed to write during his time off. The publication of a number of short stories he wrote in the army ignited his passion for writing. In the fall of 1984, after he passed the entrance examination with high scores, he was accepted into the literature department of the People's Liberation Army (PLA) Art Academy, where members of the military were trained to be writers, singers, dancers, painters, and other types of artists for the army. This was a major turning point in his life:

> There I undertook a systematic study of Chinese and foreign literary histories and read many foreign novels in translation: works by Faulkner, García Márquez, and others inspired me to concentrate on my native home. Northeast Gaomi Township became my literary kingdom; childhood memories and the people from my hometown became the material for my fiction.[3]

At the PLA Art Academy, Mo Yan wrote a series of short stories and novellas, including *Autumn Floods*, *Dry River*, and *The Transparent Carrot*. As he said after he received the Nobel Prize in Literature:

> It is no exaggeration to say that I took a considerable risk by what I wrote, and many people were shocked and affronted to learn that a military academy literature department had produced a writer like me.... Foreigners are often amazed to learn that the Chinese military has a literary component, but this has been a unique constituent of modern Chinese history. Military writers have been key in the development and transformation of China's

new literature. With bold experiments and a disdain for hardship, we have served as vanguards.[4]

While he was at the PLA Academy, Mo Yan also wrote his first novel, *Red Sorghum: A Novel of China* (1987), which was also the first of his novels to be translated into English. Its plot revolves around three generations of the Shandong family between 1923 and 1976. The narrator tells the story of his family's struggles, first as distillery owners making sorghum wine and then as resistance fighters during the Sino-Japanese War. The novel also details civil disputes between warring Chinese groups (including rival gangs and political powers), the Cultural Revolution, and the 1972 resumption of diplomatic relations between China and Japan. The work is characterized by a terse style, non-chronological storytelling, and first-person narration. It contains folktale elements that blend into myth and superstition, placing it in the magical realism genre. The novel was adapted by Zhang Yimou into the film *Red Sorghum*, which received the Golden Bear Prize at the Berlin International Film Festival in 1987 and earned critical acclaim in both Asia and the West.

Upon his graduation from the PLA Art Academy, Mo Yan was assigned to be a writer in the cultural department of a military unit. There he wrote a series of novels set in Northeast Gaomi Township, among which *The Garlic Ballads* (1988) is the most important. *The Garlic Ballads*, which was inspired by real events, demonstrated Mo Yan's powers of criticism and courage in advocating for the poor and disadvantaged. But Mo Yan did not stop at such criticism and advocacy:

> My greatest challenges come with writing novels that deal with social realities, such as *The Garlic Ballads*, not because I'm afraid of being openly critical of the darker aspects of society, but because heated emotions and anger allow politics to suppress literature and transform a novel into reportage of a social event. As a member of society, a novelist is entitled to his own stance and viewpoint; but when he is writing he must take a humanistic stance and write accordingly. Only then can literature not just originate in

events, but transcend them, not just show concern for politics but be greater than politics.[5]

In the fall of 1988, Mo Yan was admitted into a graduate seminar on creative writing jointly offered by Beijing Normal University and the Lu Xun Literary Academy. While attending classes, he wrote, among other works, *The Republic of Wine: A Novel* (1993), which penetrates deeply into the roots of corruption from a humanistic perspective. *The Republic of Wine* explores the Chinese people's relationship with food and drink and comments on government corruption and excesses. The novel's biting satire and bold experimentation shocked literary critics in China. When it was translated into English by Howard Goldblatt in 2012, however, it was widely praised by Western literary critics, one of whom heralded it as "a veritable cornucopia of comedy, ingenuity, and technical dexterity."[6]

In the following years, Mo Yan wrote many novels out of the depths of his memories. His grandfather and grandmother, father and mother, brothers and sisters, aunts and uncles, and wife and his daughter all appeared in his stories; "Even unrelated residents of Northeast Gaomi Township [...] made cameo appearances."[7] In the midst of almost crippling grief after his mother died in 1995, Mo Yan decided to write a novel for her—*Big Breasts and Wide Hips* (1995):

> In *Big Breasts and Wide Hips* I shamelessly used material associated with my mother's actual experience, but the fictional mother's emotional state is either a total fabrication or a composite of many of Northeast Gaomi Township's mothers. Though I wrote "To the spirit of my mother" on the dedication page, the novel was really written for all mothers everywhere, evidence, perhaps, of my overweening ambition, in much the same way as I hope to make tiny Northeast Gaomi Township a microcosm of China, even of the whole world.[8]

Big Breasts and Wide Hips was controversial because of the physical details that accompany its descriptions of sex, birth, illness, and violent death, and it was criticized in China for turning history upside down to glorify the Japanese fascists and the Landlord Restoration Corps. Mo Yan was not surprised at the criticism:

> Among the most frequently reviled features of contemporary Chinese fiction has been a co-optation of art by politics, narratives based on class replacing those based on humanity. *Big Breasts and Wide Hips* was a total subversion of that narrow literary concept, and its publication shocked both literary and intellectual circles to a degree current readers would find unimaginable.[9]

Mo Yan left the army in October 1997 and took a job at the *Procuratorate Daily*. During his ten years with the publication, he wrote three more novels: *Sandalwood Death* (2001), *Pow!* (2003), and *Life and Death Are Wearing Me Out* (2006). *Sandalwood Death* is set during the Boxer Rebellion (1899–1901)—an anti-imperialist struggle waged by North China's farmers and craftsmen in opposition to Western influence. This powerful novel is both a stirring love story and an unsparing critique of political corruption during the final years of the Qing Dynasty, China's last imperial epoch. Filled with sensual imagery and lacerating expressions, *Sandalwood Death* brilliantly exhibits a range of artistic styles, from stylized arias and poetry to the antiquated idioms of late Imperial China and contemporary prose. Its starkly beautiful language is masterfully rendered into English by Howard Goldblatt, who said in an interview, "I got a feeling when I was working on this remarkable, scary, hard novel by Mo Yan that in the first seven or eight novels he gave me, he was training me. He was preparing me for this novel."[10] Mo Yan was also proud of this novel because, as he noted in a lecture on "Fiction and Society" at the Kyoto University clubhouse in May 2006, "I take pride in thinking that *Sandalwood Death* led many writers toward an interest in folk culture, and this interest ultimately evolved into a craze for 'grassroots literature' that has shown no signs of slowing."[11]

In 2005, while plagued by severe insomnia, Mo Yan wrote *Life and Death Are Wearing Me Out* in the span of forty-three days. The novel is a work of historical fiction that explores China's development during the latter half of the twentieth century through the eyes of a noble and generous landowner who is killed and reincarnated as various farm animals in rural China. In his speech at the Lu Xun Museum in May 2006, Mo Yan declared, "I did this also as a direct challenge to Latin American magical realism. I used techniques from Chinese fiction and drew upon the reserves of Chinese thought."[12] He borrowed the concept of reincarnation from the Buddhist "wheel of life" to throw light on half a century of enormous changes in Chinese society, narrated from the perspective of animals. *Life and Death Are Wearing Me Out* has earned praise from critics and was awarded the inaugural Newman Prize for Chinese Literature in 2009. Mo Yan attended the award ceremony at the University of Oklahoma and gave the speech "Six Lives in Search of a Character," which has been translated into English by Sylvia Li-chun Lin and included in this book.

In October 2005, Mo Yan joined the Chinese Arts Research Institute, where he remains today. In 2009, his novel *Frog* was published. The novel is about Gugu ("paternal aunt"), the aunt of "Tadpole," the novel's narrator. Gugu performs various abortions after the One-Child Policy is introduced. Janet Maslin of *The New York Times* wrote that the conflict between the government abortion planners, who believe they are doing the right thing, and the prospective parents makes *Frog* a "startlingly dramatic book."[13] Yet Mo Yan does not think so: "I have repeatedly suggested that *Frog* is a novel about people and not about 'family planning.' In novels dealing with social issues, an author usually is absent, but in this novel I included myself as a target of exposure and criticism."[14]

On October 11, 2012, the Swedish Academy announced that Mo Yan had received the Nobel Prize in Literature for his work that "with hallucinatory realism merges folk tales, history and the contemporary." Aged fifty-seven at the time of the announcement, he was the 109th recipient of the award and the first ever resident of mainland China to receive it. (The Chinese-born Gao Xingjian was named the 2000 laureate.) In his speech during the award ceremony, Per Wästberg explained: "Mo Yan is a poet who tears down stereotypical propaganda posters, elevating the individual from an anonymous human mass. Using ridicule and sarcasm Mo Yan attacks history and its falsifications as well as deprivation and political hypocrisy."[15]

Winning the Nobel Prize brought Mo Yan both support and criticism, about which the author commented in his Nobel Lecture "Storyteller" on December 7, 2012:

> At first I thought I was the target of the disputes, but over time I've come to realize that the real target was a person who had nothing to do with me. Like someone watching a play in a theater, I observed the performances around me. I saw the winner of the prize both garlanded with flowers and besieged by stone throwers and mudslingers.

He concluded that "for a writer, the best way to speak is by writing. You will find everything I need to say in my works. Speech is carried off by the wind; the written word can never be obliterated."

Just as Mo Yan captivated his audience with his storytelling as a young boy, his speeches on literature in recent years are equally riveting. They provide rare insight into the complex thought processes of one of the most influential writers in the world. Mo Yan's passion for his work also comes across clearly in his lectures and speeches, reinforcing the strong emotions his writings evoke in his readers. Many of these speeches have been translated into Japanese and Korean, and they are now finally available in English with this book. From the writers who have influenced him to the relationship between his life and his works, these speeches provide an extraordinary window in Mo Yan's world and will help us appreciate his works even more.

Notes

1. Mo Yan, "Storytellers," Nobel Lecture, trans. Howard Goldblatt, https://www.nobelprize.org/prizes/literature/2012/yan/25452-mo-yan-nobel-lecture-2012/.
2. Ibid.
3. Mo Yan, "The Story of My Life," trans. Howard Goldblatt, https://www.nobelprize.org/prizes/literature/2012/yan/biographical/.
4. Ibid.
5. Ibid.
6. M. Thomas Inge, "Mo Yan: Through Western Eyes," *World Literature Today* 74, no. 3 (Summer 2000): 504.
7. Mo Yan, "Storytellers," Nobel Lecture.
8. Mo Yan, "The Story of My Life."
9. Ibid.
10. "The Art of Bringing Chinese Literature to the World," interview hosted by Jonathan Stalling with Howard Goldblatt and Sylvia Li-chun Lin, National Chinese Language Conference, Los Angeles, May 8–10, 2014.
11. See chapter 2, "Fiction and Society."
12. See chapter 3, "The Tradition of Chinese Fiction."
13. Janet Maslin, "Review: In Mo Yan's 'Frog,' a Chinese Abortionist Embodies State Power," *The New York Times*, February 25, 2015.
14. Mo Yan, "The Story of My Life."
15. Per Wästberg, "The Nobel Prize in Literature 2012: Mo Yan," Award ceremony speech, December 10, 2012, https://www.nobelprize.org/prizes/literature/2012/ceremony-speech/.

PART I

ON WRITING

"Whether the source of a work is a dream or real life, only if it is integrated with individual experience can it be imbued with individuality, be populated with typical characters molded by lively detail, employ richly evocative language, and boast a well-crafted structure.

"Possibly because I've lived so much of my life in difficult circumstances, I think I have a more profound understanding of life. I know what real courage is, and I understand true compassion. I know that nebulous terrain exists in the hearts and minds of every person, terrain that cannot be adequately characterized in simple terms of right and wrong or good and bad, and this vast territory is where a writer gives free rein to his talent. So long as the work correctly and vividly describes this nebulous, massively contradictory terrain, it will inevitably transcend politics and be endowed with literary excellence."

—Mo Yan, Nobel Lecture
(translated by Howard Goldblatt)

1

THE SMELL OF FICTION

SPEECH AT THE
BIBLIOTHÈQUE NATIONALE DE FRANCE IN PARIS,
DECEMBER 14, 2001

Napoleon once said it wouldn't matter if you stole his eyesight, for he could find his way to his old home, the island of Corsica, with his sense of smell alone. There is a certain plant on Corsica, you see, the special scent of which is carried in the wind.

The Soviet writer Mikhail Sholokhov also had a well-developed sense of smell, as we can see in his novel *And Quiet Flows the Don*. He describes the smell of river water, the smell of the grass covering the plains, green grass, dry grass, rotten grass, and the smell of horse sweat as well as the wafting odors of Cossack men and women. The epigraph of the book reads, "Oh, thou, our father, gentle Don!" The smell of the Don, and of the Cossack plain, is in fact the smell of his home.

Born in the waters of the Ussuri River between China and Russia, keta salmon grow to maturity far out at sea, but when the time comes, they journey thousands of miles, overcoming all manner of dangers and distractions to return and breed, and the next generation is born. The origin of this remarkable ability long eluded humans. But in recent years, scientists have found the answer: though the salmon lack an obvious nose, their sense of smell is highly developed, as is their ability to remember smells. It's this memory that helps them battle the raging waves, fighting their way upstream with no fear of sacrifice, their casualties high, the survivors covered in wounds and scars as they return to their home, there to do their duty and breed the next generation, following which they die, quietly and without rancor. The smell of their mother river not only points the way home but gives them the strength to overcome all obstacles.

In a sense, the life of a keta salmon resembles that of an author. To write is to follow the memory of the smell of home, to journey in search of home.

Today, with tape recorders, cameras, and the Internet, the art of prose description faces stark challenges. No prose style, no matter how gorgeous or how precise, can match the lens of the camera. But cameras can't record smell, or at least not yet. This is the fiction writer's final domain, though I wouldn't say it has the best prospects because before long some terrifying scientist will invent cameras that can record smell. Soon we may have films and television that can emit smell. We have to act now before it's too late—as quickly as we can, we must write fiction that is overflowing with smells.

I like to read fiction that has a smell. I think if it has a smell, it must be good. And the best fiction is the kind that has its own unique smell. Good writers are those who can fill their books with their own smell, and the best writers are those who fill books with a unique smell.

A writer might need a sensitive nose, but having one doesn't make you a writer. Hunting dogs have the best noses, but they aren't writers. And some writers suffer severe inflammations of the nose, yet they still manage to write books with a unique smell. My point is that a writer has to have a fecund imagination regarding smell. When a good creative writer works, the characters and settings created give off their own smells. Even if the thing in question lacks a smell, the writer uses their imagination to produce one. Examples like the following are numerous.

In his novel *Perfume*, the German writer Patrick Süskind tells of a murderer with preternatural olfactory abilities, who sought out all kinds of different smells and was a genius perfumer; such a person could only be born in Paris. Inside the mind of this cruel genius, all the smells of everything in the world could be found. Once he'd smelled them all, he believed the best smell in the world was the smell of young women, so he killed twenty-four beautiful young women, and, using all his considerable skills, he extracted their smells to make his perfume. When he applied the magical stuff to himself, all who smelled it forgot his ugliness and fell deeply in love with him. Despite clear evidence, no one wanted to believe he was a murderer. Even the father of one of the murdered girls came to love him, even more than his own daughter. To the end, this murderer believed that he who controlled smell controlled the world.

One of the characters in García Márquez's *One Hundred Years of Solitude* has flatulence so awful it withers flowers on the spot; another thinks the woman he wants smells like smoke, allowing him to sniff her out even in the middle of the night.

In Faulkner's *The Sound and the Fury*, there is a character who can smell cold. And although cold has no actual smell, we really don't feel that Faulkner is out of line in writing that it does; in fact, the idea rings true. That's because the character who smells cold is mentally disabled.

What these simple examples show is that in practice there are two kinds of smell in fiction, or rather, smell begets two methods of writing. One is realist: based on the author's experience, and especially the experience of home, the writer imbues objects with smell, or else uses smell to describe objects. The other relies on imagination: the writer gives smell to objects with no smell, or else gives objects some new and different sort of smell. Cold has no smell because cold isn't a material object. But Faulkner boldly gives it a smell. Death is also not a material object, but García Márquez allows his characters to smell death.

Of course, fiction is not made of smell alone. Writers have to activate all their senses, including taste, sight, sound, and touch, as well as other mysterious senses absent from the usual list. This can give your fiction the breath of life. A story is not just lifeless words but a living thing with smell, and sound, and warmth, and shape, and feeling. When we're just learning to write, we often face the problem of having a true story, with very real interest and complexity, yet when we write it down, it feels false, totally lacking in the power to move us. And some of the best stories, in contrast, are obviously fictional creations by an author, but they still move us deeply. Why? I think the key thing is that telling a true story makes us forget we are creators, so we forget to activate our senses of smell, sight, and hearing. But fictional works by great authors feel real to us because the authors write with all their senses activated, their imaginations soaring to create strange and novel feelings. That's why, for example, we all know a human cannot become a bug, but Kafka's *Metamorphosis* still holds the power to move us.

Since the advent of movies, the future of fiction has been a cause for concern. Fifty years ago, prophecies of the death of fiction were current in China, but fiction is still alive. Television's entry into everyone's homes seemed to portend a still bleaker fate for fiction, but even though television has certainly pulled away some fiction readers, there are still many more, and for the time being, the death of fiction has been staved off. At first the Internet seemed to threaten fiction as well, but I believe the Internet only offers another method of writing, a method of distribution beyond the traditional book.

As someone whose only ability is writing fiction, I am loath to acknowledge its plight despite having seen it myself; in any case, I do not believe fiction can be replaced by another art or craft—not even if someone invents a smell-recording machine. That's because a smell-recording machine would record only the smells that exist in the world, not smells that never existed at all. But the imagination of a writer can produce things that never were. Writers can use the limitless power of their imaginations to create smells that never existed, to create things that never existed and events that never happened. This is the basis of our profession's immortality.

The German writer Thomas Mann gave a volume of Kafka's fiction to Einstein, but Einstein gave it back the following day, purportedly telling him that he couldn't read it and that the human mind isn't complicated enough. That our Kafka defeated the world's greatest scientist is a source of pride for our business.

So let us boldly stir up our senses to make fiction, and may every piece have breath, have smell, have warmth, have sound, and have, of course, thought, mysterious thought.

Of course, a writer must create using language; smell, color, warmth, form are all created through language, crafted with language. Without language, nothing exists. The reason literature can be translated is that language carries specific contents. For ease of translation, the fiction writer must work hard on writing feelings, on setting up worlds with vital feeling. Only feelings can stir a reader's emotions. Fiction without vital feeling will not succeed.

Let us do as the keta salmon do, and seek the rivers of our birth, venturing forth bravely.

Let us imagine the smell of the earth in paleolithic times, when dinosaurs walked the earth, stinking to high heaven; some say the dinosaurs were killed by the smell of their own flatulence.

I'd like to offer a bold suggestion to the leadership in charge of the opening ceremony of the Olympics in China: when the flame is lit for the 2008 opening ceremony, let a strong smell waft out, one of a hundred kinds of flowers, a hundred kinds of trees, and a hundred kinds of alcoholic beverages, sending an Olympic smell surging into our noses.

Let us activate all the smells in our memories and follow the smells into our past, in search of our loves, our suffering, our joy, our solitude, our youth, our mothers...all of it, just as Proust used the madeleines to return to his own past.

Pu Songling, author of the inimitable classic *Strange Tales from a Chinese Studio*, once wrote of a mysterious blind monk who could judge writing by its smell. Many students preparing to take the imperial examinations took their compositions to the monk to smell. The monk would vomit loudly when he smelled bad writing, saying bad writing stank. But in the end, the writing that made him vomit came first in the exams, whereas none of the writing he found easy on the nose ever won any awards.

The Bunun aborigines of Taiwan tell a story about a tribe with an excellent sense of smell who lived beneath the earth, below the village. These people were expert cooks, capable of making the tastiest food imaginable. But they didn't eat; they placed the food they made on a platform, then the entire tribe surrounded it and simply sniffed it strongly, over and over. They lived on smells alone. The people above often went down there and stole the food which the tribe had already smelled. I've adapted this tale into a short story. In my story, I am a small child who goes down to steal the food below the village. I regretted it after it was published, though, because I wished I'd written from the perspective of the smell tribe, not just from the viewpoint of a normal person. If I could have imagined things and written the story as a child from the tribe of smells, the story would have really been something.

(Translated by Jesse Field)

2

FICTION AND SOCIETY

LECTURE AT THE
KYOTO UNIVERSITY CLUBHOUSE,
MAY 2006

Ladies and gentlemen, it is my third time speaking here and I must first and foremost thank Professor Yoshida Tomio for making it all possible. He is the translator of *Pow!*, which was just published, and it is his outstanding translation that has landed my novel in the hands of Japanese readers and has even made it possible for me to enjoy somewhat of a reputation as a contemporary Chinese writer here in Japan. To date, Professor Yoshida has translated three of my novels—*Big Breasts and Wide Hips*, *Sandalwood Death*, and *Pow!*—as well as my short stories —"Happy Times" and "White Dog and the Swing"—and he is currently in the process of translating my novel *Life and Death Are Wearing Me Out*. I want to express my deepest admiration for Professor Yoshida Tomio. Additionally, Professor Fujii Shozo, Mr. Yusuke Nagao, Mr. Akira Inokuchi, Mr. Masakazu Tatematsu, Mr. Takeshi Tanigawa, and Professor Kamaya Osamu have translated my novels *Republic of Wine* and *Red Sorghum* and dozens of short stories into Japanese, and I would also like to express my heartfelt gratitude for their exquisite work!

Fiction wasn't always such an elite undertaking. Its roots are in the lower classes—storytellers performed in tearooms and taverns, and tales were passed on orally, told to audiences full of cart pushers and broth peddlers. Fiction was originally a spoken art, not a written art, heard with the ears, not read with the eyes. Of course, the storytellers would also wave their arms and stomp around as they told their tales, radiant with delight, putting on a terrifically marvelous show. There are actually two different art forms that emerged from this sort of storytelling: written fiction and theatrical drama. This is all cliché by now, and if I were speaking at a Chinese university, the students would be shooing me off the stage. But tactful hospitality keeps that from happening when I'm abroad.

I was born too late to listen to the storytellers in Song-dynasty restaurants or Ming-dynasty teahouses. But in my hometown market and atop my family's warm *kang*, I got to listen to tales spun by professionals and amateurs alike. They never had a book in their hands, but each could let out an endless stream of stories. Perhaps they were reciting *huaben* (texts for storytelling) written by someone else, or they may have been compiling their own *huaben*[1] as they made up their stories. Back then, while other children were daydreaming about becoming leaders and big shots, I was hoping that one day I could become a marketplace storyteller. And I didn't just daydream about it either. I began practicing and training, constantly retelling the stories I had heard to other kids, and to grown-ups too. Whereas I was quite talented at storytelling, my labor output was lacking, and our production team leader would criticize me: "No talking, boys. You can't fill a stomach on idle chatter." Later, when I became a novelist, I wrote my stories on paper. On a trip back home I ran into my old team leader, and he apologized to me by saying, "My good writer sir, I had it all wrong! All I saw was endless yammering —I had no idea you had such a knack for writing books." "You weren't wrong at all," I replied. "I'm still a big talker. But now I use pen and paper to record all the things I want to say out loud, that's all."

I considered the storytellers my forefathers and saw myself as carrying on their tradition. This was unintentional at first, but I started pursuing it deliberately when I was writing *Sandalwood Death*. In the epilogue of that book, I wrote:

> Just as Maoqiang is performed on open-air stages for the working masses, my novel will be appreciated only by readers who have an affinity with the common man. It may in fact be better suited to hoarse voices in a public square, surrounded by an audience of eager listeners, not readers, who participate in the tale they are hearing. With that open-air audience in mind, I have taken pains to fill the work with rhymes and dramatic narration, all in the service of a smooth, easy-to-understand, overblown, resplendent narrative. Popular spoken and sung dialogues are the progenitors of the Chinese novel. Nowadays, when what was once mere popular entertainment has become a refined literary offering suitable for grand temples, at a time when borrowings from Western literary trends have all but brought an end to our popular traditions, *Sandalwood Death* may be out of keeping with the times, and might be thought of as a step backward in my writing career.[2]

These comments gave rise to intense debate. I was discussing issues of a writer's approach to writing and to narrative language, questions of how a writer mines folk culture for creative nourishment and source materials. There are many who have agreed with me, and others who have challenged me. Still, I take pride in thinking that *Sandalwood Death* led many writers toward an interest in folk culture, and this interest ultimately evolved into a craze for "grassroots literature" that has shown no signs of slowing.

This so-called "grassroots literature" is really just literature that is concerned with the lives of the lowest rungs of society, with the pain and suffering of the people. Of course, this is much more in keeping with literature's true purpose than is the sort of writing that is just frivolous songs of romantic folly, diversion for pampered noblemen and aristocrats. "Grassroots literature" has social significance; it is both reflective and critical of the restless hubbub of our world. But once a given writing style has become fashionable, things tend to take a turn for the worse. I recently went through a phase of reading quite a lot of "grassroots literature," and I found that most of the books follow the same formula in their display of hatred for the wealthy and powerful and sympathetic pity for the marginalized. Now there's nothing wrong with this per se, nor do I have the slightest doubts about the sincerity of these writers' feelings. But books in this style are basically cut from the same cloth as the "Red Classics" of the pre–Cultural Revolution era. The only difference is that the landowners and evil tyrants in the novels of yore have been replaced by the corrupt officials and filthy rich of today's world, and the poor peasant characters have been replaced by farmers, migrant laborers, and the urban unemployed. Just as the blunt class consciousness of the "Red Classics" bred overdone, cartoonish characters with no subtlety of emotion and unilateral thinking that lacked all authenticity and persuasive force—so too do today's novels reveal similar pretenses, thanks to their writers' helpless bewilderment in the face of society's intense transformations, as well as the blatant hostility they harbor toward the wealthy and powerful. The distinctive feature that these texts have in common is precisely that of superimposed suffering and bloated degeneracy, wherein the excesses and extravagance of the wealthy and powerful are exaggerated to the point of farce, and we are beaten over the head with the anguished adversity of the lower classes. As a style, grassroots literature is following the well-trodden path of our tradition of so-called "revolutionary literature," while also lifting old tricks from the tear-jerker playbook of popular literature and soap operas. Whereas it was originally supposed to be a way of staying truer to reality, the style ended up veering toward phony facades, and its original intent of criticizing corruption has veered toward stirring up animosity. So, although these books may have a certain social utility insofar as they provoke readers' hostility toward the powerful and their sympathies with the marginalized, they don't have much going for them in terms of literary value. There really isn't much literary value to speak of.

This long digression has finally brought us back around to the subject of today's lecture: fiction and society. Society is the fundamental source of fiction, or rather of literature. This is common knowledge; any textbook will tell you so. And although this isn't off the mark, the relationship between literature and society—or rather, how literature expresses and reflects society—is in fact a matter that has never quite been settled. And this "grassroots literature" that is currently so popular and in vogue is, in fact, just a revival of the ashes of "revolutionary realism," a resurgence of the creative ideology that governed Chinese literary circles and dominated the thinking of countless writers for decades.

I have always stressed that true literature is not a vehicle for playing God and delivering justice. It is not some sort of silver bullet for robbing the rich to feed the poor, nor is it propaganda to rouse the poor to rebel. True literature must transcend the narrow-minded interests of politics and social class and transcend the confines of national or regional mindsets. True literature must be philosophically and spiritually detached, lenient as it summarizes the nature of society and analyzes the essence of humanity. In simple terms, and as I see it, a good novel must have characters that are both emblematic and archetypical; its stories must come from real life but also have a rich allegorical quality that transcends reality. A good novel must use language that draws on the colloquialisms of the masses while also exhibiting the distinct individuality of language that is the hallmark of literary endeavors. A good novel must be richly thought-provoking, offering readers various possible interpretations. The duty to confront the muddled complexity of reality falls on news reporting, not on fiction. Fiction should not be used as an outlet for cursing reality or venting our hatred—that work is best left to sorcerers and to radical revolutionaries. As writers, we must sum up real life from a humanistic perspective, finding the guiding principles that help us understand the complexity of our society. There are some novelists, of course, who want to offer up solutions to society's problems. But I believe that good novels never provide solutions, or at least never provide them outright. Nor do good novelists fixate on any single societal issue. Instead, they focus on the people in our society—and on humanity's difficult struggle to break free from the desires that cling to us so stubbornly.

My novel *Pow!* focuses on the grassroots underclasses and describes real life without being tied down to it. I think its style is somewhat superior to the "grassroots literature" novels I've been talking about, and although it may be a bit shameless of me to say so, it's what I truly believe.

Pow! came out in 2003, and it describes the 1990s through the turn of the century. The differences between Chinese society then and now aren't really all that great. It goes without saying that I have seen the serious problems afflicting so many lives, the overflow of desire and moral bankruptcy, and that I, too, am seething with hatred for our society's most sinister phenomena, just as I am filled with sympathy for the marginalized. But at the same time, I am more realistic in my recognition that the marginalized and those in power are all struggling within the same quagmire of desires. The vulnerable and weak are not necessarily good and honest by nature, nor are the strong and powerful necessarily cruel and unscrupulous. Hatred of the wealthy can sometimes be envy in disguise, just as status aspirations may masquerade as contempt for those in power.

I took a fair and merciful approach in writing this book, rendering the painful struggles of all living things within the quagmire of desires. In my mind, there is no clear difference between good people and bad people, poor people and rich people. All are slaves of desire, meriting both sympathy and criticism. Not all the suffering sustained by the characters in this novel is externally inflicted, and in fact it is their own innermost essences that seem to instinctively generate the deepest distress. From a religious perspective, there is a measure of value in suffering: it is humanity's chance for self-improvement and salvation. The Earth Womb Bodhisattva's vow not to attain enlightenment as long as a single soul remained in hell and Jesus' sacrifice on the cross are both paragons of the ability to endure and transcend suffering. We need not mourn suffering with tears, and fiction's ultimate goal need not be to burden its characters with layer upon layer of suffering in order to make readers cry. A truly great, profound novel will not bring tears streaming down readers' faces. I am always keenly aware that I am writing fiction—not reporting a sociological study, and not muckraking either. And so I always place the utmost importance on the pursuit and innovation of fiction as an artistic form. With "pow" as the central image, I constructed a system of metaphors that was rooted in folklife, with a critical edge. The novel displays a complex, symbolic portrait of all living things in society, revealing the forfeiture of the treasures of our folk spirit and the distortions of humanity that have been wrought by modernization.

The book's main character is a boy named Luo Xiaotong who has the ability to communicate with meat. His life is rife with symbolism and absurdity. He has an extraordinary verbal ability paired with an irrepressible urge to tell stories, which are always full of improvisations and exaggerations. In my hometown, this kind of kid is called a "powboy." He, too, is a storyteller. He starts off as the meat-eating king, a kid who can speak with butchered flesh, and then he evolves into a Meat God. His cravings for meat are symbolic of humanity's appetite and carnal lust.

Luo Xiaotong's carnivorous appetite is born out of the hunger-driven fantasies during a period of poverty. As material conditions improve and meat becomes more abundant, his remarkable meat-eating talents gradually develop into a sort of meat worship, and people eventually sanctify him as the "Meat God." This Meat God is a cultural mutation grafted onto the body of desire, and Luo Xiaotong's carnivorous performances pander to the ridiculous nature of the times—both anti-rational and anti-sublime. The Meat God game comes to an end with the tragic death of Luo Xiaotong's mother and his father's arrest, misfortunes that amount to the end of Luo Xiaotong's childhood. But he refuses to grow up, or perhaps he is afraid to. He sits in the Temple of the Five Supernatural Powers, which symbolize virility, and, in an unceasing torrent, recounts his childhood. This narration also serves as a way for him to hold on to those years and keep them from slipping away. Whereas his body has grown into that of a young man, his spirit is still that of a boy. I have a habit of writing from a child's perspective in order to preserve the fairy-tale quality of the world as seen through the eyes of a child, to cast off the fetters of reality, and to render even more concentrated—and more deeply critical—revelations of the ridiculous modern society in which we live. I think that in *Pow!* I expanded on this and made a breakthrough.

As an adult, Luo Xiaotong is an escapist, lacking the ability and courage to face the realities of life. His younger self was memorialized—carved into a block of willow wood and placed in the Temple of the Five Supernatural Powers, where people came to bow down and worship the idol of the Meat God. And it is at this temple that Luo Xiaotong and the old monk take up the roles of storyteller and audience, representing none other than the corporeal bodies of the gods of appetite and of lust. Although they may look like two separate entities, they could be fully merged into a single whole. This old monk, with his Guinness Record–breaking ability to have sex with forty-one women at once, is more a phantom of Luo Xiaotong's mind than a man in and of himself. And it's really desire that's doing the talking, more than Luo Xiaotong himself. He gives his account as a search for absolution, but in fact it only sinks him deeper into the mires of infatuation. This is the plight of Luo Xiaotong. It is also the plight of all of Chinese society, and of the human world at large.

A few years ago, I was talking to an old monk, and I asked him if it would be possible for me to leave home to become a monk myself. He looked at me and said, "How can you become a monk when there are still so many desires in your heart?" So, I asked in turn, "How do I go about having fewer desires in my heart?" The old monk pointed to the lotus in full bloom that was sitting in the pond, and he smiled without answering. I have always wondered, was the mud in which this lotus had taken root a symbol of humanity's desires? Was the old monk suggesting that I be like the lotus and rise, unsullied by the mud? Or was he suggesting that I must first abandon myself to temptation, before resolving to mend my ways? To this day, I still haven't figured it out...which is why I still haven't left home to become a monk.

Luo Xiaotong only became a deity of meat once he had surfeited on it, and the monk had sex with thousands of women before he left home to take his oaths. What I'm trying to say is that perhaps only once humanity has been punished for its indulgent debaucheries will we be able to reach enlightenment. But this theory is still a little dubious because at no point was Luo Xiaotong free from the influence of the carnal pleasures at hand. He could never give a fully focused account; the visions he conjured in his mind were shadows of desire.

I must clear up a few things about this eponymous word "pow." Besides its association with the "powboys" I mentioned earlier, this word also sets the tone and perspective of the narrative. Luo Xiaotong is a powboy who blows his stories out of all proportion, and so is the author, Mo Yan. In contemporary Chinese society, "pow" also has a sexual connotation. Of course, the real "pow" takes place at the end of the book, and this too is a symbol: Luo Xiaotong has the upper hand against the bigwig Lao Lan, with whom he has a love-hate relationship, and he shoots forty-one artillery shells in a row. The first forty shots all seem as though they are aimed at the target, when in fact they are just blanks—it is the absent-minded forty-first shot that pierces Lao Lan clear through the middle, echoing the shot that split the viscount in two in Italo Calvino's novel *The Cloven Viscount*. Like an imaginary shot in a fairy tale, Luo Xiaotong opens fire on his desires as the desires themselves also open fire. And so amid the rumble of "pows," the characters take turns coming onstage like actors taking their bows at the end of a show, and the heavy curtains are drawn as this book comes to a close.

Now that you've heard my simple explanation, don't you agree that when it comes to fiction and life in society, my approach is a bit more compelling than those "grassroots literature" books?

(Translated by Ella Schwalb)

Notes

1. *Huaben* are short stories or novellas that are written mostly in vernacular Chinese.
2. Mo Yan, epilogue to *Sandalwood Death*, trans. Howard Goldblatt (Norman: University of Oklahoma Press), 412. The last sentence of the quotation was translated by Ella Schwalb.

3

The Tradition of
Chinese Fiction

A Discussion Drawing on Three of My Novels,
Speech at the Lu Xun Museum, May 2006

In my hometown, there are certain expressions we use to describe presumptuous behavior—wielding a hatchet in front of the master craftsman Lu Ban's workshop; flexing your muscles at Lord Guan's mighty stallion; and reciting the *Three-Character Classic* at Confucius' house. Now we ought to add one more: talking about fiction at the Lu Xun Museum. By coming here to discuss fiction, I might as well be courting my own disgrace. But it's hard to say no to a friend, so I've got to throw myself into the lion's den. I will be so bold as to talk about fiction.

Actually, ever since Mr. Lu Xun's *Brief History of Chinese Fiction*, any discussion of classical fiction is just a lousy sequel to his masterpiece. And when it comes to a homegrown author like myself, with no culture or training, it would be impossible to add anything at all. Chinese fiction has deep roots that flow long, broad, and deep: from Tang fantasy sagas to Song and Yuan *huaben,* from *Three Words and Two Hits* to *Officialdom Unmasked*, there are enough of all sorts of histories, anecdotes, gods and devils, love stories, errant knights, and crime cases to leave you dazzled. Not to mention the ever-towering presence of Chinese classics like *Romance of the Three Kingdoms, Water Margin, Journey to the West, The Scholars, Strange Stories from a Chinese Studio,* and *A Dream of Red Mansions.* A person could spend their whole life's energy on any one of these works, and their research would still be incomplete. Of course, a piece of fiction can't be studied with the same straightforward clarity as a case of appendicitis; if it could, then it wouldn't be fiction—or at least fiction worth its salt. Look no further than *A Dream of Red Mansions.* There are over three hundred years of scholarship about this novel, but the book doesn't become clearer as more research is done. Instead, it only gets more muddled. *A Dream of Red Mansions* is a million characters long, and, as articles accumulate, there may already be a few hundred million characters written about it.

In other words, reading all of those well-known best-of classics once through demands an enormous investment of energy, and finding anything new to say, or identifying any unifying pattern, is an extremely difficult task. But Mr. Lu Xun seems to have done so effortlessly—he is gifted; there's no comparison between us.

So, when a person like me, who isn't well-read and just skims the surface of books, has the audacity to start prattling on about inheriting and carrying forward the great tradition of classical Chinese fiction—doesn't it seem a bit like the rantings of a lunatic? Yes, but not entirely. What do I mean? Hold your horses, and just lend me your ears.

I think a writer's education can more or less be split up into two parts. The first takes place prior to becoming a writer, a kind of involuntary, impractical, meandering learning. For example, when I was young, I would go to the market and squeeze through the gaps between the grown-ups' legs to listen to the storytellers' performances. Or another example from when I was little is how I would scheme to find ways to get my hands on and read the few classical novels that were available across the nineteen villages of Northeast Gaomi Township. Because there was a limit to how long one could borrow the books, I had no choice but to devour them quickly. Sometimes I would make my way into a haystack and read a book in its entirety there, even though I knew my parents would punish me for it. The essence of this kind of learning and reading is a complete enchantment with stories, like a starving child's longing for food. It simply never occurred to me that I might be studying folk literature and classics, or that reading would be preparation for a creative career in the future—the feelings I got from reading were pure. Later, when I became a professional novelist, my parents said to me: "If we'd known you were going to become a writer, we wouldn't have made you tend to the cows and sheep. We should have given you time to read and given you money so you could go listen to the storytellers every market day." I said: "Well, if you'd made me go read books and listen to stories like that, I might have snuck off to go tend to the cows and sheep."

Then there is another kind of learning, when you want to study fiction-writing purposefully, and you read and listen to stories as preparation for your own craft. There is a clear-cut purpose to this type of learning, and its value in terms of technique goes without saying. But that original raw, simple feeling of being a pure reader and listener has mostly disappeared.

Personally, I think that the former type of learning is far more important than the latter. This is something I have said time and time again: A writer's style—what they write, how they write, what kind of language they use, what kind of approach they take—is basically born out of their efforts before they made a name for themselves. The efforts they make after the fact will only have an influence on the shallow surface of their writing and are unlikely to influence the deeper layers.

I was a pure young listener back then, enchanted by storytelling; I listened single-mindedly at the market, all my emotions fully charged. On the one hand, I was fascinated by the storytellers' vivid performances, their joyful movements. On the other hand, I was captivated by the fate of the characters in the stories, which struck me as even more important. At that time, there were two relatively well-known storytellers at the market

in our town. One was named Big Broken Gong. He had a husky voice, a
lame foot, a blind eye, and ears that stuck straight out like little palm-leaf
fans. He had a good memory, and he had a gift for improvising according
to the situation at hand. He handled metaphors well and frequently made
insinuations to roast anyone from the surrounding villages who rubbed
him the wrong way. As a performer, he was talented and his gestures
were exaggerated—and thanks to his knack for improvisation, he was
always able to attract an audience and generate peals of laughter.

The other storyteller was named Wang Dengke, an old man who had
taught at the community schoolhouse. His storytelling was stiff, basically
a word-for-word recitation: his intonation barely changed, his body
didn't move, and he didn't interact with the audience. It seemed almost
as if he were there just to amuse himself. At first, I liked Big Broken
Gong. Most people liked Big Broken Gong. His audience was always
packed to the gills, whereas Wang Dengke drew in only a scant dozen
or so people, mostly regulars. But as time passed, I grew weary of Big
Broken Gong because there were too many digressions branching off
from his tales. It was lively, sure, but the main storyline advanced too
slowly with all his chitchat, and his joke-repetition rate was excessive,
leaving me dissatisfied. But despite Wang Dengke's wooden delivery, the
huaben upon which he based his storytelling were already highly artful
because they had been arranged and refined by scholars and contained
the wisdom of countless generations of storytellers. So I would close my
eyes as Wang Dengke told his stories, and I would listen silently with
my whole mind and body following the tale, following the characters'
fates. This kind of listening borders on reading; it's a kind of reading
with your ears. Storytellers have always used such books to prepare, and
the stories have been refined with the storytellers' oral narrations, so
traces of speech have been left behind: "once upon a time," "his name
struck fear into the hearts of many," "meanwhile...," "tune in for the next
chapter to find out what happens," and so forth.

Often, I would recount the stories I had heard at the market to my mother and sister. I encountered severe difficulties in my attempts to retell Big Broken Gong's stories because if you weren't there in person, all his on-the-spot antics would lose their appeal. For example, once he saw that right as he was about to collect money, as he kept his listeners in suspense, someone who had been listening for a long time was stealthily slipping away. He abandoned the tale and shouted out: Hey! You, the one with the felt hat slipping away there! Slow down, or you might bump into Big White Goose's clapper sleeves—Big White Goose was a woman who was known around Northeast Gaomi Township to be a bit licentious; "clapper sleeves" was a euphemism for female genitals. This line was absolutely devastating. As the man stopped short, caught by shame, Big Broken Gong turned it around yet again, saying: "I mean, bump into some cabbage leaves!"—and the whole audience burst out laughing. But if you hadn't been there in person, the attempt to capture this kind of spectacle verbally wouldn't be funny at all. Wang Dengke was different, though. Conveying Wang Dengke's stories was really just a matter of rote memorization. Wang Dengke would rattle off his stiff recitations, and I would learn his stories by heart. I took on the role of storyteller, and even though I didn't perform, the *huaben* was still marvelous, enough by itself to enchant my mother and sister. Often they would totally forget about the needlework in their hands. And though my mother would still end up chiding me—"All right! Time for bed! Being chatty won't put food on the table!"—when the next market day came around, she would ask me yet again to tell her the stories I had heard that day.

I later went on to read a few *huaben* novels or novels that had traces of *huaben*, and over time I began to feel dissatisfied. Compared to *A Dream of Red Mansions*, *The Scholars,* and other classics of the sort, *huaben* fiction stubbornly pursued story and drama without paying any attention to character development. It sought nothing more than a complex plot, without focusing on real details. Characters' personalities were flattened, and there was a paucity of inner conflicts and friction. They didn't have much literary value and were not worth imitating.

In the 1980s, I tested into the literature department of the People's Liberation Army (PLA) Art Academy, at which point reading and writing fiction became my day job. A huge number of Western modernist novels were being translated into Chinese in those days: new French fiction, Latin American magical realism, Japanese Shinkankakuha. Then there were the works by Kafka, Joyce, Faulkner, and Hemingway. Reading so many works and genres broadened my horizons and made me sigh ruefully, wishing I had encountered these writings sooner. I thought, "If only I had known earlier, I could have written like this and I would have already become a great writer." So I dropped my books and began to write feverishly. Many critics have said that I was influenced by the literature of the Latin American Boom, particularly by Gabriel García Márquez's *One Hundred Years of Solitude,* and I've always pled guilty to that charge. It's true, I was indeed influenced by him. But to this day I've still never finished *One Hundred Years of Solitude.* Back then, after reading eighteen pages, I was possessed by such a creative fervor that I threw down the book, picked up a pen, and wrote.

I think—and there seem to be a lot of writers and critics who have said things along the same lines—that an author influences another author when a quality unique to the first author's activates, or perhaps awakens, a quality that was lying latent deep in the other author's heart. This echoes the idea put forth in Chairman Mao's "On Contradiction," that the right temperature can make an egg turn into a chick, but no temperature can make a stone turn into a chick. That's why after reading eighteen pages of *One Hundred Years of Solitude,* I just couldn't contain my deep-seated excitement. I had to slap the table and stand up because the things he expressed in that novel, and his way of expressing them, were so similar to what I had, over a long, long time, accumulated in my own heart. Like an intense beam of light, his work illuminated a part of my innermost being that had until then been shrouded in a hazy darkness. Of course, you could also say that the spirit of his novel completely destroyed my previous conception of fiction, like pushing a little boat that had been rowing along through a narrow mountain creek out into the majestic Yangtze and Yellow rivers.

I hastily picked up a pen. I always used to fret because of my inability to find anything to write about; now I had material that was coming fast and furious. I once wrote an essay describing my creative mentality of that time. I said that every time I wrote a story, there were always many others that wanted to be written, like dogs yapping madly at my heels: Me first! Write me first! Those stories spoke.

I was in school at the time—attending class during the day and running back to the classroom to write in the evenings. I still had to get up first thing in the morning to take part in the school's morning exercises. It was a military college with a militarized administration. These were the circumstances in which, in the span of two years, I wrote *The Transparent Carrot*, "Explosions," "Ball Lightning," "The Yellow-haired Baby," "Building a Road," and *Red Sorghum*—more than 800,000 characters of fiction.

This was also the period during which I came to perceive a serious problem: namely, the need to struggle free, to get out from under the shadows of García Márquez, Faulkner, and a handful of other Western writers because I could not be satisfied with imitating them. The influence of these Western writers was visible in only a small portion of my works, but critics and readers thought my works to be in large part authentic Chinese fiction—regardless, I still knew the formidable scale of their influence. García Márquez had roused those parts of my mind that were inherently similar to his mindset. But a writer's influence is like a pigment with an extremely strong, pervasive power; even those parts of my innermost being that were my own, distinct from García Márquez's, were dyed his color. I published an essay in a 1987 issue of *World Literature*, which was more or less about evading two burning blast furnaces. What I meant was that García Márquez and Faulkner were the two burning blast furnaces, and I was an ice cube. If I got too close to them, I would melt, evaporate.

But my escape wasn't complete in the slightest. I was like a smitten lover: even though we had broken up, the feelings remained. Lovers may part, but they still pine for one another. It was just too convenient to apply García Márquez's techniques, and indeed too many García Márquez-esque stories were building up in my head. It may have been a betrayal, but there was still a process I needed to go through.

Over the following dozen or so years, I nursed a rebelliousness in my writing. This was the period during which I wrote such novels as *The Garlic Ballads*, *Thirteen Steps*, *The Republic of Wine*, and *Big Breasts and Wide Hips*, as well as a few dozen novellas, including *The Woman Holding Flowers* and *Father in the Militia Company*. These pieces saw a great deal of experimentation with techniques. I was also striving to personalize my writing, and I made an effort not to rely on other people's styles. Yet traces of Western influence always remained.

Only in 2000, when I wrote *Sandalwood Death*, did I get the sense that I could be on a par with those Western writers. This is also the crux of what I want to talk about today: the creative process for my three most recent novels, *Sandalwood Death*, *Pow!*, and *Life and Death Are Wearing Me Out*, has been a matter of taking great strides backwards, toward the study of folk literature, toward understanding and experiencing the study of traditional Chinese fiction.

In an essay discussing changes in Beijing opera, Mr. Wang Zengqi once wrote: "There is a pattern in the history of literature, which is that when each and every literary form is in decline, there are just two kinds of things that save it: folk things and external things."[1]

The external things that Mr. Wang was talking about include both foreign theater and other art forms that are separate from Beijing opera; for example, fiction, poetry, and fine arts. The folk items he mentioned include folk opera, folk songs, *xiaodiao* (simple folk tunes), *gushu* (ballads with drum accompaniment), and other crude art forms, as well as the folk tales about the lives of the people, the suffering of the people.

He was talking about Beijing opera, but what he said applies entirely to fiction too. Fiction was originally popular folk material, but now it has joined the imperial court and become high art. It is ever more distant from ordinary people. This kind of distance refers not only to fiction's distance from readers but also to content that is divorced from the vivid energy, the flesh and blood, the lives of the common people. It also refers to language that is divorced from the treasure trove of popular vernacular and its exuberant, flourishing vitality. The language of fiction has become like a beautiful but pallid plastic flower that is incessantly copied from one book to another.

When I wrote *Sandalwood Death*, I proposed a return to folk culture, taking great strides backwards from the position of the so-called avant-garde. The most direct reason for this was simply my distaste for that writing style, brimming with the inflections of translation, that is so in vogue. I think this style is not only an issue of a piece of fiction's linguistic style; it also bears upon fiction's soul. Someone who writes with that kind of language is absolutely incapable of understanding the folk. And a writer who does not understand the common folk is absolutely incapable of writing fiction that reflects people's lives—all that can be said of it is that it is fiction written in Chinese. Of course, this so-called "folk" does not refer only to people in remote, desolate places and wild, mountainous terrain, nor does it refer only to people in the countryside. It must embody the lives of the lowest rungs of society in their totality. The *longtangs* (Shanghai dialect for "lane") of Shanghai, the *hutongs* (Beijing dialect for "lane") of Beijing, barrooms—all the people here constitute part of the "folk."

Sandalwood Death appears to be a historical novel, with a protagonist who is the last executioner of the Qing dynasty. For his achievements in carrying out sentences, the Empress Dowager Cixi bestows on him a seventh-rank cap badge and an imperial dragon throne and sends him home to his village to enjoy his retirement. His daughter's father-in-law, Sun Bing, was formerly the leader of the Cat Tune Opera Troupe. After the troupe disbanded, he married, started a family, and opened a teahouse to earn a living. When his family falls upon hard times, he becomes a leader in the resistance against the Germans. He learns magic from the Boxers, then rounds up the masses, along with the members of his former troupe, to face off against the German army that is constructing the Jiaoji Railway—but Sun Bing and his group are defeated and taken prisoner. To make an example of him, the head of the German army and the Shandong inspector-general, Yuan Shikai, have the county magistrate, Qian Ding, call for the old executioner, Zhao Jia, to come out of obscurity and resume his post, devising a punishment that tortures people for several days without killing them. Zhao Jia comes up with "sandalwood death," which is to be used on Sun Bing as a cautionary example for the public. Sun Bing has the chance to escape, but he doesn't. With his background in opera, he retains a theatrical mindset.

Mr. Lu Xun's works criticize coldly detached, heartless spectators, and in an oblique way his works also express the performative psychology of the condemned. I am going to take this subject of his one step further. I think that there is a trinity formed by the relationship between the executioner, the condemned criminal, and the onlooker. In this sensational drama, the executioner and the condemned are performing on a shared stage, which demands a tacit understanding between them, a coordinated rapport. If the executioner does not exhibit a perfected technique, the spectators will be dissatisfied; if the condemned is not brave, the spectators will also be dissatisfied. So, this is a murder spectacle that does away with any sense of right and wrong. The person being killed just needs to display bravery, keep a stiff upper lip, and face death without flinching —all the better if he can sing opera while being killed. Even if he is a ruthless murderer who has slaughtered people like flies, with the blood of countless victims on his hands, the spectators will still express a deep admiration for him—their cheering won't be stingy in the slightest.

In this novel, the key point I unearthed was the peculiar psychology of the executioner, Zhao Jia. Of course, his was also an abnormal psychology.

If it hadn't been for his peculiarity and abnormality, he simply wouldn't have been able to go on living...

Besides the one kernel of truth about Sun Wen's opposition to the Germans, the rest of this novel is entirely made up. This method of torture and this executioner never existed. I have always secretly thought it was actually a novel of modern times. Though the writing appears to be from the period of long, buttoned robes, braids, and bound feet, it's in fact about the modern mentality. I was extremely shocked after the Zhang Zhixin affair came to light in the early 1980s. I thought about the person who followed orders to sever Zhang Zhixin's throat before her official sentence had been carried out and about those who tortured her in the name of the revolution, in the name of the people. I wondered: What they were thinking at the time? And what did they think when they saw Zhang Zhixin thoroughly rehabilitated and posthumously recognized as a martyr of the revolution? Did they want to repent? And if they had wanted to repent, would our society have allowed them to? And then, in the 1990s, I heard the story of Lin Zhao, that bright young woman at Beijing University, and the shocking detail about how after she was executed, the government asked her mother to pay five cents for the cost of the bullet. Again I pondered the same questions, thinking about the person who invented the rubber ball to put in Lin Zhao's mouth, which would keep swelling up the more she cried out. What was this person thinking while this was happening? And to take it one step further, I wondered: If I had been the jailer watching over Lin Zhao or Zhang Zhixin at the time, and the higher authorities had ordered me to torture them, would I have carried out the orders or would I have defied them? The conclusion I came to startled me. I think, in some sense, or under certain circumstances, the great majority of us would take on the role of executioner and that too of the numb onlooker. There is a Zhao Jia hidden in the depths of each and every one of our souls.

This kind of novel cannot be separated from its nationality or folk essence. Many critics say I don't have any ideology, and frequently I admit that I don't have one. But actually I do have an ideology, though it is at times too extreme, and at other times shallow. But extreme or shallow, it is still an ideology.

The next issue I had to contend with was what kind of structure to use to write this novel, as well as what kind of language.

On the question of structure, I recalled listening to Beijing University Professor Ye Lang explain "The Aesthetics of Chinese Classical Fiction." He mentioned a pattern for the structure of fiction: a phoenix's head, then a hog's belly, and finally a leopard's tail.[2] This pattern facilitated my narration enormously, and I think it also gave my readers an easier experience.

I thought about folk opera for the question of language, about our distinctive style of opera in Gaomi that's on the verge of extinction, "Mao Qiang"—in the novel I changed it to "Meow Qiang," or "Cat Tune"—and at the same time I also thought about the unforgettable scenes I heard when I was little, listening to those storytellers at the market.

Thinking about opera and about grafting "Cat Tune" into the novel, I had a sudden revelation. This is not merely a question of language. It also simultaneously resolves the contradictory clash of fiction's innermost dramatic structure and intensely theatrical plot setup. Everything is hyperbolic, pushed to the extreme: all the bad guys are wretchedly evil; all the heroes are unswervingly loyal. Every character—Sun Bing, Qian Ding, Sun Meiniang—is covered in gaudy opera makeup. Only Zhao Jia, the executioner, is uniquely "himself." He is really the only one in *Sandalwood Death* who can stand alone, who counts as an archetypical character. Of course, all potters praise their own pots...

After *Sandalwood Death*, I wrote a novel, *Pow!*, that reflected village life in the 1990s. The novel is about a "powboy" who is very enthusiastic about eating meat. He narrates his young life to a venerable monk in a Wu Tong temple in a torrent of words, a muddy flood, so to speak.

Actually, this Pow kid is a storyteller. This was also my way of honoring those storytellers I listened to in the market back in the day.

In terms of content, this novel is about the life of the underclass; and in terms of technique, I made use of symbols. Symbolism may seem to be from the West, but it is actually also a special tradition in Chinese fiction. Think about *Journey to the West, A Dream of Red Mansions,* and *The Plum in the Golden Vase.* Symbols abound in each and every one of these works.

At the beginning of this year, I published a novel called *Life and Death Are Wearing Me Out,* which takes Buddhism's Six Stages of Samsara as the source of its ideology. I did this also as a direct challenge to Latin American magical realism. I used techniques from Chinese fiction and drew upon the reserves of Chinese thought. The novel's traditional chapter structure was no great feat and deserves no special note. *Life and Death Are Wearing Me Out* also touches upon the issue of the ultra-leftist Land Reform policies, but just like the traditional chapter structure, this is a detail that doesn't deserve too much attention. I still genuinely want to write people like Lan Lian and Hong Taiyue. I put a lot of effort into thinking about how to write people who have the kind of individuality that Lan Lian and Hong Taiyue possess. The crux of the question I am pondering is the relationship between the peasants and the land. This book is a song of praise—and it's also an elegy. After finishing *Life and Death Are Wearing Me Out,* I can finally be so bold as to say: "I wrote a rather pure Chinese novel."

(Translated by Ella Schwalb)

NOTES

1. Wang Zengqi, "On the Crisis of Beijing Opera," *Chinese Theatre* 10 (1980), 27.
2. This refers to a perfect structure for a work of fiction: a beginning as beautiful as the phoenix's head, a body as full as a hog's belly, and an ending as strong as a leopard's tail.

4

Writing What You
Most Want to Write

Lecture at Shanghai University, June 2006

The true Buddha never speaks. Who has ever seen the Buddha speak? It's just us humans who are always chattering and jabbering on.

I have some trepidation about giving a speech here today. I have no scholarly knowledge to speak of, and a place as cultured as Shanghai really shouldn't be subjected to the unorthodox ramblings of someone like me. There's no telling how many people will be swearing off me by the end of this speech. But Professor Wang Hongsheng has been a friend of mine for many years, and he extended such a warm invitation. I'm left in an uncomfortable position. On the one hand, I dare not speak for fear of being scolded because it's quite clear I don't have much of substance to say. But it's also very hard to turn down such a good friend, so I'm caught in the middle. What a mess. If you came here hoping to hear me deliver some profound insight, I can tell you right now that it's not going to happen. If, however, you're looking forward to picking apart my logic for internal inconsistencies, then you're in luck. I invite you all to prick up your ears—as soon as you hear an inconsistency, please just cut me off and shoo me off stage. I'll be glad for the chance to make off.

The so-called question of literature is said to be complicated, and indeed it is. A thousand paragraphs still wouldn't do it justice, but then again it's almost too simple for words. Especially when it's a writer doing the talking, all spoken explanations are superfluous—no amount of flowery speech can salvage a sloppy writer and turn him into a great one, just as no amount of stuttering false starts will threaten the reputation of an author who has written a masterpiece.

While I was eating yesterday, I presented a dissident view about literature, posing it as an issue with two basic points at its core, which parodies the political slogan. The first of these points is the question of *why* people write, which has been discussed for ages but has never been settled. All writers, when they first start writing, have their own personal goals—their *why*. There are those who start with lofty goals: they want to write for the proletariat, for the people, for the fulfillment of communist ideals. Others write for love or for money. Writing can be motivated by all sorts of driving forces, and everyone has one at the beginning.

There was nothing lofty about my motives back when I was first starting to write. I was part of an army unit at the time, and all prospects for my future looked bleak. Life was boring but I had time to spare, so I started writing stories. My goal was twofold. First of all, I wanted to earn a little extra cash so I could buy a wristwatch. Second, I was stoking my ambitions for fame and fortune. I figured that on the off chance my stories got published, I'd be able to change my lot in life. I was looking at things very pragmatically at the time, and I'm sure there are plenty of people out there who look at things the same way. Naturally there are many others who see things from another angle, so I can't really take my own experiences as representative. Different strokes for different folks.

It's been more than twenty years since I first started writing, and now that I am returning to the question of why I write, I can see that the answer has certainly changed. For one thing, buying a wristwatch isn't much of an incentive anymore. Wearing a wristwatch is considered tacky nowadays. Second, becoming famous holds no appeal because I've already made a bit of a name for myself at this point. Whether it's a fragrant name or a foul one, I can't be sure.

So why do I write, then, if not for money or for fame? Do I write for the betterment of humanity? For the progress of society? Of course, I am always striving for these goals in my writing. But these days my main motivation is really just the feeling that I have a lot to say. We live in a chaotic and complicated world, and people exist in an infinite array of configurations and situations, out of touch and at a loss. The complexity of our experiences is extreme, and when faced with the kaleidoscopic absurdities of our world, we all make our own judgments based on our own morals and values, based on our own attitudes to our social reality. I am a writer, and naturally I have my own tastes, my own attitudes, and my own judgments and standards for matters of right and wrong. I try to use fiction to convey my complicated feelings about all sorts of phenomena in our current society.

Then there's also my love for the art of fiction itself. Back in the day, fiction was the lowly occupation of storytellers who spun yarns for audiences of common folk in taverns, teahouses, and marketplaces. To put it simply, it was just a person telling a story. But if we allow for some shades of complexity, we will see that fiction has evolved over the course of thousands of years, as each generation of authors explores and develops it in new ways. The field of scholarship on fiction has grown so boundless that you'd never get the whole picture even with a hundred doctoral degrees.

There is a range of theories about fiction as a genre. Some say that there are no more tricks left to play, that all forms have already been tried out or, as Shakespeare once said, all the stories have been told—that a writer does nothing more than duplicate what others have done before, just frying up leftovers. This view seems a bit harsh to me. I think fiction is limitless, both in form and in meaning. It can expand to no end. So I'd sooner say that we've exhausted our writerly talents than that fiction as a medium is spent. There are still so many territories to be explored and tapped into, such tremendous room for innovation, and such vast expanses in which to experiment. Even after more than twenty years of writing fiction, the infinite variables of this form have never lost their charm for me. When I'm working on a new piece, any little innovation in ideas or imagery will get me excited, no matter how small. So I think it's fair to say that my love for the art of fiction has itself become a motivation for me.

Those are my two main reasons for writing these days. I could always tack on some loftier ideals, but they would ring hollow. Still, some may press me: "So you're saying fame and fortune mean nothing to you? Your current writing habits are completely free of all ambition? You don't take money or success into account at all when you write?" Of course, I can't stamp out ambition entirely; it still plays its role. When I write a novel, I hope that it will be widely distributed, that I'll get high royalties, that readers will like it and that critics will praise it... I'm not immune to these sorts of hopes, they're only natural. But fame and fortune just don't measure up against my main motivations for writing, which are, as I explained earlier, both to speak my mind and the simple fact that I take pleasure in the art of fiction itself and am obsessed with blazing new trails.

As I see it, the question of *why* is central for anyone who writes. It is present for all writers, whether or not they consciously take it up. A novice writer might think this question through or might choose to ignore it. But even so, it will still come into play. However, while a writer's capacity to produce work that is masterful and meaningful is certainly related to the writer's purpose, it isn't necessarily the decisive factor. There are times when a noble book is born out of base intentions, and other times when the loftiest intentions produce writing that is downright trash. Didn't our writers from the Cultural Revolution era have lofty goals for their writing? One needn't look far to find similar examples throughout the history of literature.

The second topic I want to touch upon, tired though it may be, is the question of *what* to write. Literature departments, critics, and writers have spent the past few decades puzzling over the question of what should be written and what should not be written. And now, six years into the twenty-first century, I still don't think this question has been settled. There should be no taboos around any given type of person, or any given social ill—every single being and every single phenomenon on our planet must be writeable. It's unconscionable to place artificial restrictions on what can be written. But although no subject should be off-limits, a writer's literary touch will still determine whether a given topic is written well, whether it meets aesthetic standards.

Of course some will be quick to point out: "Didn't Lu Xun say that there is no place in fiction for caterpillars, snot, or excrement?" I don't think this is necessarily so. A caterpillar transforms into a beautiful butterfly, does it not? So there's no reason we can't spare a few words for the caterpillar before we write the butterfly. And as far as snot goes, I myself wrote about a young boy who wipes the snot from his little brother's nose in my novella *The Transparent Carrot*. As far as I know, the segment didn't have any adverse psychological effects on readers, which means it must be okay to write about snot. Now, conventional aesthetic wisdom would say that excrement is indeed off limits. But I have seen performance art wherein feces were on public display in majestic locales. I've written about feces myself in *Red Locusts*, and even Rabelais and Kim Jiha pontificate about poo. Looking at it through the lens of Bakhtin's theory of grotesque realism, although it may seem unpleasant to describe the human body, and especially the nether regions, in all its fleshy physicality, these representations actually have a special fascination. Hidden meanings abound within something that might appear ugly and obscene at first glance—like a hybrid of vulgarity and virtue, of death and birth, evoking a kind of vital, maternal force. Mr. Lu Xun was not wrong, of course, but neither must his words be taken as an imperial decree.

Absolutely anything that happens in life can be put into writing. How an author handles and elaborates on a subject is closely linked to personal affinities and abilities as well as the subject matter itself. But sometimes you can't help but think that certain things just can't be put into writing. I was terribly perplexed when I first started writing, thinking that there were many lives and many topics that should never be written about. I thought one could only write radiant and uplifting novels that would contribute to reform. My writing was thus confined to an extremely narrow scope, and it turned out that the more I wrote, the further removed my words felt from life. They lacked force. Later, I gradually started looking to my own past for material—to my childhood and my adolescence. I found that as a beginning writer, if you want your writing to come out naturally and persuasively, you must start with the things you know well.

Needless to say, writing about one's personal experience can wear thin quickly. When push comes to shove, an individual's experience is finite and cannot yield a never-ending stream of writing. So where do you turn to find the material to keep going once your personal life experiences have been used up? This is the point at which you must be able to endlessly broaden the scope from which you gather your source material. You must open your eyes wide and mobilize every nerve in your body, actively attuning yourself to all sorts of information from the external world, which is then to be seized and assimilated into relevant material from your own life. By making others' lives and others' experiences your own, you will have a steady flow of source material for your work, thereby training yourself to become a professional writer. Granted, it may be difficult to wring out the same level of precision and liveliness from these sources as you would from your own experiences, but being a professional demands writing nonstop and making good use of second-hand material.

The question of what to write is undeniably important. The range of types of novels available on the market right now could boggle the mind:

some are written about the city, others about the village, some about industry, and others about war. The content varies markedly, even among books that deal with the same subject matter. Books about city life may detail white-collar existence, unemployment, bureaucratic corruption, barrooms, or big shopping malls. A wide range of writers have written novels describing practically every aspect of life, every space, and every community, which means that if we were to compile all extant writing, we could basically reconstruct the world in its entirety, with all its many, motley life forms. This also means that if everyone were to pick source material from their own accumulated experiences based on the scope of their own life, writing would always be vivid and accurate. So don't just take suggestions from others when you're deciding what to write about. Instead, prioritize your own perceptions. We shouldn't gather like a swarm of bees around each new popular subject, looking about for a charming story template, regardless of whether it has anything to do with our life or feelings. What you write must be guided by the compass of your own heart. Whatever it is that moves you most deeply, whatever it is that you most want to say—that's what you must write.

I am also of the belief that subject matter never goes out of style. There's no such thing as "old" or "new" because fiction is, in essence, a vessel for characters, and a novel's subject matter in and of itself isn't all that important. What *is* important is that our novels express human feeling, human nature, and human fate. We should mold powerful characters who forge new archetypes and leave deep impressions on our readers. These imperatives constitute fiction's most basic mission. It doesn't matter whether a text portrays rural life, modern times, or historical events. A good piece of literature is universally considered successful, no matter what the subject matter may be—take, for example, the books that brought us unforgettable characters like Jia Baoyu, Lin Daiyu,[1] Ah Q,[2] and Anna Karenina. On the flip side, a book's success is not guaranteed even if it's written about the most in-vogue, popular subject matter, like the poor treatment of teachers, for instance, which was the hottest topic a few years back. The story could be about a teacher who ends up on the street selling dumplings. Still, if the novel isn't written well, if it's imprecise and its characters are flat, and if it fails to capture the essence of the teacher's psyche, then it is effectively no different from journalism or documentary. By the same token, you could shun the contemporary and make up fictional characters from ancient times, and if you write them as so unique and memorable that modern readers can sense their personalities and presence, then your characters are actually quite modern. When it comes to fiction, the notions of "contemporary" and "historical" are incredibly vague, especially when it comes to choosing material.

The last thing I want to talk about today has to do with the question of *how* to write. The contents of a book are determined by its subject matter, of course: different subjects will beget a whole range of wildly different novels. But after many years of developments in the field of fiction, your average reader won't be satisfied with a simple tear-jerker anymore, or even just an incredible story, for that matter. Fiction's forte no longer lies in its limited capacity to tell a tale. Particularly since the advent of electronic audiovisual media like movies, television, and the Internet, using a novel as a means to narrate a story has already become considerably outdated, passé. Movies and television boast sounds and images, delivering the sensation of being right there at the scene of the action. How could a novel compete? If you've got the lay of the land in terms of the current state of artistic heterogeneity, then you're likely to agree with my evaluation that these days, it doesn't much matter what you write, but *how* you write it matters a great deal.

But this is, in fact, old hat too. Before the sea change that literature underwent during the Chinese economic reforms of the 1980s, we'd been unduly biased in our emphasis on the question of what to write, with the *how* relegated to a very secondary status. In the 1980s, though, writers like Ma Yuan and Shi Tiesheng took the lead in exploring this question of *how*, and their concerted efforts led to remarkable progress for our nation's fiction, in terms of both form and technique. But little by little, in the wake of the rise and fall of avant-garde literature, the issue of technique was put aside yet again. Especially in the 1990s, as the novel was entering its creative heyday, it seemed that telling a story had once again become fiction's primary function and that many were avoiding discussions of how one might deliberately focus on language and structure, how one might render the world with a hyperbolic, non-photographic touch. Now, six years into the twenty-first century, at a time when everyone seems to be swarming around a few hot topics, it is vital that we pay attention to questions of technique.

Whereas some might frame content and form as diametrically opposed, I think there's a sound argument to be made that they are synergetic—two opposing elements that come together to form a single unified whole. There is no such thing as form that exists completely independent of content, nor is there content that can exist completely unaltered by form. Good novels find the perfect combination of content and form, and those of us in the business should be putting a lot of effort into these technical considerations. These are immensely complicated questions, and different people will have different views. It often happens that as writers venture further in their explorations of form and become more experimental, their readership tends to dwindle, whereas a writer who tells a brilliant story will tend to have more readers. But I am a firm believer that despite their smaller audience, those novels that emphasize technique play an essential role in serious fiction. And by "serious fiction," I mean novels that go far beyond the mere portrayal of major events or the evocation of banalities like the suffering of humanity or universal love.

The very first technical element to which a writer must attend is language—polishing it so that it shines with the writer's own individuality and striving to expand our national language through such creative literary contributions. For if, in addition to producing a thoughtful novel, one is also able to push the boundaries of the Chinese language, then one can truly be considered a great writer. I reckon there aren't more than ten writers in recent history worthy of this designation. Of course, some people will disagree. When I brought this up yesterday while talking with Zhang Wei, his response was that an author's language is small potatoes, that the real meat of writing is its duty to be broad-minded and to keep a finger on the pulse of the times. He was just looking at the question of personality from a different angle. But I stand by my belief that the mechanics of choosing language carefully are indeed a vital metric. How do we distinguish our language from that of our forebears? How do we distinguish our language from that of our peers? Ultimately, it's not all that difficult to tell a new story or to write a new novel, but you could spend your whole life's energy trying to make linguistic breakthroughs in a single three-thousand-word story.

A writer's language is not determined solely by calculated efforts; our way with words is closely tied to our family background, our surroundings, and our level of education. Back in the day, I had a teacher who said that language is, in a sense, a writer's endocrine system. This might sound a bit unseemly, but what he was getting at was that even though language may look like a surface phenomenon, it is actually deeply intertwined with a writer's innate gifts and deliberate study. So from one perspective, I might feel that I am bound to write with a certain kind of language; I should just be resigned to it. But taken another way, I need not resign myself to anything because I can take every possible measure to transform my language into something else. Contemporary writers like Wang Zengqi and Lin Jinlan serve as illustrious examples, and though the books they write may not be very long, they've put a lifetime's worth of painstaking effort into their language use. Although some readers may write them off, to me Wang Zengqi's language is a clear demonstration of his discipline and development. When it comes to literary style, the scales would tip strongly in his favor, even against those of us who may have greatly exceeded him in terms of word count.

Another element I'd like to discuss is the structure of fiction, and of novels in particular. Once again, this is an important technical question that was fully appreciated in the 1980s but gradually fell by the wayside over the course of the following decade. Awash with the seeping influence of Western literature in the 1980s, we first began to pay attention to the question of structure when we encountered the "structural realism" of the Peruvian author Mario Vargas Llosa. Vargas Llosa racked his brain and put all his ingenuity into crafting distinctive structures for his novels, as is apparent in works like *The War of the End of the World* and *The Green House*, among others. Some of these structures look quite simple, as in *Aunt Julia and the Scriptwriter*, where the odd chapters tell one story and the even chapters tell another. There's nothing too complicated here, and some may dismiss it as a simple gimmick. But Vargas Llosa has written other novels wherein the structures fuse into perfect harmony with the content: the story simply wouldn't exist without its structure, and this masterful structural artistry would be impossible without the story. Vargas Llosa piqued our interest, and now here I am, twenty years later, still exploring questions of novelistic structure. By my own account, some of these explorations have been successful and others have been less so. Sometimes an imaginative structure can make things easier when I'm working with particularly challenging source material, bringing something to life that would have otherwise remained impossible, inert. The structure of a novel is also, in a sense, political. Whereas formal explorations may at times be purely aesthetic endeavors, at other times they are inseparably tied to critical questions of political structure or ideology.

What to write, and how to write it? If you want to be a writer, these are the two big questions you'll face, whether or not you choose to take them seriously. Although there's no denying that the question of what to write is important, I personally believe that in this day and age, the question of how to write is even more crucial. So, for all you students who are here today, I hope that once you've chosen a topic to write about, you won't settle for telling your story in a monotonous, pre-scripted way, and that you will prioritize considerations of language and structure.

(Translated by Ella Schwalb)

Notes

1. Jia Baoyu and Lin Daiyu are the main characters in *A Dream of Red Mansions*, one of China's Four Great Classical Novels.
2. Ah Q is the protagonist of Lu Xun's novella *The True Story of Ah Q*, which was first published in 1922.

5

Ten Major Relationships of Contemporary Literature

Speech at the Seventh Shenzhen Book Forum, November 2006

It is already so cold in Beijing that you have to put on a sweater and long underwear, yet in Shenzhen it can still be so nice and warm; the motherland is vast indeed. I've caught a little cold and the cold medicine I took has some sort of sedative in it, so I haven't been able to keep my eyes open all day. At first they just looked small, but by now my eyes have nearly disappeared.

I participated in the general assembly of the China Writers' Association a few days ago, so I didn't have time to prepare a draft for this speech today. I had no choice but to use some notes I had made for a lecture that I'll be giving after the New Year to students at Shandong University, so I'm trying it out with everyone here first. I may not be able to speak for the whole hour and a half, I'm not feeling too eloquent. But even if I can't speak for long, it will leave more time at the end for us to talk and interact. Your questions are sure to be enlightening.

"On The Ten Major Relationships of Contemporary Literature"—this title is too long and unwieldy. It will likely call to mind "Ten Major Relationships," the 1950s essay by our leader Chairman Mao. I wanted to draw from his great essay to make my own little essay, but I may be heading for a fall in trying to borrow his prestige.

One: The Relationship Between Human Literature and Class Literature

All my comrades who are a little up there in years are sure to remember this famous quotation by Chairman Mao: "In class society, everyone lives as a member of a particular class, and every kind of thinking, without exception, is stamped with the brand of a class."[1] This is true without a doubt. This framework is both an insightful exposition of the Marxist theory of class struggle and a longstanding approach to the analysis of ideological phenomena. This statement can also guide us in our pursuits of literary and artistic production and criticism. After the Yan'an Forum on Literature and Art, Chinese artists and writers deliberately kept to these guidelines in their creative endeavors, which had an enormous influence on large numbers of the literary and artistic works produced throughout the course of the revolution; for instance, *The White Haired Girl* and *Sea of Blood Deep Hatred*. These sorts of works had a remarkable impact that could almost be likened to rallying the troops. We've all heard the stories about *The White Haired Girl*. How during the war, those onstage and in the audience blended into one to the point that some soldiers watching the performance became so entranced that they got out their guns and tried to kill the actors playing the enemies on stage. Using our current perspective to look at these works from the past, it's plain that they are simplified and stylized works meant to stir up animosity among the classes and to agitate for revenge. But if we examine these works historically, we will find that they are in keeping with the demands of their era, and there's nothing to fault. Had we lived in those times, we too would have made it our supreme goal to produce writing like that.

A great amount of literature was produced in the seventeen years following liberation. If we look to fiction as our case study—as a novelist myself, I am most interested in and familiar with fiction—most works took the revolutionary war as their subject matter. By and large, the authors who wrote them had participated in the revolutionary war. There was no need for them to make anything up; everything they wrote was based on their own lives. And because their experiences were themselves so storied, so legendary, and so dramatic, their writing boasted a powerful readability. Everything the authors wrote in works like *Armed Workers Contingent Behind Enemy Lines*, *Tracks in the Snowy Forest*, and *Blazing Thunderbolt*, among others, was about their own experiences. And because these experiences were already of such legendary proportions, they only needed some minor tweaks to be transformed into highly readable texts. Those of us who were young during the Mao era went wild for these sorts of books, but if we were to reread them with our present-day sensibilities, we would surely see the characters, structure, and language as crude and simplistic. In general, they use a "binary opposition" mode in their character portrayals, highlighting clear distinctions between good and evil, beauty and ugliness—and never the twain shall meet. The good guys are unequivocally good, and the bad guys are unequivocally bad. There are practically no ambiguous situations to be found, no in-between characters. This sort of writing is particularly suited to the simple-minded youth who read them. If we nitpick the shortcomings of these Red Classics using our present-day ways of looking at things, then I believe that their most significant issue is not so much the sweetness or coarseness of their artistry, but rather the fact that the writing doesn't possess any of the author's own ideas. The thinking that guides these texts and that hangs so heavily around them is none other than Chairman Mao's, or rather Marx's, theory of class struggle. These writers intentionally took up the position of the proletariat and of the Party, using literature as an instrument of class struggle and as an instrument with which to serve the class. Although these texts may be deeply dissatisfying to us today, they were an inevitable product of society at the time, necessities of the revolutionary cause. We have no right to be too critical of our forebears, and instead we must do our best to find in these texts those things that may have been blocked from us by a past era's ways of reading. And, seeing as it's Shenzhen Reading Month, I'm going to include a few thoughts about reading in my speech here today.

I just mentioned an "era's way of reading," but what does that mean? It is simply the fact that the same book will be understood differently by two readers from different eras and different backgrounds. Lu Xun has a classic explanation of this phenomenon, in which he takes up *A Dream of Red Mansions*:

> Many Chinese people know *A Dream of Red Mansions*, or at least they know it by name. For the time being, let's put aside the question of who wrote it, and who extended it. When it comes to the essential theme of the book, readers will have all sorts of different ways of looking at things: a Confucius scholar will read this book as "changes," a Daoist scholar will read it as lasciviousness, a sentimental scholar will read it as emotionally moving, a revolutionary will read it as anti-Manchu, a gossip will read it as palace chamber secrets...[2]

A politician might read it a few other ways, and Chairman Mao would read it as class struggle. The same book will have all sorts of different effects on the different people who read it.

The second meaning of this phrase is that a single book can have a different meaning for the very same reader if she reads it at two different times. Our impressions from reading *A Dream of Red Mansions* when we were young are certainly different from our impressions upon reading it once we've grown old. As readers age and gain more experience, their interpretations of a book will change. As times change, and social mores and values too, someone reading an old book will interpret the stories and characters according to present-day sensibilities. I remember an example cited by a professor back when I was studying at the People's Liberation Army Academy. Professor Yue Daiyun talked about Auntie

Sanxian, a famous character in *Little Erhei's Marriage*. The writer, Zhao Shuli, made her out to be a negative character because she was older but still got around. She was in her forties and still dolling herself up, making herself pretty and behaving flirtatiously, even when it was her daughter's turn to be looking for in-laws. And though it was her daughter's turn to be on the prowl, Auntie Sanxian had plenty of presumptuous notions about sex, wanting to cop a feel whenever she saw a young lad pass by. Zhao Shuli was criticizing this character because her "indecent" behavior was out of step with the moral standards of the time. Rereading *Little Erhei's Marriage* today and comparing the text with our current reality, we're likely to see that Auntie Sanxian is a little over forty and that Zhao Shuli's attitude toward her is off. These days, with a little makeup and plastic surgery, I can barely tell the difference between a woman in her forties and a woman in her twenties. Is forty the cutoff point after which a woman can't make herself up or wear pretty clothes anymore? Is forty the cutoff point after which a woman can no longer want to look beautiful or think about sex? Even at seventy or eighty, a woman can still value her appearance and can still get dressed up and look for someone to marry. All of this is to say that people's moral sensibilities and value systems change with the times, and as a result, our understanding of the same character in the same book changes as well. There is also the village chief Zhang Jinfa in Hao Ran's novel *The Broad Road in Golden Light*, which was published during the Cultural Revolution era. Zhang Jinfa is an astute, worldly, and capable man with a head for economics, good at getting by. Hao Ran paints him as a negative character in the story, but reading *The Broad Road in Golden Light* again today, we'd likely say that the criticism is unwarranted. Not only that, but these days we'd say he ought to have red silk draped over his shoulders and flowers pinned to his breast and be invited onstage to give a talk.

This sort of interpretation certainly goes against the author's intention. A book's reception will keep evolving in step with society's advances. Books have their own vitality and will mature as society develops. Some books that were considered good at the time they were published will become trash, whereas others that were not valued will, in time, gradually begin to radiate their splendor.

The worldview that a reader holds while reading a book can sometimes run completely counter to the worldview they have in real life. In life, who would want a woman like Lin Daiyu as a daughter-in-law? If we had to choose a wife for our own son, it's quite likely we would choose Xue Baochai. Yet our literary critics are always criticizing the character Xue Baochai. This because she is too worldly, too practical, always urging Jia Baoyu to read, to study, to improve himself, to become an official. Meanwhile, Lin Daiyu whispers sweet nothings, she whines and moans, and she is quite serious about her puppy love. She is always hanging around Jia Baoyu, never letting him study or better himself. Reading the novel, it's only natural that we find Lin Daiyu's temperament endearing and see Xue Baochai as unrefined. My way of dealing with a problem in real life is vastly different from my view when reading a book, and yet I am the same person in both instances. As I just said, if I were choosing a daughter-in-law, I would certainly go about it just like Jia Zheng. Lin Daiyu is in poor health, consumptive, and wouldn't bear healthy children. And who could bear to wait on someone who gets upset as easily as she does? I wouldn't choose her. We've read plenty of young writers whose novels are soaked through with a rebellious outlook. The kids in the novels don't want to go to class, they defy their teachers, they won't take their tests, and they even leave school to run off and gad about. As readers, we of course think of the characters as having real personalities, and we think this sort of rebelliousness is reasonable in a novel. As we know, the reason these kids are so fed up with studying is that there are many problems plaguing our educational system and our schools. But it would be very painful for me as a parent if my own child were to defy the teacher, skip out on tests and make a mess of her report card, and ultimately leave school to go drift aimlessly. We know perfectly well that the problems facing our educational system are many, yet we do everything we can to teach our children to study hard, to listen to the teacher, and to adapt to school and get used to all sorts of rules and regulations, with the ultimate goal of testing into a good university. This all goes to show that there is a severe conflict between our selves as readers and our selves as parents.

When I become a reader, though the reader is me, he is also not me. I am one person when I'm reading a novel, and I'm a different person when I'm living or working. Reading a book can entail a splitting of the self. I think complete consistency between our identities as readers and our identities as social beings will be the telltale sign that we have reached the height of civilization because it will mean we have all become genuine and pure, people with integrated personalities. But reaching that point will be no easy feat, for when we criticize the myriad hypocrisies of our society, we are in fact criticizing ourselves.

We'd better get back to our topic, which is class literature and human literature. Looking back and thinking about these writers from the past, we see that they had rich experiences, having lived through all sorts of legendary ordeals. Some of them had solid foundations in writing and outstanding literary skills. So why doesn't their writing satisfy us today? I think it's because of the limitations placed on them by their era. The ideology of class struggle and class literature became the orienting guidelines for writing—their talents were confined by politics. In the society of the time, everything had to be in the service of class struggle, everything was prescribed by class, and everything deferred to Maoism. Writers' ideas were enfeebled because the greatest ideal and glory lay in their analyses of Maoism. Although there is a certain artistry to the Red Classics written in the seventeen years before the Cultural Revolution—we must concede their success at least in terms of their powerful readability—they have a major flaw, which is that none of these books feature the author's own ideas.

We're in the twenty-first century, and the class-struggle program has been cancelled for over twenty years now. We've met other allegedly socialist countries on the battlefield and then restored friendly, neighborly relations. We have extremely close ties with allegedly capitalist countries on all sides. Back in the day, the Kuomintang leader's animosity toward the Communist Party was completely irreconcilable, but now he has shaken hands with the General Secretary of the Communist Party at the stately Great Hall of the People, burying the hatchet. The rousing rendition of "Grandpa, You've Come Back At Last" that was performed for the occasion has swept both sides of the strait as a funny, sappy fad. It even reached the point where the song became a popular ringtone for a while. All of this is to say that the buzzwords of class struggle that guided China's major policies and its people for decades have become relics of a former era, and literature from that period is now maligned. In these new historical circumstances, our writing must take up a higher position, which is not to say that we are superior to our forebears, but only that we have been given this opportunity because of the times we live in. We must be even more open-minded in our writing, incorporating even broader visions—seeing humanity from above, positioning ourselves to cover its full breadth. Of course, in these new times we may still depict class and class struggle, along with all the intense bloodshed of resistance that happens throughout the process of vying for political power. But I think that today's writers should place themselves at a standpoint that transcends class, rather than extolling one class and criticizing another. When one class eradicates another, we must not treat it as some sort of great victory, singing its praises. We must recognize this as the horrible truth that it is, standing at the heights of humanity and looking sorrowfully upon the blood of the people. War should be regarded as an inevitable part of the evolutionary process of human society, but it should also be regarded as an enormous, painful tragedy. From the perspective of the history of the Chinese people at large, the atrocity is grievous no matter whether the Communist Party has killed a hundred thousand Kuomintang members or the Kuomintang has killed a hundred thousand Communist Party members. When they were alive, the dead were all just ordinary people, and I think that it is only through a certain elevated distance that one can write genuine human literature. Only then can a writer pen moving and influential works that will resonate with readers from different nations, different classes, and different social strata. This is the only way to avoid losing your own sense in the changing tides of politics.

The history of socialist literature counts among it a few texts that transcend narrow concepts of class. For example, a lot of great writing came out of the Soviet Union in the 1920s and 1930s, such as *And Quiet Flows the Don* by Mikhail Sholokhov, *The Forty-First* by Boris Lavrenyov, *Flight* by Mikhail Bulgakov, and *Red Cavalry* by Isaac Babel. Soviet society in the 1930s was full of terrible political strife: spies ran rampant, and the Red Terror reigned. Many writers, artists, and high-ranking military officials in the Red Army were secretly arrested and murdered, and many intellectuals were sent off to be imprisoned in concentration camps. Yet Sholokhov still managed to write *And Quiet Flows the Don*, even in this state of affairs. He was subjected to fierce criticism as soon as the book was published, and some higher-ups in the political crowd even went so far as to say that the book was trying to curry favor with the White Army and was sure to meet with enthusiastic praise from the Western bourgeoisie. Stalin sent many distinguished writers to their deaths, but he gave Sholokhov a way out. What made him want to protect Sholokhov? It's a difficult enigma. *And Quiet Flows the Don* portrays Grigori, a politically vague archetypal character born into a family of small-time landowning farmers. He was part of the Red Army, spent a period stranded with the White Army, but regardless of the side he was on, he was always a skillful fighter and gallant commander, able to charge ahead and kill the enemies. He ultimately got fed up with war, so he dismantled his rifle and braved the threat of execution to make his way home. When he got back, he saw that he and his lone son were the only ones left of the Melekhov clan, which had been so numerous in the olden days. The war and the revolution had destroyed everything he had. For a character like this to appear in a work of Soviet literature at the time is an extraordinary marvel. Stalin still authorized its publication, even in the face of so much controversy. He killed so many and did so much evil, yet the way he handled *And Quiet Flows the Don* shows that Stalin truly understood literature.

There's also Larenyov's novella *The Forty-First*, which was translated into Chinese in 1928 by Cao Jinghua. Lu Xun thought very highly of this novella, and in the 1970s it was adapted for the screen and won an award at the Cannes Festival. The story describes a female soldier in the Red Army named Maryutka who was born into extreme poverty and whose staunchness in her views is second to none. She is an exceptionally brave fighter, and after killing forty White Army soldiers, she is ordered to take on the task of escorting the captives. While she is responsible for conveying a golden-haired White Army officer, her boat capsizes and the two of them are stranded on a desert island. There is a log cabin on the island, and inside there is enough food, firewood, and tinder, so they go along living there, with no way to predict when they will be rescued. Surrounded by the boundless sea, the seagulls are their only company; they are fundamentally isolated from the world. And in this setting, she gradually begins to shed her defining class nature and to recover her human nature. The young couple fall in love and start living together. But one day, a White Army vessel appears out of nowhere upon the blue waters, and the officer runs over toward his ship. Maryutka's concept of class is suddenly reawakened, and it dawns on her that this young man running toward the ship is actually her enemy. And so she shoots. Her heart is overcome with sorrow, and she cries bitterly as she holds his corpse, her class nature and human nature wrestling fiercely within her. This story serves as a laboratory for the human soul: what sorts of struggles and trials will emerge between human nature and class nature in such unique circumstances? What manner of changes will ultimately take place? Though the situation is fictional, the results of the experiment are truly compelling. It's quite likely that such a situation never occurred at any point in the interminable revolutionary war, but the writer was able to conjure it up, placing two people in this imaginary situation to put them to the test. It is logically sound because he showed the most rational aspects of human nature, which made the story tremendously persuasive. I later found myself thinking that perhaps the difficulty of the experiment he put to their souls was not great enough—he should have made Maryutka give birth to an incredibly cute little baby with blond hair and blue eyes because then, when the White Army ship appeared, the gun would have weighed even heavier in her hands as she watched the man—who was not just her lover but also the father of her child—running toward the ship. And then, when he fell beneath the barrel of her gun as the little boy whimpered, crying out for his father, we would see the shape of Maryutka's soul once and for all.

Sholokhov, who wrote *And Quiet Flows the Don*, came from an incredibly poor peasant family, which would ordinarily have placed him squarely with the proletariat, writing proletarian fiction that took a clear-cut stand. But the things he heard and saw throughout the course of the revolutionary struggle opened his eyes to the narrowness of class as a lens through which to view the world, and to the universality of human nature. He heeded the call of his conscience and took up a position that transcended class, impartially portraying the different social strata that existed along the Don River region, showing them all without prejudice. On the most fundamental level, he wrote about people, making their fates known and describing their charm.

Mikhail Bulgakov is known for having written a great novel, *The Master and Margarita*. But in the 1930s, he actually put most of his energy into writing plays. *Flight* and *The Day of the Turbins*, both of which portray the Soviet civil war, led to great controversy in the Soviet Union and ultimately perturbed Stalin. Notwithstanding fellow writer Maxim Gorky's pleas in their defense, it proved difficult for these plays to avoid getting banned. Bulgakov, too, wrote from a human standpoint, seeing the humanity in the so-called "villains." The White Army's commanding officer in *Flight* is like Khludov—he is a murderous fiend in wartime, yet he protects a woman and has an intensely guilty conscience after he hangs a soldier. After losing the war and getting exiled, he reminisces with his former troops about the motherland, yearning for the streets of

Saint Petersburg, its streetlights in the bright white snowy mantle ... he is a complex, three-dimensional character. He is a historically realistic character, but he is even more realistic in terms of his humanity. And though the text was banned, in the end the play was still allowed to be performed. Chinese writers didn't have the courage to write anything of the sort after liberation, and even if such writing had been permitted, it's quite likely that it wouldn't have reached the same depth as Soviet writing, which drew from Russia's deep well of great humanist literature. The far-reaching influence of great masters like Tolstoy, Dostoevsky, Turgenev, Kuprin, and Bunin helped Soviet writers to write real literature, risking their lives in the face of political repression and gag rules. Meanwhile, the chronicles of Chinese literature are almost entirely blank in the period between *A Dream of Red Mansions* and the founding of the People's Republic of China, with the exception of a few muckraking books, romance novels, books about martial arts, and some fiction from the May Fourth Movement that dealt with brutal investigations of the soul in man's search for essence, faith, and deliverance. Feudal culture in China yielded no traditions of literature that touch the soul. We have too much literature and too many teachings about vengeance, but no traditions of forgiveness and repentance. There weren't too many legacies we'd inherited in terms of ideology, so when the narrow concept of class struggle came to dominate literature, the majority of writers were not only oblivious to the pain of the restrictions it placed upon them but also earnestly took this framework as their guiding standard.

By and by, as we reread the texts we have criticized, we will find to their detriment proof of the harm that the parochialism of class ideology inflicted upon literature. Take, for example, *The Rice Sprout Song* by Eileen Chang. *The Rice Sprout Song* portrays land reform on the mainland. Chang relied on other sources to write this novel because she didn't live through these events herself. Her position is extremely clear; her emotions side with the Kuomintang, and as a result, she makes a mistake that other Chinese writers have made as well: she fails to write the Communist Party village official and the land reform team members as real people.

Needless to say, her descriptions of the invasions and expropriations to which the rich peasants are subjected are still breathtaking. She brings to light many secrets of human nature; for example, when she narrates the feelings of a starving woman as she sneaks a few bites of pilfered food, and the sense that the sound of her own chewing is deafening, so loud that she fears others will hear. This description captures a psychological reality and leaves a strong impression.

The long and short of it is that in our new historical era, you can still write fiction about class struggle, about the War of Resistance against Japan, about the War of Liberation, and about land reform. But if these books are to have a wide appeal, if they are to arrive at a profound understanding of humanity and to be for all of mankind, authors must stand at the heights of humanity and write human literature from a human standpoint. This is precisely where a writer can fully express all that is called compassion and humanistic concern. I think that descriptions of the physical annihilation of one class by another in celebratory terms cannot be reconciled with our present era's value of seeking harmony. Perhaps, too, such writing threatens any harmony we may have already achieved.

Two: The Relationship between Literature and Politics

Twenty years ago, I wrote a novel called *The Garlic Ballads.* In the novel's preface, I wrote, "Fiction writers always want to steer clear of politics, but fiction makes you get up close and personal with politics. Fiction writers are always considering the fate of humanity, but they neglect to concern themselves with their own fate. And therein lies their tragedy." I had the nerve to attribute this quote to Stalin. I felt Stalin must have said something along those lines. Later, the editor asked me for the chapter and page it came from in Stalin's collected works, and I told them it's not in there. They went on to say it would be better not to cite Stalin, and instead just leave it as a "famous quotation." All the while, I was the one who had written it. It is one of the conclusions I had come to at the time while considering the relationships between literature and politics and between writers and politics.

The Turkish writer Orhan Pamuk, this year's winner of the Nobel Prize in Literature, recently said that even though politics has always influenced his life, it has not influenced his writing, and he always strives to distance his work from politics as much as possible. Of Pamuk's books, I have only read *My Name Is Red*, which was published in September before the favorable reception he enjoyed among Chinese readers in the wake of the Nobel Prize announcement. About a month ago, I participated in a symposium about the novel that was convened at the Turkish embassy. At the meeting, I said that the greatest feature of Pamuk's novel, or rather that which is most worthy of our attention as Chinese writers, is the way he puts a special emphasis on the craft of fiction. His native Istanbul is geographically unique, straddling Europe and Asia. It is a place where Islamic cultures and Christian cultures coexist, getting along peacefully and influencing one another. There's a cathedral on one side of the street and a mosque on the other. Muslims in white headscarves walk around shoulder to shoulder with Christians wearing crucifix pendants around their necks, everyone enjoying one another's company. Istanbul is, in effect, the confluence of European and Asian cultures. At the meeting, I talked about how when cold and warm air currents meet, there's bound to be heavy rain. The places where warm and cold ocean currents flow together are often the richest places in the sea, where fish breed most actively. And the places where many cultures blend together and coexist will always make possible the emergence of new ideas and new art. So it's no accident that Istanbul gave rise to a writer like Pamuk. His work really doesn't describe politics directly. *My Name Is Red* describes the lives of a group of painters, miniaturists. The book has a subplot about a murder case, and he lets us hear the voices of trees, dogs, dead people, rooms, and objects—there is a multitude of narrative perspectives. He is a writer who places high value on both craft and tradition, and he takes great pains to avoid describing and criticizing present-day politics. This is his approach to writing fiction. But in his appearances as a public intellectual, he is a fierce critic, a political activist who pulls no punches. In a recent interview with a Swiss newspaper, he said publicly that a million Armenians and Kurds had been massacred throughout Turkish history. The Turkish government was greatly displeased with this assertion and brought him to court on charges of libel and insulting the nation. He was later let off, but only after there was international pressure (Turkey was trying to join the EU at the time). During the symposium, a newspaper reporter asked a Turkish embassy official, "How do you all regard Pamuk? How do you feel about his winning the prize? What about the lawsuit against him last year?" I remember the embassy official saying, "That we are hosting this symposium is an explicit declaration of our attitude. He is the pride of the Turkish people, and of the Turkish nation." All of the writers present were deeply moved by this proof that the Turkish government was still so open-minded. The official didn't demonize this writer who had aired his own country's dirty laundry and instead recognized the honor and glory that Pamuk brings to Turkey. This speaks to the open-mindedness of Turkey, and of its people. Turkey's history of massacring Armenians and Kurds is a demonstrable fact, whether or not the country acknowledges it. What I am trying to say here is that there are all kinds of positions authors can take on politics as well as on the relationship between their writing and politics.

These days, there is a lot of fiction that meddles directly in politics, taking political life as its main subject matter; for example, books on anti-corruption and about legal issues. These sorts of books enjoy a wide audience; the authors are highly esteemed within the hearts and minds of readers, and they are praised for expressing the "main theme" of society by some government departments. Still, there are many writers who do not write such books. Everyone has their own dreams, and you can't force them to do as you say. Personally, I am loath to describe current political activity directly. I prefer to describe historical life, crafting symbolic texts that are based on the present. Fiction is art, after all, and it shouldn't be burdened with the role of a news dispatch or an incident report. Fiction should still be made up, maintaining a certain distance from real life. It should be symbolic and capable of profoundly elucidating the mysteries of human emotion, of human nature. Of course, I know it's impossible for literature to be completely independent of politics. To be a writer, to be a citizen, you cannot live on the moon. Everyone still lives in a certain country, in a certain social environment. As a person, you are subject to the conditions of your environment as administered by society. Your personal life will inevitably be affected, either directly or indirectly, by politics. Some may render current events directly, through either rhapsodic praise or bitter criticism, taking an intense approach to meddling in reality. But I think we must set our gazes a little further off instead of shortsightedly pursuing instant gratification. We must leave room for more objective, flexible forms of literature that keep far away from the realm of politics.

I may sound very detached myself, but I am nowhere as coolheaded when it comes to my own creative practice. Looking back at my writing over the past twenty years, you will find many texts in which I made fierce interventions into politics. My 1987 novel *The Garlic Ballads*, for instance, was originally inspired by an event in real life. As some may know, in 1987 there was an incident involving garlic shoots in a county in southern Shandong that was well-known for its garlic production. Local protectionism, corruption, and bureaucratism among officials resulted in millions of *jin* of garlic shoots—which had been painstakingly grown and picked by farmers—to be left unsold, and they ended up rotting away. Angry farmers went to the county offices to demand a settlement from the head commissioner and local magistrate, but the head commissioner hid and sent people from the public security bureau to drive away the masses. For his safety, he even pulled wire netting over the courtyard wall of his home. As a result, the conflict grew more acute and the farmers used rotten garlic to block up the entrances to the county offices. Wild with rage, they charged, setting fire to the offices and destroying the facilities. Many farmers were ultimately arrested, and local officials were given administrative punishments or Party discipline. When I read about all this, hot-blooded rage surged through me. Though I live in the city, I am still a peasant at heart, with peasant blood flowing through my veins. All that is rural, all that is peasant, is as much a part of me as my very breath. I stand firmly with the peasants, beyond the shadow of a doubt. The weight of all my affections lies on their side. Given the situation, I wrote the whole novel in a month's time. The book mounts a sharp anti-bureaucratic attack, portraying a political instructor at a military academy. He is a Marxism-Leninism instructor, and you can practically see him as an embodiment of myself. He argues in defense of his father and of fellow villagers in the court of law, giving a lot of impassioned speeches, saying, "If a party or government does not care about the welfare of the people and instead becomes a tyrant, domineering from on high, then it is the people's right to overthrow them." At this point, the judge demands that he shut up, saying, "You need to take responsibility for what you said." I think of the impassioned speech that the instructor of politics at the military school delivered in this court as my inner voice, as the author himself speaking. On account of my extreme familiarity with rural areas and rural people, I didn't investigate the county where the garlic shoot incident took place. I just transplanted this incident to the village I knew, writing my uncles and fellow villagers into the book. While the novel makes a vehement intervention into politics, my deep-rooted experience of rural life and my knowledge of peasants and their emotional states saved this book from turning into a shallow political rag. *The Garlic Ballads* molds quite a few characters with distinctive personalities, accurately capturing the peasant mentality and depicting the atmosphere of village life in such a way that people can get a strong sense of it. This is all to say that even though I know full well that fiction should steer clear of politics, or at the very least maintain a certain distance, in reality all sorts of situations will arise that make it impossible to hold yourself back, that make it impossible to restrain yourself from ferociously lashing out against the injustices of society and the dark side of politics.

My later novel *Republic of Wine* also contains incisive political criticism. The novel is an expression of my implacable hatred of corruption. *Republic of Wine* was a relatively early anti-corruption novel within this new wave of literature, but for some reason it hasn't been included as part of the canon. In my view, it is a bit better than the later novels that took up the anti-corruption theme. Rather than writing in a realistic manner, it allegorizes the story, taking it as a symbol. The book's events and characters—in fact, everything in the book—can be seen as symbols. And beneath it all, despite the intricate style, a deep ire toward corruption and corrupt officials is expressed throughout. I think this sort of book offers a more proper form of handling an author's conscience and the relationship between politics and literary work. If a novel does nothing but denounce, criticize, and shout slogans, then even if it looks like a means of giving vent to hatred, it is in fact powerless. Events are quick to grow outdated. It is only art and characters that achieve some measure of immortality.

In the winter of 1987, I wrote a novel called *Thirteen Steps*. There was a saying going around in those days that "wielding a surgical knife isn't as good as wielding a barber's blade, and making missiles isn't as good as selling tea eggs." At the time, teachers were still a vulnerable population with low wages and poor treatment, and many people were calling for a reevaluation of the status of teachers in society. There are teachers in my own family, so in this novel I effectively spoke on behalf of teachers, but when I look back at this book now, I feel that the subject matter is already terribly antiquated. Teachers haven't been a vulnerable group for a long while. Now they're very wealthy—elementary, middle school, and university teachers alike. Of course, there are still incredibly poor rural substitute teachers in the Northwest, but I also know that in big cities like Beijing, Shanghai, and Shenzhen, many middle school teachers have all sorts of ways to get rich. They no longer need to work as private tutors, and instead can make money by getting a few people together to teach summer classes or by editing textbooks. University teachers have it even better. Those in the social sciences and literature can write or edit books while they teach, and scientific researchers can apply for all sorts of funding for themselves and can serve as consultants and program designers for others.

In short, teachers today are no longer among the ranks of the poor. As a group, teachers are no longer vulnerable, and their portrayal as such in *Thirteen Steps* is already obsolete. Fortunately, *Thirteen Steps* features a great amount of literary experimentation, exploring all kinds of perspectives in Chinese-language narrative, and so the novel does not lose its value just because the incident it describes is dated.

In a word, I think the relationship between literature and politics is a tangled skein that can't be straightened out, and the relationship between an author and politics is characterized by both the desire to dissociate from politics and the impossibility of doing so. Even if you write something that is wholly removed from reality, the influence of politics can never be discounted. What I mean is that writers should be constantly reminding themselves to keep their writing detached. Even if they want to describe politics, it's best not to do so directly. Only when the writing symbolizes events and stylizes characters will it be true literature. If it is too heavy-handed in its political content, it will be swiftly denounced and swept away by the changing times.

THREE: A BRIEF DISCUSSION OF THE RELATIONSHIP BETWEEN PRESSING CLOSE TO LIFE AND TRANSCENDING LIFE

Because it's getting late, I'll have to be brief in talking about this major relationship. Given the opportunity, I will explore them in more detail with you all.

"Pressing close to life" is a phrase that's on everyone's lips these days. When it comes to amateur fiction writers living among the people, the question of pressing close to life simply doesn't exist. If I want to write literature about wage labor and I'm a young factory worker, how can I possibly get any closer than that? I am already inside the life; I can't get any closer. This kind of slogan applies to those of us literary professionals who live in the ivory tower, who've already made a name for ourselves and don't have to worry about putting food on the table.

As a group, we began our careers in the 1980s, and after twenty years of hard work, we've earned some fame and achieved a certain level of success. Now that we have moved up and enjoy a relatively comfortable life where we need not worry about basic necessities, how can we maintain an exuberant vitality in our writing? How do we make sure our work preserves a strong flavor of life? How can we grasp this current era accurately, staying in step with the common people? The question of how to press close to life and stay familiar with the current reality, and in particular with the lives of those on the lowest rungs, is certainly there before us, but finding a solution is quite difficult. Because it's hard to press close to life when you make a special point of doing so, there's always a layer of skin in between. A contrived and pragmatic press will never be as good as real life because the experiences of real life are always more sincere and precise. For example, if I want to write a story about a miner, I can of course descend into a mine and dig coal. But it will be hard to rid myself of the subconscious knowledge that I'm a writer. My face could be smeared and jet-black, my clothes covered in soot, but deep down I won't be able to forget my identity, and the emotions I experience may not be authentic. So while going out to have experiences for myself can serve as a partial answer to the question, I still think that my own experience will be different from that of a real-life worker, dripping with sweat as he labors inside the mine. There's no way around it; everyone has their own limits. So how do we save ourselves from this trap? How can we maintain, as best we can, a bit of vitality in our work? We just need to be constantly calling our attention to these limitations and calibrating for our own identity and position. We must refrain from always seeing ourselves as "engineers of the human soul," as intellectuals, as head and shoulders above the average person. Instead, we must lower our regard for the profession of writing a bit. It is not all that sacred, nor is it all that dignified, so we must not think we should get special treatment. Lu Xun cleverly satirized the issue when he said that Heine thought poets were the most noble, and because God is so just, when poets die they go and sit around God, who offers them lots of candy to eat. You won't necessarily be at God's side when you die; a great writer must never have high expectations of going to heaven, and in fact must be prepared to descend into the maw of hell. It's a given that you must not forget your roots—you must calibrate your position in society without sanctifying yourself. You must not forget your past and where you came from, recognizing deep down that you come from the ordinary people. This is the only way to keep your fiction alive and sincere. And although this can't solve the root of the problem, we must make little improvements however we can. "Slumming it" will always inherently be a corrupt artifice. But in our current state of things in China, no one is untainted by the pervading fishy stench, so whoever goes around making unjustified denunciations of others must at least refrain from going overboard and must do their best to be aware of their own conscience.

And once you have your source material, how do you write about it? The most important thing is to never forget that fiction's primary mission is to mold archetypal characters, taking the writing from the level of realism to the level of symbolism, transcending parochial, pragmatic ideas and small-minded moral outrage. You must not fix your eyes so firmly on the problems of society that you neglect actual people. That is, you can pay attention to social problems, but your writing should go beyond merely reporting on them, treating these problems as the context in which to mold your characters. It goes without saying that we cannot count on fiction to solve society's problems. As I said at a symposium at Shanghai University this winter, "Literature must not be made into a tool for carrying out the just will of God, nor must writers become heroes pleading on behalf of the fate of the people." There is certainly nothing wrong with the fact that we writers and critics are making appeals out of concern for the common people or the fact that we want to understand their lives, especially those of marginalized groups. But I think that when it comes to writing, we cannot stop at merely portraying suffering and evil. We must go even further, using events to tell about people. The ultimate goal of what we call "pressing close to life" is in fact to transcend life. Literature must be written to symbolize life, to show the philosophical theories that are found within. It is not enough that a piece of writing simply renders life as it is. Fiction cannot be worth reading only in the present but must be worth reading in the distant future as well. In other words, we must emphasize the artistry of literature and play down its political elements; we must take an interest in current social issues, but an even deeper interest in eternal issues. And what are eternal issues, exactly? They are questions of humankind, of existence, of death, of where we come from and where we are going.

Four: The Relationship Between Writers' Ideas and the Ideas of Their Writing

I wrote the following in the afterword to my novel *Pow!* in 2003: "I always used to take pride in my lack of ideology, especially when writing fiction." This line has frequently been taken out of context and skewed, getting fierce criticism. Of course, I know it's impossible for a person to be devoid of ideology. Writers are no exception, and it's equally impossible for a book to be devoid of ideology. I said it in order to push back against what everyone else was saying. I wanted to resist the sort of ideology that feigns depth while really just playing to the lowest common denominator or passing off others' ideas as one's own. I wanted to resist the sort of ideology that cries out for rural justice from the back of a limousine. No matter how simple and unadorned your ideas are as a writer, so long as they are your own, they are valuable. If they're not your own, if they come from someone else, then you are just following the herd and are left with false ideas, which is worse than having no ideas at all.

When it comes down to it, does the writing process demand preexisting ideas, which are expressed through made-up stories after the fact? Or does life itself sprout the seeds of ideas, which are then synthesized and refined, and finally expressed through the actions of literary characters? It is the latter, without a doubt. Our literary production was governed for several long decades by a call to place "theme above all," squandering the talents of generations of writers and leaving us with a huge amount of trash that lacks any literary value whatsoever. We must be careful not to reinstate this standard that compels us not to weave our stories until we have our thinking solidly in place. Instead, writers must first be moved by life, by a vision of a character, following the threads of new ideas that peek out from the abundance of our world, and then must refine and improve upon these ideas. Some writers will find these new ideas and others will not. Throughout literary history, the majority of writers have not even been conscious of all the ideas on display in their work. All writers are subject to the limitations of their era and their upbringing and may be unaware of the true meaning of what they have written. There are many novels and many pieces of art that have more imagery than ideas. That is, the ideas contained within a writer's work go beyond the writer's own ideas. As a matter of fact, a great novel always transcends its time.

Let's take *A Dream of Red Mansions* as an example. When Cao Xueqin was writing, I don't think his intention was to portray the political struggles between the four big families in the novel, nor for his book to be a dirge for feudalism. And he surely wasn't thinking that the seed of bourgeois democratic thought would manifest in the character of Jia Baoyu. These interpretations have all been retroactively superimposed by critics and readers. More than anything else, I think that Cao Xueqin wrote *A Dream of Red Mansions* as a kind of wistful nostalgia for a bygone life of wealth and prestige. His true goal probably wasn't to bemoan the extinction of his class and of feudal society. In writing this book, his heart's true desires revolved around the progress of his descendants, his hope that one day his clan would experience a resurgence. So from this perspective, I believe Gao E's continuation in the last forty chapters is fundamentally in keeping with Cao Xueqin's original idea. You can't fancy Cao Xueqin a democrat, and certainly not a communist. He was subject to the limitations of the era and deeply lamented the fading of his family's high position and great wealth.

Then there's Pu Songling, who failed the imperial examinations and ridiculed the imperial examination system throughout his stories. Deep down, I think he was obsessed with the imperial examinations and with scholarly honors. Not long before his death, he commissioned an artist to paint a portrait of him wearing the costume of a *jiansheng*.[3] It may be easy to take a photo nowadays, but having such a portrait done in those days would have been an enormous undertaking. He had to pay the artist's commission fee in addition to providing food and accommodations. Ranking as a *jiansheng* was barely considered a scholarly honor—it could be secured with a donation or with some rubber stamping by some officials who decided to humor an old scholar because they felt bad that he kept failing his exams. It didn't count for anything, but Pu Songling still attached a great deal of importance to it. Many of his novels end with the protagonists doing brilliantly on their exams, and even if they miss the mark themselves, their descendants make the cut. Doing well as a candidate for the imperial civil service and living in luxury with a whole bevy of wives and concubines must have been the highest ideal among intellectuals at the time, and this was the life that Pu Songling longed for, deep in his heart. Had the emperor offered him a first-place ranking in exchange for burning his book, Pu Songling wouldn't have thought twice. In hindsight, had he passed the exam and placed into national, regional, or even local service, then *Strange Tales from a Chinese Studio* surely would not exist. Pu Songling had a gifted mind, but it was all in vain because he still didn't pass the exam. So when he wasn't teaching, he would sit at the head of his *kang* as the cold wind whistled outside and the ink froze over on his slab. A penniless old scholar who had fallen on hard times, he was deeply miserable and had no way out; he was perpetually grumbling. A deep contradiction is evident in his personality: on the one hand, he was an unrecognized talent with a bitter loathing of the dark disorders of the imperial examination system, but on the other hand, he could not shake off the fetters of his era, and so he envied the lucky dogs who passed the exam with all his heart. This is a deep conflict that gives his writing with a certain duality, granting it eternal worth.

I think the artistic value of his work would be reduced had he been a diehard critic of the imperial examination system, though of course the same would be true had he been a firm supporter or beneficiary of it. So I would venture to say that the artistic value and expressive power of a piece of writing do not correspond directly to the level or scope of a writer's ideas. A higher level of thought by no means guarantees writing of greater artistic worth.

All great fiction is grander in ideas than in imagery because the book's ideas go beyond the images of its characters and beyond even the author's own ideas. If a text achieves this double feat of "going beyond," then I think there's no doubt that it's a very good piece of writing. By looking at the behavior of characters in these novels, we can glimpse of the dawn of a new era, the first glimmers of new ideas. And when we look at the novel as a whole, we can see the ways it transcends the thinking of its author. There are many people these days who go around criticizing writers for their lack of ideas, but these people aren't necessarily right. A writer does not need to become a philosopher or a thinker first. It goes without saying that Lu Xun's thinking is incredibly deep, that he is a great thinker. But his great ideas aren't particularly well-matched to his fiction. The incisive scrutiny of the ideas that Lu Xun spearheaded in his later essays surely surpasses the level of thinking in his earlier novels; for various reasons, he never wrote a novel that matched the thinking of his later period. Conversely, there are many writers whose thinking is clearly not very advanced or profound, who don't deliberately assume the role of "thinker," and yet their writing is actually incredibly valuable. Are Shen Congwen's ideas advanced and profound? Eileen Chang's? But aren't they splendidly successful fiction writers all the same?

FIVE: A BRIEF DISCUSSION OF THE RELATIONSHIP BETWEEN THE PERSONALITY AND THE WORK OF A WRITER

Critics these days frequently bring this topic up, and authors are fond of talking about it too. It has also been used as a weapon against people.

There is a certain competitiveness that exists between writers in the marathon of literary production. We're all writing, but when all is said and done, who will go the farthest? Who will write the best books? Who will write with a vitality that outlasts that of the others? Popular wisdom has it that the force of a writer's personality determines the final outcome. This idea isn't wrong, but I have some other ways of looking at things.

First, a writer with a lofty personality is not necessarily capable of writing a lofty novel.

Second, what is a lofty novel, after all? There has never been a single, universally accepted criterion. The English author D. H. Lawrence's novel *Lady Chatterley's Lover* was banned after its publication for promoting sex and violence, for being vulgar and obscene. But the socialist George Bernard Shaw thought it was a lofty novel and believed it should be used as a textbook for girls when they reached marriageable age. These two evaluations are as different as night and day. So what is lofty fiction? The question remains open. *The Golden Lotus* is still banned to this day; the unabridged version cannot be sold publicly in bookstores. Apparently they still print the whole thing, but solely for the eyes of high-ranking officials. That's because they're so high-minded that reading it won't lead them to sin. Evaluations of *The Golden Lotus* have always been very much at odds. Some think it a book of great compassion, whereas others see it as a fearful scourge. So I think that for many pieces of literature, a relatively clear conclusion can be reached only after a considerable number of years. It often happens that a book that at the zenith of its popularity was read by more than half the planet is, as the years go by, left forgotten. And sometimes, little by little, books that stank like human waste, or were dismissed as such by critics, have come to be highly regarded—a transformation from poison grass to fragrant flower.

Third, there are many writers who have written great books but have personalities with no shortage of obvious flaws. Nobody is perfect; everyone has faults. Some are always criticizing others and making public denouncements, but if they were to search their souls in the still of the night, they probably wouldn't dare to claim impeccable moral integrity even for themselves. Dostoevsky wrote *The Brothers Karamazov, Crime and Punishment, Notes from the Underground,* and *The Possessed*— I don't think there's anyone out there who would call into question his literary accomplishments. Nevertheless, he had many personality flaws, according to the biography written by his wife. He was a gambler, and it seems he suffered from depression and had a rotten temper—a textbook case of personality disorder. This was also the case for James Joyce, author of *Ulysses.* Some of the bookstore owners and publishing house editors with whom he was in contact hated him to the bone, yet he still wrote great literature. Sometimes the quality of writing is just completely incongruous with the writer's personality. No one could say that Pushkin, Hugo, and Tolstoy were morally irreproachable. In fact, they were quite despicable. Pushkin's journals were published in Russia a few years ago, detailing his dysfunctional relationships with women, the darkness of his heart, and the depravity of his sexual proclivities. It is hard to see the link between all that and the exquisite grace of his poetry. Tolstoy's relationships with the slave women of his estate probably weren't so noble or virtuous either, were they? Yet these things have no effect whatsoever on the eternal splendor of their masterpieces.

Then there are authors who are of noble character, good and honest to others, morally beyond reproach. There's nothing to criticize in their personal lives, and yet they lack artistic talent, imagination, a deep foundation, and unique psychological experiences, and so they are forever relegated to the ranks of mediocrity. When we have lofty goals for our writing, more often than not we end up preaching. On the flipside, some of those authors with personal flaws and missteps in their lives end up writing books that are handed down for many generations, never to be forgotten. Treating the quality of a work as being directly correlated to the writer's personality is an unscientific endeavor. I think the question should be dealt with on a case-by-case basis. Of course, we may hope that every writer has a noble personality—virtuous, kind, talented, and capable of producing great work. In a word: perfect. But this sort of person is rare indeed. You can make any demands and appeals you want, but when you're dealing with real people and real writing, you have to work with what's there, and you especially can't project criticisms about a writer's personality onto the work because these are two entirely different things. We must not treat the work and the personality of a writer as one interrelated whole, and we certainly should not equate characters in the book with the author. This may be the most basic of common sense when it comes to criticism, but a few of our critics can't seem to make peace with their disgust or hostility toward certain writers and have no scruples about violating this principle, ascribing the thoughts of the book's characters to the author's own mindset. But the pen is in their hand, and how they write is their prerogative.

Six: A Brief Discussion of Carrying On Traditions and Innovating Within the Process of Literary Production

Last week at the National Congress of China Federation of Literary and Art Circles (CFLAC), Chairman Hu Jintao spoke on this topic. He said,

> All writers and artists who have dreams and ambitions must devote major effort to bringing their spirit of creativity into full play, actively breaking new ground in the fields of literature and art and spurring on the expansion of our culture. Innovation, built upon a foundation of tradition, is key. Carrying on tradition and making innovations are the two major wheels that drive the propagation of any people's culture. Past and present, near and far, every single legendary, universally acclaimed work by a world-famous artistic or literary master is the result of an aptitude for both carrying on traditions and making innovations. Without an aptitude for carrying on traditions, there is no foundation upon which to innovate; without an aptitude for innovation, the carrying on of traditions will lose its luster. The best forms of carrying on a tradition tend to be those that yield innovations.

Artists and writers far and wide should radiate their creative fervor, stirring creative forces.

Why am I recounting these words by Chairman Hu Jintao? There was a common sentiment shared by everyone at the National Congress of China Federation of Literary and Art Circles: at no previous summit had any leader talked about innovation in such a positive light. In the past, more emphasis tended to be placed on the carrying on of tradition, and innovation wasn't mentioned much. I think of it as a change that innovation was now being talked about as a point of vital concern, the revelation of a new message. Although we continue our fine national cultural traditions, carrying them forward is no longer the goal in and of itself. Instead, the goal is to innovate on the basis of these traditions to produce something new. Otherwise, we'd just be perpetual clones of our predecessors. So I think the fact that innovation was spoken of so highly at the National Congress of China Federation of Literary and Art Circles really provides us with a guarantee from the policy side of things, encouraging all sorts of art forms and all sorts of explorations. To my mind, even failed innovations are more valuable than a mediocre reprisal of an inherited tradition.

SEVEN: A BRIEF DISCUSSION OF THE RELATIONSHIP BETWEEN PERSONALIZED WRITING AND POPULARITY

Literary creation is indeed a special kind of labor. It is highly individualized. I have said repeatedly in many of my talks and lectures on writing that maintaining individuality in one's work is one of the most fundamental requirements for a writer. If writers neglect to individualize and pursue individuality in their works, then they are not all that valuable as writers. A work of art that is thoroughly unique is effectively the product of a writer's toiling to individualize. It is the artistic expression of the writer's unique life, as refined by the writer. A text must have personality to have value. The reason we need so many writers, so many poets, so many artists, and so many musicians is that each person's work is different. And why is it different? Because each person's temperament is different, as are the life experiences they have accumulated and the education they have received. Artists' work is only valuable when they value themselves and their individuality highly. Some may challenge this way of thinking by saying, "Self-expression means writing the individual rather than writing the collective. Our mantra has always been that we must sing the praises of the people, write the people, that we must stop focusing on ourselves and our self-expression. We must write of the radiance of society and life, of sunshine and fresh flowers and never the dark sides that linger in the depths of the individual soul, and certainly no ugly, deviant thoughts." Generally speaking, these sorts of appeals aren't wrong, but I think if writers don't use themselves as starting points, their writing will simply never get off the ground. My point is just to say that writing should start with the self. There is a sort of destiny to it. Because if a writer's personal experience, personal life, and personal suffering are consistent with all of society and its common people, then this individual's writing can achieve a sort of universality—a popular, mass appeal. If such suffering is solely the writer's, or shared only by a very small group of people, then the value of his work and its universality are knocked down a few notches. Of course, a writer can make a deliberate point of trying to understand society, grasping its structures, keeping a finger on its pulse, finding out the mindsets and desires of common people, and, as much as possible, integrating the ideas born of the writer's personality and of the sufferings shared with society, with the majority of people. But at its root, I think there's no way such an effort could really resolve things. After liberation, at North China University, Shen Congwen tried to completely remold himself in the new novel he wrote. But the characters were "dead"; he just couldn't blend in with the times and was left to drag himself along on the margins. Similarly, Lao She and Cao Yu may seem to have blended in, but in fact they were still just floating on the surface. Their pen strokes bloomed in color only when they described the past; when they tried to write about the present, the words immediately took on a dull and heavy pallor because the lives they were writing weren't their own, and forcing it never works.

Literary creation is cruel like that. If your pains, joys, and impressions are out of step with the times, then using yourself as a starting point will yield writing that doesn't resonate. There was much fanfare surrounding *Red Sorghum* when it was published in the 1980s, but had I written that same book in 2006, I would have heard crickets. *Red Sorghum* was made into a movie in 1987, which caused a great stir yet again. But were this movie to come out in today's world, no one would bat an eye. So why did *Red Sorghum* provoke such a reaction in the 1980s? I think it's because it happened to line up with the needs of society at the time; the ideas expressed in the book and the emotions highlighted in the movie corresponded well with the mental state of the common people. Although freedom of thought was ramping up in the mid-1980s, a lot was still off-limits. There was intense repression of people's personalities in the decades after liberation. We were not so liberated after all. It was as though *Red Sorghum*'s enormous flaunting of personality and its booming venting of emotions happened to echo the popular attitude at the time, long-repressed and thirsty for release. So, just like that song from the movie, it reverberated for a moment all over China. In fact, this too was an instance of common people letting loose and exposing themselves. Singing was a way to free all the emotions that they'd been bottling up for so long. This sort of thing is a historical coincidence, and any author who happens to fall upon it is graced with a celestial crown of light.

EIGHT: THE RELATIONSHIP BETWEEN EMBRACING WESTERN LITERATURE AND KEEPING OUR OWN NATIONAL LITERARY TRADITIONS ALIVE

There is, of course, an eighth point about the relationship between embracing Western literature and keeping our own national literary traditions alive. But I've already touched upon this issue a lot, and I'm pretty much out of time, so I've got to quit being so verbose.

Nine: A Brief Discussion of the Relationship Between National Literature and World Literature

After eight comes nine: these days we are putting special emphasis on the need to write texts with Chinese characteristics, with a Chinese air, with a Chinese style. Chinese literature is a component of world literature, and yet it must stand apart from the thicket. I think of this as a major issue that all of us writers are faced with: How can we write books that manifest distinctly Chinese characteristics and style, while also ensuring that we are accepted by readers from countries all around the world? As I see it, we have no other choice but to find a suitable middle ground between the particular and the universal. We should be constantly deriving nourishment from the soil of our deep national cultural traditions and injecting this into our descriptions of our surroundings and lifestyles, in the molding of our characters and portrayal of their psyches, and in our pursuit of novelistic language and form. But we cannot forget that fiction's most fundamental duty is to write people, and so we must reveal the secrets of the human soul and the commonalities of human feeling, which is to say that there is a national character to certain aspects of being human, but other aspects transcend nationality altogether, such as the love of a mother or a father, or the love between a man and a woman. These elements may be expressed in different styles—enthusiastic, outrageous, or laden with hidden meanings—yet in essence they are all the same. So long as we write that which is universal and eternal in human nature, our writing can head out into the world and take up its place in world literature. Just like the Red Classics I mentioned in my first point about the relationship between human literature and class literature—they weren't bad per se, but their focus on class obscured many of the truest parts of human nature, and so they ended up narrow, works that would never join the grand ranks of world literature at large. At this point, we already have all the necessary conditions for creating world-class literature, but we have to do a good job of balancing the relationship between nationalism and cosmopolitanism. In other words, we must pay special attention to the relationship between the particular and the universal. The most fundamental point, I think, is that we must never forget human beings. As a writer, you must consider the understanding, research, and expression of human beings to be your most important duty. Because only when you show a deep and accurate understanding of people, richly describing them in colorful, extraordinary ways, will your literature be given the green light to move out toward the world.

TEN: THE RELATIONSHIP BETWEEN LITERARY PRODUCTION AND LITERARY CRITICISM

Finally, a brief discussion of the relationship between literary production and literary criticism in the context of a market economy. I think that the healthy participation of literary critics is necessary for the healthy development of literature. I've always felt that literature would be incomplete if it were only writing and no criticism.

It's no secret that the role of literary criticism has become quite complicated within the market economy. The behavior of a few bad apples has crashed clear below the lowest bar of critical ethics and brought shame upon the endeavor of literary criticism as a whole. A great many essays have, in one way or another, forgone their principles of critical impartiality. This sort of criticism does nothing to promote literature's healthy development; in fact, it is toxic. Writers should maintain sufficient respect for critics who promote normal literary health and should see serious critics as a source of help. But only those critics who have an innate sense of right and wrong should be seen as true friends. One must be tolerant of everything they say, no matter how sharply ear-piercing or unkind the words may be. Writers should expand their minds and broaden their horizons—comparing present-day situations with historical contexts and looking at things as they are with an eye to the future. In so doing, you will see through the facade of things, understand a lot, and come to realize what's truly valuable and what's just fluff.

I have received a lot of pointed criticism over the course of my literary career, and sometimes it's hard for me to keep a cool head about it. At times I've been too extreme in my rejoinders, so I'm hoping that as I age, I will be able to stay calmer when faced with criticism of my writing, and of other things as well. I also hope that our critics will be able to neutralize the influences of the market economy on their work, along with the interference of personal grudges. Critics should analyze texts with a genuine intent for literary criticism, taking a dialectical approach to the writing at hand and distinguishing between writers and their writings. The critic must focus on the work, not on the person who wrote it. Biographies, of course, are another story. So I think of the two camps, writers and critics, as both friends and enemies. Debate, even intense debate, is necessary, but it should not stir up hatred toward any individual, nor should it compromise the jointly held true, fair standards for evaluating literature.

I've gone over my allotted time for speaking here today. I am sorry, everyone, for giving such a dry, dull speech.

(Translated by Ella Schwalb)

NOTES

1. Translation from Mao Zedong, "Analysis of Classes in the Chinese Society," *Collections of Mao Zedong* (Beijing: People's Press, 1951), 5. See also https://www.marxists.org/reference/archive/mao/works/red-book/ch02.htm.
2. Lu Xun, "On A Dream of Red Mansions," *Collections of Lu Xun* (Beijing: People's Literature Press, 1980), 169.
3. *Jiansheng* designates a low-level scholarly rank.

6

My American Books

Lecture at Tattered Cover Bookstore,
Denver, Colorado, March 20, 2009

Before I start, I should mention my American translator, Howard Gold-blatt. My novels could have been translated by someone else and published in the United States, but the English versions would never have been so beautifully translated if not for him. Friends of mine who know both Chinese and English have told me that his translations are on a par with my originals. But I prefer to think they've made my novels better. I admit that some people, with dubious motives, have told me he's added things absent in the original, such as descriptions of sex. These people were ignorant of the fact that he and I have an agreement that he'll translate sex scenes in ways that will appeal to American readers, which is why the English and Chinese versions may seem different.

Howard and I began our collaboration in 1988. We've exchanged more than a hundred letters and spoken innumerable times over the telephone. The sole purpose of such frequent contact is to perfect the English translations. Often, we confer over a phrase or an object with which he's unfamiliar. Sometimes, I have to call upon my primitive drawing skills to sketch something for him. From this you can see that he is not only a talented translator but also a serious and conscientious one. It's my good fortune to be able to work with someone like him.

My first novel that was translated into English was *Red Sorghum*. Before it was rendered into English, it was made into a movie by China's renowned director, Zhang Yimou, and won a major prize at the Berlin International Film Festival. The novel became famous because of the movie. In China, when my name is mentioned, people say, "Oh, *Red Sorghum*!" Forgive my immodesty, but, as a matter of fact, *Red Sorghum* evoked strong reactions in China before it was made into a movie. So Zhang Yimou benefited from my novel; then my novel benefited from his movie.

I wrote *Red Sorghum* when I was still at the PLA Art College. It was the early 1980s, the so-called "golden age of contemporary Chinese literature." An enthusiastic readership inspired writers to become passionate about literature. People were no longer content to create or read stories written in traditional styles. Readers demanded that we be more creative, and we dreamed of nothing but becoming more inventive. A critic quipped that Chinese writers were like a flock of sheep being chased by a wolf, a wolf whose name was innovation.

At the time, I had just crawled out of mountain ditches and didn't even know how to use a telephone, let alone possess any knowledge of literary theories. So the wolf of innovation was not chasing me. I hid out at home, writing whatever I felt like writing. Now that I have some rudimentary knowledge of theory, I realize that slavishly following trends is not true innovation; real creativity is writing honestly about things you're familiar with. If you've had unique experiences, then what you write will be unique. And being unique is new. If you write something different, you will have developed a unique style. It's like singing: training can change your technique, not your voice. No matter how diligently you train a crow, it can never sing like a nightingale.

In other talks I've given, I've brought up my childhood. While city kids were drinking milk and eating bread, pampered by their mothers, my friends and I were fighting to overcome hunger. We had no idea what sorts of delicious foods the world had to offer. We survived on roots and bark, and we were lucky to scrape together enough food from the fields to make a humble meal. The trees in our village were gnawed bare by our rapacious teeth. While city kids were singing and dancing at school, I was out herding cows and sheep, and I got into the habit of talking to myself. Hunger and loneliness are themes I've repeatedly explored in my novels, and I consider them the source of my riches. Actually, I've been blessed with an even more valuable source of riches: the stories and legends I heard during the long years I spent in the countryside.

In the fall of 1998, when I visited Taiwan, I participated in a roundtable discussion on childhood reading experiences. The other writers on the panel had read many books in their childhood, books I haven't read even now. I said that my experience was different because while they read with their eyes as children, I read with my ears. Most of the people in my village were illiterate, but such words flew from their mouths that you'd have thought they were educated scholars. They were full of wondrous stories. My grandparents and my father were all great storytellers. But my grandfather's brother—we called him Big Grandpa— was a master storyteller, an old Chinese herbal doctor whose profession brought him into contact with people from all walks of life. He was very knowledgeable and had a rich imagination. On winter evenings, my brothers, sisters, and I would go to his house, where we'd sit around a dusky oil lamp, waiting for him to tell us a story. He had a long, snowy white beard but not a single hair on top. His bald head and his eyes glinted under the lamplight, as we begged him to tell us a story. "I tell you stories every day," he'd say impatiently. "How many do you think I have? Go on, go home and go to bed." But we'd keep pleading, "Tell us a story, just one." And finally he'd give in.

I've memorized some three hundred of his stories, and with minor changes, every one of them could become a pretty good novel. I haven't even used fifty of them. I doubt I could ever use up all the stories he told us. And the ones that haven't been written are far more interesting than those that have. It's like a fruit peddler who tries to sell the wormy fruit first. Someday, when the time is ripe, I plan to sell those stories of his.

Most of my Big Grandpa's stories were told in the first person, and they all sounded like personal experiences. Back then we believed they were his own stories, and it wasn't till much later that I realized he'd made them up as he went along. His stories sprang from the fact that he was a country doctor who often saw patients in the middle of the night. They always started like this:

"A couple of nights ago, I went over to Old Wang the Fifth's house in East Village to check on his wife. On my way back, as I passed that small stone bridge, I saw a woman in white sitting on the bridge and crying. I said to her, 'Big Sister, it's the middle of the night. Why are you out here all alone, and what are you crying about?' She said, 'Mister, my child is sick, he's dying. Would you go take a look at him?'" My Big Grandpa said, "I know every woman in Gaomi, so this one had to have been a demon." He asked her, "Where do you live?" The woman pointed under the bridge, "There." My Big Grandpa said, "You can't fool me. I know you're that white eel demon under the bridge." Seeing that her ploy had failed, she smiled, covered her mouth, and said, "You got me." Then, with a jerk of her head, she leaped under the bridge.

Legend had it that a white eel the size of a bucket lived beneath the stone bridge. It had transformed itself into human form to seduce my Big Grandpa. We asked him, "Big Grandpa, why didn't you go with her. Since she was so pretty..." He just said, "Dopey kids, if I had, I'd never have come back."

Then he went on to another story. A few nights earlier, he said, a man came to see him, leading a little black donkey with one hand and holding a red lantern in the other. The man said that someone in his family was very sick. Now my Big Grandpa was a very conscientious doctor, so he got dressed and left with the man. The moon was out that night, and that little black donkey shone like fine silk. After the man helped him onto the donkey, he asked, "Sir, are you all set?" My Big Grandpa said he was, so the man slapped the donkey on the rump. Big Grandpa said, "You can't believe how fast that little donkey flew. How fast? All I heard was the wind whipping past my ears, and all I saw were trees on both sides of the road whizzing backward." We were dumbstruck. That donkey must have been like a rocket. He said he knew something wasn't right, and he must have run into demons again.

What kind of demons? He didn't know, so he made up his mind to wait and find out. Before long, the donkey descended from the sky and landed in a magnificent mansion, all lit up by lamps. The man helped my Big Grandpa down as a white-haired old lady came out of the house and led him to the sickroom. It turned out to be a woman about to give birth. Country doctors had to take care of every illness in the world, so delivering a baby was no big deal. He rolled up his sleeves to help the woman deliver her baby. He said this woman was also very pretty, unsurpassably beautiful—that was his favorite phrase in describing a pretty woman. And not only beautiful, but amazingly fertile. As soon as he grabbed hold of a furry baby, out came another head. My Big Grandpa thought, "Hey, twins!" But then another furry head poked out, and he thought it must be triplets; then out came another. Just like that, one after another, she delivered eight babies, all furry, with little tails. Cute as can be. It suddenly dawned on him. "Foxes!" he shouted, but the word was barely out of his mouth when ghost-like cries and wolfish howls erupted, as darkness descended around him. Scared witless, he bit his middle finger—a fabled way of exorcising demons—and wound up in a tomb, surrounded by furry little foxes. The adults had fled.

I also heard stories from my grandmother, my father, and other talented storytelling relatives. I've committed many of them to memory. Since they were told by different people, they have distinctively different flavors. If I were to relate all the stories they told, my talk today would be as long as the Great Wall. So now I'll tell you about my novels.

On the surface, *Red Sorghum* seems to be about the war against Japan. But in reality, it's about the folklore and legends told by my kin. Of course, it's also about my longing for the contentment of love and a life of freedom. The only history in my head is the legendary type. Many famous historical figures were actually ordinary people, folks like us. Their heroic accomplishments were nothing but the result of embellishment over a long period of oral transmission. I've read some American reviews of *Red Sorghum*. They struck a resonant chord when they viewed my novel as folklore. This story, which I wrote in the ancient form of storytelling, has been viewed by Chinese critics as a fantastic, new innovation, and I can't help but chuckle to myself. If this is innovation, then being innovative is the easiest thing in the world.

My second novel in English was *The Garlic Ballads*, which I wrote in 1987. In the early summer of that year, a major incident occurred in Shandong County, a place famous for its garlic. The farmers had a great harvest that year but were unable to sell their crops, owing to the corruption of officials. Tons of garlic lay rotting in the fields. So the outraged farmers trashed the county government building. There was widespread fallout, with lengthy newspaper reports. In the end, the officials were dismissed, but the farmers who led the rebellion were also arrested and jailed. This incident enraged me. I may look like a writer, but deep down I'm still a peasant. So I sat down and wrote the novel; it took me a month. Of course, I moved the setting to the kingdom of my literary production: Northeast Gaomi Township. In reality, this is a book about hunger, and it is a book about rage. I wasn't thinking about innovation when I wrote it; I just felt the need to vent the anger welling up inside me. I wrote it for myself and for all my peasant brethren. But after the book was published, critics continued to insist that I was striving for innovation. They pointed out that the novel was told from three perspectives: first, that of a blind man, a balladeer; second, the objective viewpoint of a writer; and finally, the perspective of the official voice. And they called that innovation!

In my hometown, there were indeed balladeers, most of them blind men. They generally performed in groups of three: one to play the Chinese lute, one to beat a drum, and the third to sing. Some were very talented; they wove current affairs into their songs and improvised as they went along. As a child, I admired them greatly, and considered them to be true artists. When I was writing *The Garlic Ballads*, their hoarse, sad voices echoed in my ears. That, not innovation, was my muse.

My third novel is the recently published *Republic of Wine*. I began writing it in 1989 and finished it in 1992. It was published in 1993, to deafening silence. The clamoring critics had suddenly turned mute. I guess these noisy "experts" were shocked. They had been promoting innovation all along, but when true innovation arrived, they turned a blind eye to it.

There are still many improvements that could be made on both *Red Sorghum* and *The Garlic Ballads*, and if I were to rewrite them, I believe they'd be better. But with *The Republic of Wine*, I couldn't improve it, no matter what I did. I can boast that while many contemporary Chinese writers can produce good books of their own, no one but me could write a novel like *The Republic of Wine*. Deep down I know that even though I may look like a middle-aged man on the outside, my heart is still as young as when I was listening to my Big Grandpa's stories. I realize I'm getting older only when I look in the mirror. When I'm facing a piece of paper, I forget my age, and my heart is filled with the joy of a child. I hate evil with a passion. I ramble; I mutter as if dreaming. I rejoice. I raise hell. I'm getting drunk.

That's about all I have to say about *The Republic of Wine*. Please read this novel, which Howard and I created together. The sex scenes are from the original; he didn't spice it up one bit.

Now, he's translating my next novel, *Big Breasts and Wide Hips*, a book as thick as a brick. If you like, you can skip my other novels, but you must read *Big Breasts and Wide Hips*. In it I wrote about history, war, politics, hunger, religion, love, and sex. I tell you, if he asks me to cut some of the juicier parts, I won't do it. That's because the sex scenes in *Big Breasts and Wide Hips* are among my most gratifying accomplishments. After he finishes the translation, you'll see how well I've done!

I'm pretty drunk now, so I'll stop here.

(Translated by Sylvia Li-chun Lin[1])

NOTES

1. *World Literature Today* 74, no. 3 (Summer 2000): 473–476

PART II

ON LITERARY INFLUENCES

"I must say that in the course of creating my literary domain, Northeast Gaomi Township, I was greatly inspired by the American novelist William Faulkner and the Columbian Gabriel García Márquez. I had not read either of them extensively, but I was encouraged by the bold, unrestrained way they created new territory in writing, and learned from them that a writer must have a place that belongs to him alone. Humility and compromise are ideal in one's daily life, but in literary creation, supreme self-confidence and the need to follow one's own instincts are essential.

"At one time, I was a diligent student of Western modernist fiction, and I experimented with all sorts of narrative styles. But in the end I came back to my traditions. To be sure, this return was not without its modifications."

—Mo Yan, Nobel Lecture
(translated by Howard Goldblatt)

7

MYSTERIOUS JAPAN AND MY LITERARY JOURNEY

LECTURE AT KOMAZAWA UNIVERSITY IN JAPAN, OCTOBER 1999

MOTOJIROU KAJII'S LEMON

This is my first time setting foot on Japanese soil, despite the fact that I have described Japan's mountains, creeks, rivers, and local customs many times before in my novels. Those descriptions were all made up, crafted privately without ever checking them against reality. Now that I'm here, it's plain that my imaginary Japan was worlds apart from the real Japan. I had written a literary Japan, the likes of which can be found nowhere on this earth.

So far, my brief visit to Japan has been chock full of literature. But it might be even more apt to say that this trip has been full of mystery.

We got to the interior of the Izu peninsula, with all its hot springs and hotels, the day before yesterday just as dusk was falling. The water roared through the depths of the Nekkogawa in the hazy twilight, and the narrow road was flanked on either side by countless climbing vines and giant, dripping trees. I had the sensation that many mysterious spirits were moving about.

Mr. Kamaya Osamu of Komazawa University took me around, and our first stop was Yumotokann Inn, the small hotel where Kawabata Yasunari wrote "The Dancing Girl of Izu." I don't know what sort of sweet talk Mr. Kamaya used, but he managed to persuade the elderly gatekeeper to let me look around Kawabata's former room. I took a picture sitting on the staircase that led to his room and one on the mat he used to sit on, hoping that a little spark of genius might rub off on me. The stairs must have been authentic, but the mat was surely fake. The room was tiny but exquisitely elegant—a perfect match for Kawabata's temperament. It was as though the room had been arranged especially for him.

We left Yumotokann Inn and walked across a winding stretch of the gloomy mountain road until we reached the small hotel where Motojirou Kajii stayed while writing his story "Lemon." Kajii was a prodigy but died spitting blood at a young age, not long after finishing "Lemon." Mr. Kamaya said that "Lemon" is a brilliant story, and he remarked that it was such a pity that there are still no Chinese translations of it to this day and that even the majority of Japanese readers are unfamiliar with it. He went on to say that seventy years ago, there was no electricity here, nor was the area connected to any transportation. It was a desolate place where signs of human life were few and far between. Every night, sheltered by either the starlight or the moonlight that filled the sky above his head, Kajii would follow the twists and turns of the mountain road until he reached Yumotokann Inn, where he would discuss literature with Kawabata deep into the night. Then he would walk home alone. I wondered whether Kawabata ever saw off his pallid young guest: two literary spirits, one old, one young, walking together through the dead of night on the winding mountain road in the twinkling starlight. Mr. Kamaya said he didn't know because there was no documented account of it. Still, I stubbornly clung to the belief that this moving scene had indeed taken place.

According to Mr. Kamaya, Japanese writers established a lemon festival to commemorate Kajii after his death. Writers would come from all over the country to take part in the festival, which convened every year on the anniversary of his death. But it seems that these days the festival is on the wane, that Kajii and his lemon have been forgotten and people will no longer make the long and arduous journey to participate in his festival.

Mr. Kamaya led us from Kajii's hotel, following the steep trail as it climbed up the hill, to go see Kajii's tomb. A streak of blood-red sunset was illuminating the purple stone tablet that stood lonely, marking his grave. Something yellow glimmered atop the stone tablet. It was a lemon. Mr. Kamaya wondered aloud in amazement, "What's a lemon doing here at this time of year?" And I thought to myself: Who rushed to put this lemon here before I arrived?

Kawabata's Ghost

That night, we stayed at the Green Amagi Hotel, not far from Yumotokann Inn. It was a little bigger and more modernized than Yumotokann Inn, but there were very few travelers; it seemed we were the only people there. After dinner, each of us went off to our own room to turn out the lights and retire for the night. The rushing water sounded all the louder with just a window between me and the Nekkogawa. I was followed into dreamland by a slight nip in the air and by a slight faint-heartedness. When I got up in the middle of the night to go to the bathroom (the rooms in this hotel didn't have their own bathrooms), I was blasted head-on by a gust of cold wind, which seemed to be carrying a strong scent of perfume. A wave of tension came over me, like fear, or rather excitement. As I passed through the long, long hallway on my way to the bathroom, I heard the delicate sound of wooden-clogged footsteps on the stairs behind me. I stopped and waited, looking back with the hope of catching a glimpse of a demure Japanese beauty descending the stairs, who, like a white lotus flower, had found the cold wind too much to bear. But nobody appeared. The sound of the wooden clogs faded away too, and all that was left was the thunderous flow of the Nekkogawa. It was as though there had been no other sound at all, as though it had all been a figment of my imagination.

I entered the bathroom, a little cloud of regret hanging over my head. There were quite a few stalls, and as I pushed one open I heard the gurgle of a toilet flushing. The wooden clogs on the stairs a moment earlier may well have been a figment of my imagination, but that flushing toilet was absolutely real. I kept listening, and the sound of the water as it filled up the tank was still going, proof that there was someone else who'd gotten up in the night. Surely he'd come out soon. But for the whole time I was in the bathroom, no one came out. So, at the risk of offending someone, I opened the door to the stall where the sound was coming from—and, as I'm sure you could've guessed, there was nobody there. Back in my room, I couldn't fall back asleep. I kept listening for sounds of something astir, but other than the creek outside, there was nothing to be heard.

Later, as daybreak approached, a few rooster crows rang out from some far-off place and I found myself overcome with emotion. It had been years since I'd heard the sound of a rooster's cry, and never in my life had I heard one in such a serene and solitary environment in the mysterious hours of the early morning. The cry sounded so distant that it seemed as though hundreds of years stood between us. I recalled the line "The rooster's crow: a moon over the cottage-inn / The travelers' footprints: the frost on the plank bridge,"[1] along with similar images from the Chinese classics. Roosters used to be the alarm clocks that heralded the break of day. Hot water for washing your feet was called "tang" back then, and water for bathing was surely called tang as well. And, wouldn't you know, the character for tang is found in the Japanese script for Kawabata's former residence, the Yumotokann Inn. Our hotel had a wonderful hot spring spa on the ground floor, and a few of us had gone in for a soak the night before. Inside, the steam was curling up along the walls, the tang burbled out through the cracks in the stones, and the smell of sulfur hung heavy throughout the baths. Seeing as I couldn't sleep, and I would soon have to bid farewell to Izu and its lovely hot springs, I could see no reason not to take another dip.

I had gone downstairs to the baths alone, and since there was no one else around, I hadn't even bothered to close the door between the hot spring and the changing room. I lay back into the water and thought about the night's events in a daze. Just then, without so much as a creak, the sliding door closed before my eyes. I thought it might be a hotel worker shutting the door for me, but it had closed so gently and so silently that there simply couldn't have been anyone there.

When I went to recount my adventures to my travel companions, they didn't believe me. They said the door probably had an electric sensor. But when I went down to check, there was no sensor to be found. What's more, it was clear that the door was very seldom closed. It took quite a bit of effort to push it shut by hand, and it produced a groaning creak.

I brought it up again at breakfast, but my friends were still dubious. They thought I was trying to pull the wool over their eyes. Just then, a pair of disposable chopsticks that was set out in front of me split themselves open with a pop. This happened in full view of all my friends, and even so they still weren't ready to believe.

But I was ready to believe. If the curious events of this past night hadn't been Kawabata himself making his presence felt, then surely they were the presence of Kaoru, the little dancing girl from "The Dancing Girl of Izu."

Inoue Yasushi's Snow Bug

Yesterday morning, Mr. Kamaya took us to tour Inoue Yasushi's former home and elementary school. Off to the side of the playing field behind the school stood a tablet with a poem engraved in Inoue's own handwriting. I can't remember the words now, unfortunately, but needless to say they were marvelous. There was also a set of statues beside the pond in front of the school—on the left, a big-headed little boy with a backpack, holding a maple leaf in his hand and looking up, chasing his snow bug. (Inoue has a famous story called "Snow Bug," which, according to Mr. Kamaya, is an exceptionally beautiful insect. In late autumn when the maple leaves turn red, these bugs dance in the breeze like fluttering snowflakes, one after another. Later, at the Izu forest and literature museums, I saw snow bug specimens. It's a little transparent insect, and it is indeed utterly gorgeous. They say that when Inoue was little, he ran to chase after a fluttering snow bug on his way home from school, and that his story "Snow Bug" is a slice of his own childhood.) To the right of the boy was an older woman, either Inoue's mother or his grandmother. She was seated, and her raised hand seemed to be at once beckoning the boy home and encouraging him to wander further off. I was deeply moved by these sculptures. I felt transported back to my own childhood and felt, too, as though I could really see young Inoue Yasushi on his way home from school, chasing after a snow bug with a maple leaf in hand.

We went back to Tokyo that night. I got a call on the hotel phone from Mr. Kamaya, who told me that he had just had a mystical encounter of his own: When he got home, he opened the newspaper only to find an article about the snow bug of the Izu peninsula, with illustrations to boot. The article said that the late autumn evening sky used to be filled with the fluttering of these magical little bugs in decades past, but now they've gone extinct.

I'd collected three new short story titles so far: "Kajii Motojiro's Lemon," "Kawabata's Ghost," and "Inoue Yasushi's Snow Bug."

FOX-GIRLS ON THE STREETS OF TOKYO

The Izu peninsula was a graceful literary muse, and inspiration was brewing. But by the time we got to the bustling streets of Tokyo last night, a third of that inspiration had already slipped away, and by the time we got to Shinjuku, I was left with a mere ten percent of what I'd started with.

The streets were alive with fox-like young women, their hair dyed every color you could imagine, their platform shoes even taller than the thick-soled boots of an opera performer. Their faces were dotted with glitter, and they had on silvery lipstick, all of which sparkled under the glow of the city lights. Everything about their gestures and facial expressions made me think of foxes. And that's when I recovered my fugitive inspiration—of course it was no longer a muse of the Izu variety. This was pure Tokyo. And so I came upon my fourth short story title: "Fox-girls on the Streets of Tokyo."

Besides these fox-girls, I also found a flock of raven-teens outside the gates of the university. They were all wearing pitch-black clothes and black hats with bright brims. I didn't make the connection to ravens when I first saw them marching past on the street. The school leader had been bowing and crowing over and over throughout the parade, but it wasn't until the parade was over and he lowered the strap that had been holding the school banner that I felt in a flash how they were just like a flock of ravens, similar not only in the sounds they made but also in their dress and appearance as well. I guess that makes "Raven-teens at the University Gates" my fifth short story title.

It seemed to me that while the Japanese youth were amusing themselves, turning into foxes and ravens out on the streets, the older generations were hard at work. The highway fare collector was elderly, as were the road maintenance workers, the taxi drivers, the garbage collectors, and the scholars of Chinese literature. I thought this must be some new Japanese philosophy of life: you play your heart out when you're young, and then you start working once you can play no more. But that's enough nonsense for now. I'd better start talking about serious literary matters.

Yesterday around noon, Mr. Kamaya, Comrade Mao Danqing, and I went through Amagi Tunnel, the one made famous in Kawabata Yasunari's short story. We happened to be walking through at the same time as a group of girls from Numazu Middle School, who all began shrieking simultaneously. One girl in particular seemed to carry on for a full three minutes, and the shriek itself could have been roughly subdivided into three parts: it began in excitement and transitioned into distress before landing in a state of frenzy. A tripartite shriek that embodied three profound themes of human existence. I think I have my sixth short story title: "The Shriek of the Middle School Girl."

In fact, while I was passing through the tunnel, my mind was still stuck on "The Dancing Girl of Izu." Before going to Izu, I had dreamed of meeting a beautiful geisha in her first blush of love, just like Kaoru. I already had my brush with Kaoru's ghost, and now in the tunnel I happened to be walking alongside a group of middle school girls who were close to her in age. The parallels between the world described in the story and the one in reality were earth-shattering.

WALKING ONE OF KAWABATA'S DOGS

One day in the middle of the 1980s, I read a line from Kawabata's novel *Snow Country* that went something like this: "A powerful black dog stood on the stones by the doorway, lapping at the water."[2] A clear image appeared before my eyes, as though I could feel the warmth of the water and the dog's breath. "How about that!" I remember thinking, "It turns out you can go right ahead and write about dogs. And even the warm water of a river or the stones by the waterside can be the makings of a novel."

The first line of my story "White Dog and the Swing" goes: "Northeast Gaomi Township once produced a species of large, gentle, white dogs, but now after several generations it's very difficult to find a purebred."[3] This is the first time the phrase "Northeast Gaomi Township" appears in my fiction, and it's also the first time I make any reference to the concept of "purebred." Ever since then the genie's been out of the bottle—most of my stories now take Northeast Gaomi Township as their setting. It's my homeland, the place where I lived for over twenty years, and where I spent my whole youth. Ever since "White Dog and the Swing," it's been like the floodgates have opened. I used to think I didn't have anything to write about, but now it feels like ideas are rushing forth in a never-ending stream. It often happens that before I've finished writing one story, ideas for a few other stories start sprouting up, waiting to be written. I probably wrote a million stories during the years between 1984 and 1987. The stories from this period feature a lot of personal experiences, and many of the characters are modeled after real people.

IMAGINARY EXPANSIONS OF MY "HOMELAND"

I wrote a fragment of my own life experience in *The Transparent Carrot*, the work that made me famous. At the time, I was working not far from home at a construction site for a bridge, where I operated the bellows for a blacksmith, forging iron by day and sleeping in the construction pit at night. The production team had a jute field just outside the construction pit, and next to the jute field was a radish patch. One time, during a lull, my famished state (and gluttonous tendencies) drove me to sneak off and nab myself a radish. But alas, I was caught by the radish guard. He was very experienced. He peeled off my shoes and handed them over to the foreman. My feet were a size 30 at the time, but I sported a size 34 so that I'd be able to get a few more years of wear out of them. Kids' feet grow very quickly, you know. I used to look just like Charlie Chaplin, waddling around out there in my oversized shoes. I couldn't run fast at all, otherwise that old radish guard would have never had a chance of catching me.

The foreman of the construction site had hung up a portrait of Chairman Mao, and he made all the workers gather round it, packing themselves in like sardines. He denounced my transgression in front of everyone, and then made me stand before Chairman Mao to beg his forgiveness. The repentance process consisted of the wrongdoer first reciting a Chairman Mao quote and then confessing his crime. I remember that I recited "Three Rules of Discipline and Eight Points for Attention," which included the clauses "Do not take a single needle or piece of thread from the masses" and "Do not damage crops," which were actually quite fitting, despite the fact that I was just a hungry little urchin and not a revolutionary soldier. Weeping bitterly, I said to Chairman Mao: "Esteemed Chairman Mao, I have let you down. I forgot your teachings and I stole a radish from the production team. But I was really so hungry. From this day forward I would sooner eat grass than steal another radish from the production team...." When the foreman saw my good attitude, and that after all I was just a kid and it was a small infraction, he gave me my shoes back and let me go.

But my older brother had witnessed my big public apology to Chairman Mao. He escorted me home, beating my backside every step of the way. This sort of nasty display was typical for an adolescent kid with some good dirt on his little brother. Back home, he gave an account to our parents, and my father was livid. He felt I had caused our family to lose face. The whole family took a hand in setting me straight, with my father acting as Bruiser-in-Chief. It seemed he had learned a few tricks from the movies: he went to fetch a cord which he soaked for a bit in the brine jar for pickling vegetables, then he told me to take my trousers off—he didn't want to tear them—and flogged me with the briny rope. The party members in the movies would rather die than surrender, but here I was crying out to high heaven because of a bit of rope. My mother couldn't bear to see the ruthlessness of my father's blows, so she ran right over to her sister-in-law's house to call for my grandfather. And my grandfather came to the rescue. He said to my father, "What the hell! So the little boy nabbed a radish—what's the big deal? Does it really warrant such a beating?" Right from the get-go, my grandfather had never taken kindly to these sorts of ideas from the people's commune. He himself had stealthily worked a little unused land, and he refused to participate in production team labor. As early as 1958, he had predicted that the people's commune won't last as long as a rabbit's tail. And sure enough, his prophecy came true. But at the time he was seen as a stubborn old man, resisting the progress of history. I wrote the short story "Dry River" and the novella *The Transparent Carrot* based on this painful experience.

The character Wang Wenyi in my novel *Red Sorghum* is actually modeled on an old neighbor of mine. Not only did I write about his story; I also used his real name. I know it's not right, but at the time it felt like the words I penned would never come alive unless I used his real name. At first I was planning to change it once I finished writing, but when that day came, every name I tried felt wrong. Wang Wenyi was literate, so when the book and movie were out in our village, he both read the book and saw the movie. When he saw that I'd written his death into the book, he was furious. Leaning on a rod, he made his way over to my house to look for my father. "I'm still alive and well," he said, "but your third-born son wrote me dead in his book. I've never done anything wrong to your family, and we've been neighbors for generations. Who does he think he is, insulting me like that?" My father responded, "The first line of the novel refers to me as 'My father, a bandit's offspring.' Surely I'm no bandit's offspring. It's fiction." Uncle Wang replied, "I don't care about your family business. But I'm still alive, so I'm upset about being written dead." My father said, "Once a boy is grown, he doesn't listen to his father anymore. You'd better sort it out amongst yourselves when he gets back."

On my next visit home, I bought two bottles of wine and went to pay Wang Wenyi a visit, thinking I could apologize. "Uncle Wang," I said, "I built you up—I made you into a great hero in my book." He replied, "What kind of great hero covers his ears as soon as he hears a gunshot, shouting to his commander that his head has fallen off?" "But didn't you end up valiantly sacrificing your life?" I asked. Uncle Wang was forgiving: "In any case, it's already been written. We're grown men and we don't need to bicker about it. Why don't you go out and get two more bottles, eh? I heard you made a good deal of money from this novel of yours."

After this phase, I found that I shouldn't invariably stick to representations of my own experiences and hometown. Other people may not have been bothered by it, but it bothered me because I felt my

Northeast Gaomi Township should be an open concept, not a closed one—it should be literary, not just geographic. I created it to access the cultural and geographic environment that is so intimately linked to my childhood experiences. Northeast Gaomi Township has no fence around the perimeter. It doesn't even have national boundaries. If we say that Northeast Gaomi Township is a literary kingdom, then as its founding sovereign, I must be constantly expanding its domain. This was the line of thinking that led me to write *Big Breasts and Wide Hips*.

In *Big Breasts and Wide Hips*, I moved mountain ranges, hills, swamps, and deserts into "Northeast Gaomi Township," not to mention all sorts of plant life that had never grown in the region. When Mr. Yoshida Tomio, who translated this book, came to my homeland looking for some of the things I put in the novel, he saw that it was flat in every direction—there were no mountain ranges or hills, no deserts or swamps, and certainly none of that exotic vegetation. I know he was extremely disappointed. Mr. Fujii Shozo, who translated *Republic of Wine*, came to Northeast Gaomi Township a few years ago to see the red sorghum and didn't see that either. He'd been duped as well. But of course this expansion is not limited to enhanced geography or vegetation; more important is the expansion of thought. It is a transcendence of my homeland that I've been proposing for a few years now, and to put it in grand terms, it's a profound philosophical question. In my heart, I have a general understanding of it, but it's very hard to explain precisely in words.

Fifteen years ago, when I started writing literature in earnest, I wrote an essay called "Bold Imagination" in which I posited that a writer's most precious quality is an extraordinary imagination, the ability to imagine things as more beautiful than they really are. For example, the ocean as rendered by a writer who has never laid eyes on the sea might turn out even more majestic than an ocean as written by a fisherman's son because the one who has never seen the ocean will make of it a laboratory for his imagination.

A few days ago a reporter asked me about the reason behind the beautiful depictions of romantic love in my novels. I responded that I actually couldn't think of a single book of mine that had any such beautiful descriptions of romance. Based on the experience of some other Chinese authors, if you write beautiful love stories, you'll receive lots of fan mail from young ladies, some of whom even include charming photos of themselves as keepsakes. But to this day I haven't received any letters of the sort. I did receive one sappy letter back when I was a university student, but I later found out it was just a male classmate playing a trick on me. I responded to the reporter, saying that if he believed my novels had beautiful descriptions of romance, then who was I to disagree? And as for this question of why, it is simply rooted in the fact that I've never fallen in love. Love tends to turn dull and insipid when written by someone with a generous background in romance. I believe a novelist's emotional experiences, or imagined emotional experiences, are worth even more than real experiences. Personal experience is limited, after all, but imagination is limitless. You can court a thousand women in your imagination and even share the same bed with them. But in real life, one woman is more than enough to keep you busy.

I think it's quite likely that from now on, some of these Japanese sights will make appearances in my books. The fox-girls and the raven-teens may become characters in my stories, and if I feel like it, I might transplant them right into my very own Northeast Gaomi Township. Of course, they will be transformed, perhaps even changed beyond recognition.

"The proletariat have no nationality" used to be a booming refrain, but now it sounds hollow and sentimental. Maybe we could say: novelists have nationalities, but novels have none. The fact that I can sit here today talking such rubbish is partial proof of the truth of this statement.

Thank you all for wasting so much of your precious time to come hear me speak.

(Translated by Ella Schwalb)

Notes

1. Lu You Ji, 26: 2232, quoted in Huaichuan Mou, "The Secrets of Wen Tingyun's Life and Poetry" (PhD dissertation, University of British Columbia, 1998), 26.
2. Kawabata Yasunari, *Snow Country*, trans. Edward G. Seidensticker (New York: Knopf Doubleday Publishing Group, 1996), 46.
3. Mo Yan, "White Dog and the Swing," in *Worlds of Modern Chinese Fiction*, ed. Editor Name, trans. Michael S. Duke (Armonk: Sharpe, 1991), 41. Quotation modified by the translator.

8

The Infinite Merits
of Translators

Lecture at the opening of Peking University's
Institute for World Literature,
October 2001

Not long ago, at the summit for Moscow's application to host the Olympics, a member of the Olympic committee asked the China delegation a question: At the 2008 Olympics, would China have enough foreign-language talent to take on all the translation work? I thought the question was pretty funny. China may still have some problems in other areas, but when it comes to foreign-language talent, it can boldly say: "Yes, we've got it." China has many universities and university departments devoted to foreign-language study, as well as the Institute of Foreign Literature at the Chinese Academy of Social Sciences, and now it has an Institute of World Literature. As for the foreign-language talent needed for the Olympics, there's likely no need to even look for workers around the country when the teachers and students of Peking University could suffice—am I right? And if Peking University's foreign-language talent were not sufficient, well, mobilizing all the foreign-language talent in Beijing would likely result in a severe surplus!

I believe there is no other country in the world with a team of translators as large and excellent as China's. A few years ago, President Clinton came to Peking University to give a lecture, bringing a Chinese translator, and I believe he was one of the most excellent Chinese translators, but his Chinese carried a strange accent, his grammar was bad, and his vocabulary was markedly insufficient, whereas our stock of fluent English speakers in China is truly overflowing. And more than just English-language talent, we have vast groups proficient in French, German, Spanish, Russian, and Japanese. Why, we even have masters of the minor languages, the ones so obscure that most people have never even heard of them. Although China might not be as economically developed as Western countries, in terms of languages, we are the strongest in the world.

Translators have an enormous impact on literature, for if there were no translators, the very term "world literature" would merely be an empty placeholder. It's the creative labor of translators that allows for the emergence of literature's worldliness. Take away the labor of translators, Tolstoy's books would belong only to Russia; take away the labor of translators, Balzac would be only France's Balzac; take away the labor of translators, Faulkner would belong only to Anglophile countries, and García Márquez only to the world of Spanish. In the same way, without the labor of translators, Chinese literature would not be accessible to Western readers. Without translators, literary relationships across the world would not exist.

As a writer coming of age in the 1980s, I personally experienced the importance of studying foreign literature. If outstanding translators had not translated such voluminous amounts of foreign literature into Chinese, writers like me who don't read foreign languages would not have been able to understand the incredible achievements of foreign literature; without the creative labor of translators, Chinese literature wouldn't look at all the way it does today. Of course, some writers deny the influence of foreign literature, as if this were a good way to show how different they are from the rest. But this is, in fact, unnecessary vanity. Acknowledging the usefulness of foreign literature does not make you a lesser writer; no translator will think you any less for it. Lu Xun made great use of foreign literature, as did Guo Moruo, Mao Dun, Ba Jin, and Cao Yu. Even Zhao Shuli, that model "peasant writer," made use of foreign literature. This in no way makes them less great as writers, and perhaps it even helped them to become great. And some might retort that Cao Xueqin knew nothing of foreign literature, not even in translation, yet it was he who wrote the great *A Dream of Red Mansions*. I would reply that Cao Xueqin was a genius, and a genius of course may produce without using any models. And if we really want to quibble about it, we might remember that Cao made much use of Buddhist thought in his novel, which is, in fact, a foreign literature.

Of course, the 1980s' passion for studying foreign cultures also brought some negative phenomena. I myself had to undergo a process of change, from clumsy imitation to a subtler use of models. That's because our cultural literacy was insufficient to begin with, so when this deluge of great works from foreign countries started to come down, we were so dazzled by it all; many of us had the same feeling García Márquez describes when he read Kafka in Paris: "Damn! We can write stories like that!" Back then I read a single chapter of García Márquez's *One Hundred Years of Solitude*, then threw the book down, thinking to myself, "I can write like this!" But I quickly realized that even though I could write like that, if I did, I'd never find my own voice. If I wanted to be a good writer, I'd better learn from his work, liberate my ideas, and learn to do my own thing. If I'd gotten stuck at the "We can write stories like that!" stage, then I'd never have made it out of the "I can write like this" stage. I remember the metaphor Professor Fan Wenlan used in his great history of China: studying foreign cultures is like eating mutton; it's a matter of absorbing nutrients, not pasting pieces of meat to your body. When we study foreign writers, we eat them, absorb their nutrients, and then excrete them. Of course, we eat their work. We eat with our eyes, eat with our hearts, and not with our mouth or teeth.

Not long ago, I participated in a conference on the form of the novel in Dalian, and at this conference Professor Chen Sihe of Fudan University raised the questions: Did foreign literature translated into Chinese still count as foreign literature, or did it count as Chinese literature? Is the language of the fiction that of the original author or of the translator? For writers like me who don't know foreign languages, the translations of Latin American literature by Zhao Deming, Zhao Zhenjiang, and Lin Yi'an brought changes to our own storytelling language; so were we influenced by Latin American literature, or were we influenced by Zhao Deming and others? I can answer without hesitation that it was Zhao Deming who influenced my language, and not the Latin American writers. And who was it who was influenced by the Latin American writers? It was Zhao Deming.

Professor Chen Sihe's verdict was that in terms of literary form, translations of the greatest foreign fiction have become part of Chinese literature. And I agree with this verdict. I believe that an excellent translator must not only be an expert in foreign languages but also a master of the literary forms of that person's mother tongue. The two combined make for a grand master of language study. Their remarkable labors not only help us understand the stories and the storytelling techniques of foreign writers, illuminating intellectual concerns, but also develop the richness of the mother tongue. Their work truly deserves infinite merit. In this sense, the Peking University Institute of World Literature is an institution not only for the research and translation of foreign literature but also a cradle for the nurturing of Chinese literature; not only a place for the research and translation of foreign languages, it is also a lab for formal experiments to bring fresh substance to the Chinese language.

It has been said that the twenty-first century will be the century of the Chinese language. There's a prophecy out there that Chinese will become the most widespread and most fashionable language. Not only will Chinese continue to absorb nutrients from abroad to enrich itself, but foreign languages will enrich themselves on the nutrients of our Chinese language. But in its present state, besides ranking first for population of speakers in the world, Chinese exerts only a weak influence. When I go abroad, I'm often embarrassed and ashamed that I don't know any foreign languages, but I've discovered that no one feels ashamed that they don't know Chinese. It's as if Chinese people ought to learn foreign languages, but foreigners do not need to know Chinese. We are so friendly to foreigners who do not understand Chinese, but those foreigners are so cold to us Chinese who do not understand foreign languages. I brooded on this unfairness at first, but now I think I understand. It wasn't the foreigners who made Chinese weak; no, we did. We closed off the country, as proud and as smug as the Yelang king, refusing to learn from foreign countries, and as a result, we fell behind others in all areas. I think a great nation requires a spirit of studying other nations well, and to study other nations well is first and foremost to study their languages. Language is the heart of the nation, the soul of the nation, and the style and substance of the nation. A mark of our prosperous ages, the Han and the Tang dynasties, was our foreign-language talent. The magnificence of Han and Tang literature came only through the absorption of foreign influence. Li Bai, the great poet of the Tang dynasty, mastered foreign languages. Rich and bustling talent is a clear sign of a country in prosperity, or at least an auspicious omen of a country about to prosper. It is the mark of enlightenment, the mark of progress, the necessary condition for development, and also the mark of a nation's growing self-confidence. I believe that only when the majority of Chinese people have the facility for foreign languages will Chinese become a strong and influential language. When Chinese becomes an influential language, China will become a strong country to the world. When that happens, foreigners will feel shame and embarrassment that they do not understand Chinese. When that happens, foreign writers will pay their respects to Chinese writers. When that happens, a young foreign writer will perhaps say: "I was influenced by the Chinese writer Mo Yan." In this sense, the Institute of World Literature is not only for Peking University, and not only for China, but for all humankind.

I once said to a county chief back in my native Shandong that I would trade half my fiction to have his job. Now I can also say that I would trade the other half of my fiction to be fluent in another language. If both trades were a success, then I'd be a county chief fluent in a foreign language, with a career that would surely be glorious. But the man just said, "You wouldn't get my position with half your work or even all of it; at most, I could see you earning the position of village head with it." And I don't think I'd get a whole language in exchange for all my work; at most, I could see getting a few words. That's because I know that anyone can write fiction, but foreign languages are not so easy to master. My grandfather once told me that back in 1900 when the Germans were building the Jiaoji railway, they recruited some of the more clean-cut Chinese kids and taught them German. Grandpa said the Germans would first work on training the kids' tongues—you know, like when you train birds to talk, you first snip the birds' tongues. So you can see from that just how hard foreign languages are to learn. That's why I want to express my respect and admiration for all the experts who have mastered foreign languages. The tongues on you guys are so nimble, and your brains are so complex!

(Translated by Jesse Field)

9

Ramblings on Strindberg

Speech at Beijing University Forum on Strindberg, October 2005

Ladies and gentlemen, I am very honored to be a part of this conference, and furthermore for the chance to speak.

I did some online research in preparation for this speech, and over forty thousand search results came up for Strindberg. There's so much written up on him already that plenty of other popular writers are left in the dust. Strindberg, the "most blazing flame of Sweden," has clearly blown up in China too.

Both online and in the papers, I've seen many accounts of Mr. Ljunggren Börje, the Swedish ambassador to China, saying that "Strindberg is the Lu Xun of Sweden." It's a compelling comparison, helping those who aren't very familiar with Strindberg to get a good sense of his position, both within Swedish literature and within the broader scheme of world literature.

As it turns out, today is the anniversary of Lu Xun's passing. Here at this conference, in addition to commemorating Strindberg, we are, in a sense, commemorating Lu Xun as well.

I am neither a Lu Xun scholar nor a Strindberg scholar, yet I have felt for many years now that these two writers are connected somehow, distant echoes of one another. Not only do Lu Xun and Strindberg occupy parallel positions within Chinese and Swedish literature, respectively, but their spirits also seem somehow linked.

According to written accounts from Lu Xun's diary, in October of 1927 he bought several of Strindberg's works— *A Dream Play*, *To Damascus*, *The Defense of a Fool*, and *Black Banners*, among others. Although we cannot conclude from this fact that Lu Xun was influenced by Strindberg, we can be sure that he was indeed very familiar with Strindberg's work.

Both Lu Xun's and Strindberg's works express a tenacious determination never to make compromises with dark powers. They were both solitary fighters, thinkers who could see humanity's soul with profound clarity. They both had restless, uneasy souls and were screaming heralds whose messages were loud enough to be heard by the deaf.

Both writers challenged old art forms and created new ones. They were both masters who made contributions to the languages of their people.

Both were true modernists, avant-garde prophets who transcended their times. Many of the questions raised in their works are the very same questions facing us today, and the work they did in their time remains unfinished to this day. Their writing still has real, serious implications.

When introducing Strindberg to Chinese readers, Ambassador Börje said that Strindberg is the Lu Xun of Sweden, and I think that a Chinese ambassador introducing Lu Xun to Swedish readers could very well say that Lu Xun is the Strindberg of China.

When I read Strindberg's novel *The Red Room* in the 1980s, I felt it was rather dry and dull. Structurally, it shared some similarities with the Chinese classic *The Scholars*, but there was nothing extraordinary about it. Before long though, after reading his plays *The Father* and *Miss Julie*, I got the full sense of his writing's depth and grandeur. By and by, I ended up rereading *The Red Room*, and there, too, I saw a sort of psychological force that was worlds apart from the traditional novel. It did not draw its readers in through its plot but instead grabbed readers close through its incisive intellectual analyses.

I have been reading more Strindberg lately, thanks to Li Zhiyi's outstanding translations and Renmin University Press' five-volume publication of *Strindberg's Collected Works*. I've been deeply scorched by this "blazing flame," though of course what he is burning is not my flesh but rather my soul.

Strindberg was born in 1849; if he were alive today, he would be 156. If we estimate that human generations are spaced apart by twenty years, he should be of my great-great-grandfather's generation, a distant ancestor. But when I read his works, I don't feel in the slightest that these are by an ancestor. It feels much more as if he were from my same generation. His suffering and his ire make me think of my own suffering, my own ire. In other words, his writing resonates intensely with me.

I get the feeling that he is a rumbling contradiction, spinning round and round. Not only is he a blazing flame, he is also a river, rolling with waves. His spirit contains many opposing elements in conflict, colliding, crumbling, combining. Like silt, pebbles, weeds, animal carcasses, fish, and prawns being swept along, rolling down a river. Like a lion, a tiger, a vicious wolf, and a sheep, all locked up in the same cage at the zoo. And what's more, these rapids are constantly threatening to burst the river dam, these animals are constantly trying to break through the bars of their cage. Writing serves as a way to drain this immense energy, and so his work is really a cry sent out from the depths of his soul.

He dares to make tortuous interrogations into the souls of others but none more so than his own. His blaze has scorched many, but the one who was burned most severely was Strindberg himself. For no good reason, I have the feeling that Strindberg dressed in black and had pitch-black skin, like coal or steel. He is just like the character Mei Chien Chih in Lu Xun's story "Forging the Swords." Yan Zhi Ao Zhe says, "I bear on my soul so many wounds inflicted by others as well as by myself, that now I hate myself."[1] This saying of Yan Zhi Ao Zhe is a precise portrayal of Lu Xun's mood at the time he wrote it. It seems to me that Strindberg's feelings in his later years were extremely similar to Lu Xun's feelings in his later years. Strindberg, too, endured slander and attacks, and he, too, had a take-no-prisoners approach in his fights with enemies; both men detested their enemies and themselves simultaneously. To some degree, Strindberg's self-hatred surpassed Lu Xun's. Strindberg frequently made the case that the executioner suffers more than the executed. He considered some of his writings to be "vivisections," and rather than dissecting others, it would be better to say that he was dissecting himself. I received a lot of criticism for my own novel about the executioner and the executed, *Sandalwood Death*, before having read Strindberg so thoroughly. People said that I lacked compassion and that I was making an exhibition of cruelty. I was unable to accept these criticisms because I see myself as having a compassionate spirit and because I feel that the real cruelty lies in covering up atrocities. However, I never came up with a powerful weapon with which to refute those critiques. Now I have found a weapon in Strindberg's claim that the executioner suffers more than the executed, and if the executioner wants to mitigate that suffering, he has no choice but to look for a way to absolve his soul. In his later years, Strindberg frequently dreamed of being put on the dissection table at the Uppsala University Medical School, which is symbolic of how he had the guts to take himself apart.

I think of Strindberg as a writer who took himself as his starting point. He used personal experience as his creative source material, which was extremely abundant due to the many abnormalities in his nature and the intricate complexities of his personal life. A great deal of artistic energy was inherent in his personal experiences. His own life was tangled up with the life of society, and his own contradictions and suffering happened to fit well with the contradictions and suffering of the era. So although his writing has a dense autobiographical hue, it also moves beyond the narrow circles of personal experience and achieves universal societal significance. This rallying cry arose from the depths of his soul and turned into a cry of the people, for the people.

Strindberg, I think, tended to indulge in wishful thinking, frequently mixing up fantasy with reality and mixing up his characters with himself. As he himself said, "It's like I am walking in a dream. Imagination and life seem to have merged into one."[2] So he wrote his autobiography into a novel, and he wrote novels and drama into his autobiography. Some of his writing imitated his life, and his life, at times, imitated his writing. There were indeed many people who caused him suffering, but I think that the suffering he inflicted on himself was graver than any pain inflicted by others. This sort of person would really have a much harder time if he weren't a writer.

I also think that Strindberg's whole life was in fact his greatest work. His romance, his marriage, his struggle, his resistance, his honor, his humiliation, his writing, his research, his short-lived riches and prestige, his drifting, his myriad fans, then his finding himself utterly isolated... all of this constitutes a grand symphony. This is both *A Dream Play* and *The Ghost Sonata*, but more than that, it is the incomparably rich history of a soul.

In commemorating Lu Xun, the celebrated Chinese poet Zang Kejia once wrote, "Some people die, yet they live for eternity; some people live, yet they are already dead."[3] This statement about the first group is entirely fitting for Strindberg too. Strindberg and Lu Xun may be dead, but they are eternal. They live forever through their writing, making each generation of readers feel as though they are their contemporaries.

(Translated by Ella Schwalb)

Notes

1. Translation from https://www.marxists.org/archive/lu-xun/1926/10/x0
    1.htm.
2. *August Strindberg: Selected Essays*, trans. Michael Robinson (Cambridge
    University Press, 1988), 232.
3. Zang Kejia, "Some People," *Selected Poems by Zang Kejia* (Beijing:
    People's Literature Press, 2003), 136.

10

One Man's Bible

Speech at an Amos Oz symposium,
September 2007

In the preface to the Chinese edition of *A Tale of Love and Darkness*, Mr. Amos Oz writes, "If you made me describe all the stories in my books using a single word, I would say: family. And if you permitted me two words, I would say: unhappy family." Ten years ago at the Chinese release of his five-book volume, he said, "My novels examine the inscrutable mysteries of family life."

It's true. Throughout Mr. Oz's extensive writing career, he has maintained a passion for exploring family life, shrewdly exposing the stirring secrets and ghastly shocks that lurk within our commonplace, everyday existence. After reading Mr. Oz's work, and especially after *A Tale of Love and Darkness*, I felt that he was being too modest. The novel spans more than five hundred pages, and in it Mr. Oz has crafted a rich saga of everyday family life and a hundred years of history. Through it all, he placed his own family—a sample cell of Jewish society—within the context of Jewish and Israeli history and reality, creating the breathtaking effect of a panorama as seen through its tiniest minutia. This microcosmic style is a perfect showcase for Mr. Oz's extraordinary talents as a novelist; it is also a magnificent specimen for other writers to learn from. Beyond his accomplishments as an author, Oz is also a lucid voice on various issues currently facing society. Although he doesn't make a special point of flaunting his extra-literary expertise, his insight into questions of nationality, linguistics, and international relations is evident throughout this novel.

I read *A Tale of Love and Darkness* as though it were pure fiction, despite its heavy autobiographical overtones. The issues of Palestine and of Israel's relationships with its Arab neighbors may very well be the thorniest and most complicated in the world. Portraying these issues, relationships, and contradictions in literature is an immensely difficult challenge. It is, in a sense, the arena in which the human soul is most dramatically on display, the site where humanity's glory and disgrace both reach their fullest manifestations. It is certainly a rich deposit that ought to yield great literature, yet somehow it is still rare to see problems this big tackled in writing. Mr. Oz took it upon himself to be the literary spokesperson for these people and for this country, fulfilling literature's historical mission. As he so boldly put it in his book, "Where you are is the center of the universe."[1] Our global gaze follows Mr. Oz's pen into the world of the Jewish family as depicted in his novel. Shrouded in darkness, everything his pen touches seems to sparkle and glow.

I am a fiction writer myself, so when I read a novel, I tend to look at it first and foremost from a technical perspective. Mr. Oz molds his characters masterfully. He brings each one to life with exquisite, precise language and countless vivid details that seem to roll off the tongue. We can almost see and hear each individual character that is led out before our eyes. On his father's side, we meet the funny, vivacious grandfather (a real Romeo) and the cheerful, cordial grandmother with her daily cleaning and sweeping, the erudite great-uncle and the kindhearted, affectionate great-aunt; on his mother's side, we meet his magnanimous grandfather and long-winded grandmother. We meet his intelligent, feeble father whose talents remain unused, and his beautiful, ice-cold mother, melancholy and moody, with a heart as unfathomable as the sea. And lest we forget the steely, domineering General Ben Gurion.... In fact, dozens of household names make appearances in this book, and Mr. Oz paints even those who show up only once with that crucial, final touch, giving them the breath of life.

Mr. Oz is good at building a scene. His characters are always in motion, and their behavior, language, and rich sentiments are woven into an unbroken tapestry of life and history, rife with symbolic details. As his pen skips across the page, we follow his characters all over Jerusalem. We go into Joseph Klausner's study and follow red-faced Aunt Galita through the maze-like clothing store, getting a whiff of mothballs in the dark storeroom. We see the Arab father with two big bags under his good-natured eyes, the tape measure draped around his neck. We follow these characters into the wealthy Arab quarter where we see the girl Aaisha, with her thick unibrow, and see her little brother too. We follow the protagonist as he climbs to the top of a tree and feel his youthful effusion of affection and vanity, followed by the remorse and shame he feels when he accidentally hurts the little boy.

We follow these characters into that soul-stirring night of the United Nations vote. The stars glitter and the air trembles above the Jews who stand as still as stone out on the dark street, up against the wall, but full of hope; and then that catastrophic cry; we see his father—a refined, cultured polyglot—standing there howling, a howl without words, "as though language were not yet invented."[2] His mother and father might as well have been strangers, but now we see them embracing one another for the first time, as the fate of the nation and of the people fuses poignantly with the fate of the family. Beyond the Jewish quarter, countless Arabs silently prepare to meet the tragic fate of exile. And prepare, too, for bloodshed, for struggle, and for sacrifice—this scene was destined to be a classic, Mr. Oz's most hallowed contribution to world literature.

Later we follow our protagonist to the sun-drenched kibbutz, through the chicken coop and the meeting room, and through the smells of the communal dining hall. We see the sooty dust kicked up by the tractor as it bumps along, and then his father's embarrassment when faced with the willful insolence of his sunburned son. We follow Amos, trembling with fear, into the bare-bones office of the iron-fisted Ben Gurion and are struck by the general's singular charisma, at once frightening and magnetic. We follow Amos and his mother to the library as they look for his father, getting a taste of this dysfunctional marriage, as well as of the love and warmth that still manage to survive amid the neglect and hostility of such an oppressive family. His mother's death is the crux and the climax of the whole book. Through a loyalty that runs as deep as chromosomes, Oz reconstructs her two long walks through the rain, like a long take with the lens trained on the life of this one woman. She was always too beautiful, too smart, too sensitive, and too lovesick ever to find her place on this strip of war-torn, blood-soaked land. She departs for a distant place, like the one whence she came, and we are left speechless as her silhouette recedes.

It's clear from this book that Mr. Oz knows Jerusalem—a city exalted and jinxed in equal measure—like the back of his hand. He knows every avenue and alley, every building, every tree. And of course, above all, he knows the people who've lived there, past and present. *A Tale of Love and Darkness* has both the subtlety of Proust's *In Search of Lost Time* and the precision of Joyce's *Ulysses.* Just as Proust evokes the life of nineteenth-century French nobility and Joyce reproduces the city of Dublin, so too can reading *A Tale of Love and Darkness* make those of us who have never been to Israel feel as though we are long-time residents of Jerusalem, as though we are old family friends of the Klausners.

Beyond Mr. Oz's exceptional craftsmanship, I have an even greater admiration for the broad-mindedness that shines through his writing. He is tolerant, rational, and full of compassion. Standing at the heights of humanity, he looks out upon this piece of land and the fighting, struggle, and bitter survival of its peoples. He writes,

Now, you would think that two victims would immediately develop between themselves a sense of solidarity—as, for instance, in the poetry of Bertolt Brecht. But in real life, some of the worst conflicts are precisely the conflicts between two victims of the same oppressor. Two children of the same cruel parent do not necessarily love each other. Very often they see in each other the exact image of the cruel parent. And this is precisely the case not just between Israeli and Palestinian but between Jew and Arab.[3]

Mr. Oz is Jewish, yet his vision stretches far beyond the Jewish people; he is an Israeli citizen, yet he embraces all of humanity. Jewish peoples have wandered in exile for thousands of years, massacred by Hitler and Stalin alike. Arab peoples have suffered the depths of misery, too. The Jews established the State of Israel with the hopes of having a bit of land on which to settle down and live in peace. A reasonable, just request. Yet the Palestinians' defense of their homeland is itself a dignified endeavor. The ensuing resentment has led to rivers of blood in an entanglement of successive wars that drag on with no end in sight. The two sides, both suffering, seem as deadlocked as two mountain goats in a standoff on a narrow cliffside path.

Mr. Oz writes with clear-headed wisdom, and a spirit of repentance and forgiveness pervades his novel. The book has no bona fide bad guys, but it may very well be that the suffering good people inflict on one another is even harder to stomach. As the author himself writes, "This is not a black-and-white kind of novel. It couples tragedy and comedy, happiness and longing, love and darkness."[4] These pairings are no less than the makings of truly great literature.

It seems to me that the honesty and tolerance in *A Tale of Love and Darkness* has a sort of biblical quality to it. It is Mr. Oz's personal bible. And maybe it would be the bible for all kindhearted people because in this book we might find the secrets of our own souls.

(Translated by Ella Schwalb)

NOTES

1. Amos Oz, *A Tale of Love and Darkness*, trans. Nicholas De Lange (London: Vintage, 2005), 5.
2. Ibid., 96.
3. Amos Oz, "Between Right and Wrong," in *How to Cure a Fanatic* (Princeton, NJ: Princeton University Press, 2006), 3.
4. Amos Oz, *A Tale of Love and Darkness*, 8.

11

THE ANXIETY OF INFLUENCE

LECTURE AT THE
CHINESE-AMERICAN LITERARY FORUM,
OCTOBER 2008

The theory of economic globalization has been around for over a decade, but in the past it was always a theory and nothing more. There were no concrete effects whatsoever on ordinary people, or rather not everyone had felt the effects yet. But things are different now. The US subprime mortgage crisis triggered a financial crisis that has swept the globe, and its effects have reached ordinary people in China as well. The United States caught a cold, and now the whole world is sneezing. Our stocks are all held up, and even though they're in the bank, our funds are shrinking, losing value day and night. Those in high places are having a tough time of it, and ordinary folks are having an even tougher time. That said, this bleak period may be a perfectly opportune moment to discuss literature—after all, it is desolation, and not high spirits, that has produced the majority of good literature.

In the past few years, scholars have started to worry that globalization would lead to the homogenization of world cultures, which would naturally include the homogenization of world literature. In June 2003, I gave a lecture called "Stoic Resistance" with Wang Anyi at the Shanghai Library. "Resistance against what?" you may ask. Resistance against the homogenization of world cultures within the context of globalization. I gave the following example as part of the lecture: There are approximately seven thousand languages in the world, but they are dying out at a rate of one every two weeks. And this rate will steadily increase in the wake of scientific developments and the expansion of high-speed communications. It won't be long before there are only a few languages left on the planet. From an economic perspective, this is a good thing. But it is tremendously distressing from a cultural and artistic perspective. If economic development comes at the cost of sacrificing our cultural diversity, then this sort of economic boom is actually bad news for humanity, which would mean that "globalization" is bad news too. But reality has an iron grip, and it's not up to us to decide if we want it or not. When it comes to the economy, all we can do is grin and bear it. When it comes to culture and literature, though, there's still some room to express our own ideas.

Thanks to constant scientific advances and the ever-increasing speed and convenience of communication systems, things that used to take weeks or months to get done can now be accomplished in the blink of an eye. Just a few decades ago, it was such a grand occurrence for a Chinese person to visit America or Europe that it practically merited its own memoir—now it's no big deal. This is the context that supplies the necessary conditions for the spread and propagation of trends. Twenty years ago, a study was done on the movement of fashion trends. The researchers found that if red skirts were popular on the streets of Paris, they would become popular on the streets of Tokyo three months later, popular in Shanghai one year later, and popular in Qingdao one year after that. By the time red skirts became popular in Qingdao, the Parisian fashions would have already transitioned from red skirts to blue skirts, and then to black skirts. But nowadays, if red skirts are popular in Paris today, you'll see them on the streets of Shanghai by tomorrow. This sort of thing can even happen such that if red skirts are all the rage in

Shanghai, the skirts in Tokyo and Paris will follow suit. These days many cities are starting to look more and more alike. A few days ago, I flew from Germany to Hong Kong and then to Seoul, and I noticed that the young people were dressed almost identically. They all seemed to be wearing the same thing, down to the expressions they wore on their faces. Such circumstances present an enormous existential challenge to individuality in both literature and art. Our resistance is vital, but it is to no avail. Just as a desperate government's last-ditch bailout schemes do nothing to curb plummeting stock markets, neither can the resistance of writers and artists prevent the growing waves of artistic cloning and inbreeding. We see that Chinese and American movies are increasingly similar, that paintings and sculptures are growing harder and harder to distinguish by nationality, and that day by day it seems that the bestselling novels worldwide are all concocted according to a single formula, as though they were canned beverages.

This is by no means a new problem, nor is it a particularly big one. As a matter of fact, it is inevitable at a certain point in the development of human society. As a country, we cannot seal ourselves off from contact with the outside world on account of the present economic crisis, and neither should Chinese writers and artists use the threat of literary and artistic homogenization as a reason to reject exchanges with foreign peers. As our current circumstances become more deeply entrenched, we should seek out connections with our foreign counterparts ever more enthusiastically and audaciously, proactively learning from one another with even more openness. We should have higher standards for the ways we learn from one another than we had during our exchanges in the 1980s because we've had more than twenty years of practice at this point, gaining plenty of experience—and achieving remarkable results— along the way. In the 1980s, we may have been kneeling at the feet of our foreign peers, looking up at them in admiration. But now we can, and indeed we must, sit with them side by side and talk on an equal footing. Of course, I have many friends who hold our literature from the 1980s in low regard, and although I personally don't agree, I respect their point of view.

One of the main reasons that is often given for this low regard for writings from the 1980s is that they lack originality because of the influence of Western literature on them. I would argue that whether a piece of writing was influenced by Western literature or not has no bearing at all on its originality. It's true that our ancient literary masters Pu Songling and Cao Xueqin were probably not influenced by foreign writers because according to contemporary sources, it appears that neither of them knew any foreign languages. Cao Xueqin definitely knew Manchurian, but it's up for debate whether that counts as a foreign language, given that the Manchurians had already assumed control of the empire by then. Nevertheless, almost all of the writers from Lu Xun's generation knew other languages and were clearly influenced by foreign literature. One can plainly see the influence of foreign fiction throughout some of Lu Xun's earlier novels, but no one would argue that a work like *Diary of a Madman* is unoriginal, despite the clear traces of borrowing. We need not be so fearful of the influence of foreign literature, nor must we stigmatize it. To be sure, I had to go through a process myself before I could arrive at this sort of acceptance. In the 1980s, I never liked to hear others say that I had been influenced by foreign writers. I published an essay in *World Literature* about how I wanted to escape the blaze of García Márquez and Faulkner. I wrote that they were burning blast furnaces and I was an ice cube; if I got too close, I would melt, evaporate. My way of thinking has changed in recent years, and I now feel that there's no reason to be so anxious. García Márquez is a human being, and Faulkner too. It goes without saying that the reason García Márquez and Faulkner became masters is that their writings were original and had distinctive personalities. But their abilities to write such original work is inseparable from the ways they broadly and boldly learned from their peers. García Márquez often spoke about the influence Kafka and Faulkner had on him, regarding Faulkner as a mentor. And when, in a Paris loft, he read Kafka's *Metamorphosis,* a story that had long been familiar to writers from around the world, García Márquez was so excited that he pounded the table and rose to his full height. So it seems clear that the influence of foreign literature, or the lack thereof, must not be treated as the determining factor upon which a writer's quality is judged. One might even go so far as to say that in our present conditions, if you want to write something original, something that has personality, you must read foreign writers as much as possible, and you must do your best to thoroughly understand and master the dynamics of world literature. Of course, this isn't a hard-and-fast certainty; we can't rule out the possibility of a Pu Songling for our times.

Brilliant writers can navigate foreign literature freely and easily—as soon as they jump in, they cast off the superficial layers and get right to the marrow. And as soon as they jump back out, they put the unique sources they have gathered to good use as they make the most of their own special talents. Shen Congwen himself never spoke about being influenced by foreign writers, but he was certainly no stranger to foreign literature; even though he didn't know any other languages, he surely read plenty of works in translation. Still, there is an individuality and originality to his fiction and prose in terms of language and source material, as well as in his views on life and society. In the early 1980s, Shen Congwen's student Mr. Wang Zengqi started writing in an utterly distinct style with Chinese characteristics, in which the influence of foreign literature is completely undetectable. Nevertheless, Mr. Wang himself has said that he learned a few things from the languages of Chekhov, Hemingway, and Saroyan. These influences left no trace in his works, and therein lies his prowess. So why is it that some writers leave visible traces of those who have influenced them whereas others leave no traces at all? This question dangling before us is, I think, badly in need of answers.

I believe a brilliant writer's ability to write without showing a trace of influence by foreign peers or fellow countrymen is rooted in a strong sense of self that the writer is always careful to use as a cover, overlaying the objects of study. In addition to a writer's personality and natural gifts, this "self" also embodies a writer's life experiences and sentiments, in that the writer's existence is roused by the writings of others. So, even if the writer's creative inspiration is sparked by the words of their peers, it is the writer's own life that is illuminated by this divine light. Ultimately the works of such writers are driven by their experiences, and rather than cloning other writers in an attempt to move readers, they put into writing that which moved them the most in their own lives.

Moreover, brilliant writers do not kneel and worship at the feet of their foreign peers, regarding every word they've written as a precious gem—to engage in true study is to engage in critical study. Every piece of writing, no matter how great, has its imperfections. In the 1980s, we read foreign literature to seek out what to emulate, but we should now be looking to identify its shortcomings as a signal of our own progress. I read *One Hundred Years of Solitude* in the 1980s, and after just a few pages, I was struck by an immediate and uncontrollable urge to write. I often reached for *One Hundred Years of Solitude* as time went on, but I never read it all the way through. It wasn't until last June that I spent two weeks reading it from cover to cover—and this was because I knew I would very likely be meeting García Márquez at a conference in December. I felt a flurry of excitement when I finally finished because I saw that there were still shoddy parts, even in this book that was undeniably a classic. There are twenty chapters in the book, but García Márquez's stamina starts giving way by the eighteenth—you could almost say that he was just going through the motions in those last two chapters. I am by no means a brilliant writer, but after seeing the flaws in García Márquez, I was able to pay attention to my own progress.

In an essay about Beijing opera, Mr. Wang Zengqi once wrote, "There is a pattern in the history of literature, and that is there are only two things that save a literary form in decline: folk things and external things."[1] The homogenization of world literature can be understood as a decline, and these two magic weapons are our only possible responses. I have already roughly presented my own views on learning from foreign literature—that we must take more initiative and "take" more boldly from others' writings, all of which must be followed by earnest research and analysis. Although we must continue to study and draw on artistic commonalities—looking to writing that focuses on human beings, pressing closely to their core, and going deep into their minds—our charge is to develop an artistic personality, that is, our own touch. And what is "touch," exactly? I think it stems from the customs of our people, the psyches of our people, and the languages, histories, and feelings of our people, all of which come together to form our resplendent existence. Writings with our own touch express and reflect this existence through our unique perceptions.

Wang Zengqi once called into question a saying: "The more it represents a certain nation, the better it represents the world." I don't think there's anything wrong with this saying in and of itself, but there's a problem if this slogan is applied to reinforce national arrogance, or if national identity is reduced to the courting of exotic, contrived, or even counterfeit customs.

In short, literary diversification is impossible without bold forays into learning from foreign literature, and it's also impossible without vigorously learning from folk culture, seizing creative sources of inspiration from a robust folklife.

(Translated by Ella Schwalb)

NOTES

1. Wang Zengqi, "On the Crisis of Beijing Opera," *Chinese Theatre* 10 (1980), 27.

12

LITERATURE IS THE WORLD'S

SPEECH AT THE OPENING CEREMONY
OF THE FRANKFURT BOOK FAIR,
OCTOBER 2009

There are a lot of people in China. This is one of the most basic features of the country. A lot of people, and a lot of writers. This is another basic feature of the country. It would seem that this is the first time China has been the guest of honor at the Frankfurt Book Fair, and now, all of a sudden, there are over a hundred Chinese writers lined up here. This speaks to the fact that Chinese writers take this book fair seriously and that they've been looking forward to the chance to participate. It is a sign, too, of their humble open-mindedness, wanting to use this opportunity to learn from their peers in world literature, and from their German peers in particular. Of course, it's also evidence of the desire to take advantage of this opportunity to show off their creative ambitions to international publishing circles, to colleagues in world literature and international readers alike—not to mention that many will take this as an opportunity to tour Goethe's former residence, hoping to learn more about his background and to get a sense of the cultural and geographic atmosphere that nurtured this great soul.

When I was here last month, I told a well-known story about Goethe and Beethoven meeting a member of the Austrian royal family, and I shared a few thoughts. The story goes that Goethe and Beethoven were walking together on the street when they came across the royal procession. Goethe stepped aside to the curb and took off his hat to pay his respects, but Beethoven took no heed and went right along with his head held high. They say that he boldly pronounced: "There are and will be a thousand princes; there is only one Beethoven."[1]

When I was young, Beethoven's contempt for the higher-ups garnered my fullest admiration, whereas Goethe, who had bowed down and paid his respects, was the object of my fullest contempt. As I've gotten older, I've come to better understand Goethe as he appears in this story. It may be that Beethoven's swaggering, arrogant nonsense isn't all that difficult to pull off, whereas the lowly posture that Goethe assumed in showing respect to authority is in fact no easy feat. What I want to get at here is that when Goethe took off his hat to pay his respects, it didn't mean he was giving into or ingratiating himself with the higher-ups, nor did Beethoven's bluster prove that he didn't have a mind to butter up the aristocracy. Most artists live in two worlds—they are both ordinary people living in the ordinary world and extraordinary people living in the imagined, virtual world of art. If you step into this imaginary, virtual world without ever coming back out, that's not talent—that's just lunacy.

The attitude an artist adopts when confronted with a member of the royal court isn't important; what's important is the work the artist creates. Beethoven's greatness lies in the masterful quality of his symphonies, not in his attitude toward the royal procession. Had Beethoven spit or thrown rotten eggs at the royal procession, such audacity wouldn't have earned him the great status he enjoyed because of his masterful symphonies. And the greatness of Goethe's writing meant that even kneeling down before the flag wouldn't have tarnished his reputation. What's more is that I've always doubted the veracity of this story. There are plenty of well-known stories about famous figures that ought to raise suspicions.

During their lifetimes, great artists use the masses as creative source material; after they die, they become source material for the masses.

The great Chinese writer Cao Xueqin died in 1763, when Frankfurt's own Goethe was fourteen. Ten years later, the young German channeled his emotions from his experiences into his world-renowned novel *The Sorrows of Young Werther*. At the time, it would have been completely unthinkable for this book—brimming with resistance against feudalist rule and courting a spirit of individual freedom—to have had any sort of connection with the essence of Cao Xueqin's *A Dream of Red Mansions*.

The Sorrows of Young Werther and *A Dream of Red Mansions* are novels with two wholly different forms, yet both are classics in world literature. Judging from this, we see that literature is the integration of individuality and universality. The literature of any ethnic group will have that group's literary personality, setting that nation and its literature apart from other nations and their literatures. Literature's capacity to resonate with readers across countries and ethnic groups, to break through national and ethnic boundaries, depends on how well literature showcases the universal values that transcend such boundaries.

In Goethe's later years, he repeatedly brought up the concept of "world literature," without ever giving the phrase a straightforward definition. However, his correspondence with friends and conversation records prove that in Goethe's mind, "world literature" referred first and foremost to a kind of "intercultural dialogue and exchange." Through extensive academic reading and translations of texts, Goethe hoped to get to know the perspectives of the world's various cultures, and, with a tolerant and open mind, to understand the unity and harmony that are embodied in all living creatures, despite their differences.

Goethe's visions of world literature have rich implications for us even today. His ideas have long since broken through and extended beyond the scope of literature—his pursuit of common ground, mutual understanding and inclusion, respect for diversity, and defense of diverse ideas have been widely adopted as core doctrines in international relations.

In a newspaper interview last month, I talked about the ways foreign readers appreciate contemporary Chinese fiction. First, I hope that people overseas can read our books from a humanistic perspective, looking at the kinds of characters we mold in our writing, the mysteries of emotions we make known, the rich individuality we portray, and all that we reveal of the circumstances and fates of people's lives in history. Beyond that, I hope they appreciate our fiction from an artistic, technical standpoint, looking at the structure of our novels, for example, or getting a sense of the symbolic implications in our writings. And of course, if it's done well, the language transfer mechanism of an excellent translation can very well help them imagine the linguistic styles of our works in their original form.

Our participation in this book fair is the effective fulfillment of Goethe's theoretical concept of world literature. In this era that promotes exchange and dialogue, such interactions among writers are absolutely essential. It is a form of exchange to sit and talk face to face, and it is an even more important form of exchange to read one another's writing. Contemporary Chinese writers are no strangers to their German counterparts: Günter Grass, Heinrich Böll, Siegfried Lenz, Martin Walser, Peter Handke.... We are very familiar with these names and have delved earnestly into their important works. I can't speak for others, but for me personally, these German writers have had a profound influence on my own work. This sort of study will not drown out our individuality; it will only strengthen it. And of course, the shared human values in our fiction will be fortified as well.

One hundred years ago, two theories about Germans were floating around my hometown: one was that Germans didn't have knees, and all you had to do was push them over and they wouldn't be able to get back up. The second was that Germans had bifurcated tongues, and if you wanted to learn German, you'd have to cut your tongue open first. The Germans were building the Jiaonan-Jinan railway through my hometown at the time, and they wanted to enlist a group of children to study German. Almost all the parents tried to hide their children for fear that their tongues would be cut open.

In the 1980s, a few German students who were studying abroad at Shandong University came to my hometown, and my grandfather was completely mesmerized as he checked out their knees and their tongues. He asked me quietly: their knees look all right, and their tongues aren't split either... are they really German? When I told the students about my grandfather's doubts, they looked like they didn't know whether to laugh or to cry. So I asked them: A hundred years ago, when Germans who had never left their villages imagined Chinese people, what did they think they were like? The students didn't know what to say. I told them that once, on the island of Sicily, I saw a fresco that was over a hundred years old. Painted on it was a Chinese man with a long braid trailing down his back; he had a long, pointy mouth and was perched in a tree, looking very much like a bird. I reckoned the Germans' views of the Chinese in those days weren't so good either.

My point in telling this story is to try to explain that in centuries past, the people in my homeland demonized the Germans in their imaginations, and the Europeans did the same with their ideas about the Chinese. Had Goethe's fiction been translated into Chinese at the time, or had Cao Xueqin's novel been translated into German, there's no way the people who read those books would have come up with such strange ideas about one another. Exchange and dialogue are the most effective methods to eliminate misunderstandings and get to know one another properly—which I think may be the most fundamental goal of the Frankfurt Book Fair, and a crucial goal for those of us who are here.

So, let literature manifest its rightful effect on the interactions among nations, ethnicities, and people. And let us writers, in this time of dialogue and exchange, play our rightful roles well.

Thank you all!

(Translated by Ella Schwalb)

Notes

1. Maddy Shaw Roberts, "10 of Beethoven's most stirring quotes about music," Classicfm.com, January 25, 2021, https://www.classicfm.com/composers/beethoven/best-quotes-about-music/.

13

Fiction's Function Is Greater Than Social Criticism

Speech at the Foreign Literature Award Conferral Ceremony, December 2009

Ladies, gentlemen, friends:

Christmas season is just around the corner, and Martin Walser has come to China. All he needs is a little makeup, and he could be Santa Claus. To use a typical Walserian sentence pattern: those who want to become Santa Claus may not necessarily become Santa Claus, whereas those who don't want to become Santa Claus can't help but become him. The gift that this Santa Claus has brought for us is his new novel, *A Man in Love*. Awarding this novel the Foreign Literature Prize is our gift back to Santa Claus.

Martin Walser is a contemporary German writer with whom Chinese readers are very familiar. His novels *A Gushing Fountain, Runaway Horse,* and *Death of a Critic,* among others, have been translated into Chinese and have left deep impressions on readers. In this era of flourishing information, not only do we know of Mr. Walser's literary success, we also know of his lofty position within German literary circles and the large impact he has had on German society. Though he may never have thought of himself as having had an influence on German society outside literature, his writing has influenced Germany and, even more broadly, the world at large.

Just as Mr. Walser said in his speech moments ago, "Our first impression of a country is determined by its literature." Chinese readers' first impressions of contemporary Germany were formed through reading Günter Grass, Martin Walser, Siegfried Lenz, and other contemporary German writers. Although we can get a more direct and accurate sense of German society through electronic media these days, and even though the Germany we see there may be quite different from what we had imagined through literature, we still prefer to maintain our impressions of Germany as gleaned through literature. This is because a literary impression has an emotional hue and is built on emotional resonance. We create these impressions together with the author.

At the Frankfurt Book Fair, I once said: "Writers may have nationalities, but there are no national boundaries in literature. Literature cannot be divorced from politics, but good literature is more than politics." In his speech just now, Mr. Walser also said, "Fiction's function is greater than social criticism. The critiques of reality that inevitably show up in fiction frequently become something quite different from social criticism."[1] I think that often the primary motive that drives writers to create is not a societal event, but rather the people who are part of these events, the rich implications of their experiences and expressions, and their unique personalities. It's just like in Mr. Walser's novel *A Gushing Fountain*, for those of us who have read it. What makes this genuine literature is not just how the mother joins the Nazi Party but also her distinct ways of doing things and her unique expressions. Events will quickly grow outdated, but humanity always stays fresh.

Walser said that people who write fiction give an account of their own experiences with the help of the characters they pen. Writers publish their novels because they want to know if other people have had the same life experiences, because they want to find out if they are alone. And when readers pick up these books, they are reading their own life.[2] Although these words may seem simple, they are in fact a revelation of all the secrets of the profession of writing. A writer may write about all sorts of characters. The personalities of these characters may be as different as can be from the writer's own personality, and their feelings in the events of the novel are not direct reflections of the writer's own feelings. But for writers to make themselves fictional characters in the fictional events of their novels, they must rely on powerful imaginations and rich life experiences, on profound understandings of human nature and the ability to put themselves in other people's shoes. Just as Flaubert was able to write the flirtatious young Madame Bovary and Tolstoy was able to write the naive young Natasha, so too can Martin Walser, who is not Goethe, render Goethe vivid and lifelike.

A Man in Love shows Goethe in his later years. It is not Martin Walser, and it's certainly not Mo Yan. Still, while reading this book, I frequently felt as though I were experiencing it all myself, despite the fact that I haven't reached Goethe's level of literary achievement or his noble status, nor do I have his extensive breadth of knowledge. Be that as it may, much of Goethe's psyche and behavior in this novel were understandable to me, an ordinary Chinese writer. What's more, it even brought on a knowing smile. The contradiction between Goethe's young spirit and his aging body, as well as the resulting psychological distress, is precisely what we are all going through. And even if we don't check ourselves out in the mirror as Goethe does in the book, we've probably all done something just as laughable at one point or another. Of course, this book is much more than just a love story between two people in their twilight years. It also recounts a human predicament and the resulting mental anguish, struggle, wrestling, and ultimately transcendence. This is the literature of real people, a literature that can bring readers deep enlightenment of the spirit. Though we are not Goethe, we understand him. We see ourselves in Goethe as rendered by Walser, and even if we cannot conjure a preposterous love affair to launch us into literary greatness, we still see in this character the mysteries of humanity and the ways people make the immortal out of the absurd. Moreover, reading this kind of book can help us to understand ourselves and to understand others.

The dialogue between Chinese writers and foreign writers has been increasing exponentially in recent years, and these dialogues certainly promote understanding and fellowship. I believe, however, that the best dialogue is to read one another's literature. Though living writers may not always be dressed to the nines, each and every writer is keen on wearing some kind of clothing when out in public. But in their books, writers are like Goethe in *A Man in Love*—bare naked, without a stitch to cover them. Don't trust biographies of authors, and certainly don't trust their autobiographies. All the secrets of authors, especially the secrets deep in their hearts, can be found in their books. So I will say that even if I can't communicate with Mr. Walser directly, from having read his books, I feel as though I already know everything about him.

Finally, let's congratulate Martin Walser on receiving the 2009 People's Literature Publishing House Foreign Literature Award. And let's thank him too because though he didn't mean to, he couldn't help but become our Santa Claus, bringing us good luck and happiness.

(Translated by Ella Schwalb)

NOTES

1. "Weishanhu Award for Best Foreign Novel Announced," http://pku.
    cuepa.cn/show_more.php?doc_id=255097.
2. Ibid.

Part III

On My Own Life

"My most remorseful memory involves helping Mother sell cabbages at market, and me overcharging an old villager one *jiao* (dime)—intentionally or not, I can't recall—before heading off to school. When I came home that afternoon, I saw that Mother was crying, something she rarely did. Instead of scolding me, she merely said softly, 'Son, you embarrassed your mother today.'

"A person can experience only so much, and once you have exhausted your own stories, you must tell the stories of others. And so, out of the depths of my memories, like conscripted soldiers, rose stories of family members, of fellow villagers, and of long-dead ancestors I learned of from the mouths of old-timers. They waited expectantly for me to tell their stories. My grandfather and grandmother, my father and mother, my brothers and sisters, my aunts and uncles, my wife and my daughter have all appeared in my stories. Even unrelated residents of Northeast Gaomi Township have made cameo appearances. Of course, they have undergone literary modification to transform them into larger-than-life fictional characters."

—Mo Yan, Nobel Lecture
(translated by Howard Goldblatt)

14

THE MYSTERIOUS
COW OF MY HOME

LECTURE AT KYOTO UNIVERSITY,
OCTOBER 2003

Ladies and gentlemen,

Time is like an arrow; the days and months are like spears. The last
time I came to Japan seems like it just happened, but if I count the time
that has since passed, it's already been four years. The little puppy that
was born the last time I went to Japan is already a big dog who rules our
house; the little sapling I helped plant at the Shonen temple in Chiryu
is now a big tree. In these four years, I have gotten about a centimeter
shorter, my hair has been reduced by about three thousand strands, and
the number of wrinkles in my face has increased by about a hundred.
Sometimes I look in the mirror and can't stifle my distress at seeing the
ravages of time. But when I see the faces of all my Japanese friends, four
years seem not to have left the faintest trace. They are still strong and
healthy, their bodies still sturdy and compact, and they are still so full of
lust for life. So then I begin to feel better immediately.

On the road of literary creation, I am still a young acolyte. Using the method of writing, I can re-create my youth. With writing, I can turn back the clock. Writing is my tactic to resist time. I turn time into fiction, which I can then put to one side. Time passes, and the fiction by my side gradually piles up. In this sense, the writer can forget how old he is. A person who writes may age in body but will always remain young in spirit.

In November of 1999, I flew from Osaka to Shanghai, deplaned, rented a car, and then drove straight off to an awards ceremony in Hangzhou. My novella *Cow* had just won an award there. This was a story written from a little boy's point of view, based on my own experiences as a boy. In the early 1970s, the peasants of China still lived in a system of people's communes, with no individual freedom of movement. And the cows, which had been the peasants' partners for thousands of years, became an important livestock resource for the people's communes; the peasants were put into production teams, with no individual freedom, for the collective breeding and care of the animals. Back then, cows were sacred and not for slaughter, and even cows that had died of illness could only be distributed to commune members for food after inspection by the commune veterinarian. Because there was a lack of pasture grass, during the coldest part of winter, the production team would send me along with an old man to herd the cows out onto the fallow plains. The land was covered in icy snow, the withered grass deep beneath. In these forbidding conditions, the cows went wild again to survive. They used their mouths to dig through the piled-up snow in search of grass to fill their bellies. They used their hooves to break the ice and get at the frigid water to quench their thirst. Even now, I can't forget the sound of cow hooves knocking against the ice: "choo...choo...jang-jang!" And I can still remember how the cows' mouths would spurt milky white steam when they drank the ice water. When spring came, with its warmth and new flowers, the ice and snow melted, and all the land went green again. The cows, who had hung on bitterly all winter long, recovered their verve and vigor, fattened up, and became more active. The director of the production brigade had a good understanding of cows and gave us a solemn order: the cows must not be allowed to breed. The production brigade leaders knew that ten cows were sufficient to meet the production needs; any more would be too many to feed. Because they couldn't be sold, and they couldn't be killed for food, the cows actually became a burden. But it's not easy to stop cows from breeding. No matter how many ways the old man and I thought up to stop them from breeding, by the end of the herding season, all the female cows were pregnant; every single one carried a calf. There are some great stories about these calves. Because time is tight, I cannot relate all of these stories, but I hope that before long, my novella can be translated into Japanese for you all to read.

At that awards ceremony, I remarked that during the fifty years since the People's Republic of China was established, cows and fiction have shared a similar fate. Both were raised for a time to an important but impractical position, totally under the control of others. By the 1980s, with the collapse of the people's communes, the peasants won their freedom, and the number of cows began to increase after being very low, just like the number of works of fiction during this period. But with advances in mechanized agriculture, cows have gradually been edged out of the production process, so fewer and fewer peasants keep cows, just as the fiction of this period has gradually become a quick and simple form of entertainment, like karaoke bars, or the television dramas that also crowd the entertainment field. Now, of the peasants who keep cows, half do so to fatten them up to sell for slaughter, and the other half do so because they love what's good about animal husbandry. An old man in his dotage can mumble to his cow all he wants. Such a scene is partly saddening, partly warm and reassuring. And now, of those who write fiction, some think to profit from it, whereas others want to use it to express themselves. I, of course, am of the latter group. I can find no true friend to whom I can tell all my life's troubles, so I make fiction my friend, and it listens to me, for writing is telling, just as the farmer might confide in his old cow. The reason I speak so much here on cows is that in my next story, there will be a cow that becomes a spirit.

In the summer of 2000 I finished the novel *Sandalwood Death*, and it was published in the spring of 2001. This novel was like many of my works in that it provoked quite a lot of intense controversy. People who liked it thought it was a great work, opening new directions for twenty-first-century fiction in China. Those who didn't like it thought it was a pile of dogshit. The controversy centered on the executioner, Zhao Jia, and the scenes in which he administered torture. After the book was published, I was interviewed by reporters, and I urged women with sensitive natures not to read the work. But later events proved that many women of sensitive natures did read the work, and not only did it not give them nightmares or stop them from eating, but ironically, many seemingly strong and manly men cried like little girls and complained that I had wrecked their nerves. From this, one can see that the nerves of women are stronger than those of men. A woman wrote to me to say, "I wish you could come deliver the sandalwood death to my cheating husband." I wrote back saying, "My dear lady, although your husband's cheating heart is likely contemptible, it hardly merits the sandalwood death, and moreover such barbaric punishment has long been relegated to history. Besides, the characters in books should not be identified with their authors. I may have written about a cruel and heartless executioner, but in real life, I am quite benign, even timid. I cannot even see a chicken killed without my calves quaking."

Regarding the scenes of extreme violence in *Sandalwood Death*, I believe they were necessary; that is, artistically necessary, though not necessary for my own psyche. I think the reason these descriptions disturb some readers so much has to do with the revelation that such darkness and violence really did exist in history. The descriptions uncover an ugly and aggressive side deep in the human soul, and of course we must castigate the politicians who depend on such barbaric methods to maintain their dark and corrupt governments in an authoritarian society.

Some critics think that *Sandalwood Death* has only savagery; others say it's filled with a spirit of compassion. The latter description is closer to my original intent. Writing a book like this, I frequently face bouts of deep despair from which it is hard to extricate myself. I think to myself, Why are humans like this? How does it happen? Why would anyone punish someone of their own kind so cruelly? What gives anyone the right to torture others? Why do so many people, who seem well-meaning and humane, rush off to watch such scenes of torture as if these were part of a theater production? What is the relationship between the tyrant and the executioner? Between the executioner and the prisoner? Between the prisoner and the spectator? I found these questions very hard to answer, and my confusion caused me great and deep pain. I think there *is* confusion, not just for Northeast Gaomi Township but for all of China, and even for all of humanity. What force drives us humans, who should all be under God's hand, to perpetrate such violence? This violence has not lessened in the least even with scientific progress or advances in civilization. For this reason, while *Sandalwood Death* may seem mired in history, it truly is relevant to the world today.

Still other people say that *Sandalwood Death* is a grand fable, and I agree with this view. Yes, this particular punishment, the sandalwood death, has disappeared, but as a dark, black state of the mind and spirit, it has lasted much longer. In other words, in a certain dark part of our consciousness, some would still deal out the sandalwood death to others, some would gladly accept it, and others would just love to watch. As I wrote this work of fiction, I was the executioner Zhao Jia one moment, and the next moment I was the opera singer, the prisoner Sun Bing. One moment I was in Gaomi County, in the cracks and gaps of government, raising money, and the next moment I was the young woman Mei Niang, the nymphomaniac. On the road of human life, each person will perform different roles at different times; one can be an executioner, a learned man, and a spectator. If, after reading the book, the reader can sense the different mindsets of these kinds of characters and thereby give deeper consideration to history, the present, and human nature, then I have reached my goal.

Sandalwood Death was my first effort to marry the narrative techniques of fiction with the Mao-style opera of my home region. I wanted to create a unique form of writing that would be different not only from every other form but also from all of my earlier work. For I hoped I could make a unique voice. And the structure of the novel borrows from Chinese traditional fiction's method of "phoenix head, pig stomach, leopard tail." The plot design and character relationships are all rendered as high drama, with sharp contradictions and intense conflict. Ties of kinship and punishment link the major characters, unfolding a grand and heroic tragedy. This is dramatized fiction and fictionalized drama. The characters in the drama live less in a realistic world than in a dramatic world. At certain points, even they themselves cannot say what is drama and what is real.

The "Mao style" in the novel is basically my own invention, but Shandong does in fact have its own regional opera form. I grew up on the melodies of this minor regional opera, so as I wrote *Sandalwood Death*, these melodies rang in my ears the whole time. When I found the right narrative style for this work, the writing flowed out like river water. But I know that such language and such a style must have imposed tremendous suffering on the work's translator, Professor Tomio Yoshida. I do not know how Mr. Yoshida managed to effect the exchange.

After *Sandalwood Death*, I wrote the short stories "Snow Beauty" and "Upside Down," and these were reprinted in many journals and periodicals.

Between 2000 and 2002, I traveled to the United States, France, Sweden, and Australia, working to market the English and French versions of *The Republic of Wine* and the Swedish edition of *The Garlic Ballads*. At the end of last year, I returned to Taipei for a month as writer in residence. During these two years, I wrote very little, but I had many dream-like flights on planes. When I'm up in the air tens of thousands of feet high, I look out the cabin window under the airplane wing, at the white clouds and the dark green earth, and frequently dark feelings of despair float up into my heart and mind. The universe is so large, and humanity is so small; time and space extend forever, but human life is so short. But to think always of these problems is simply to make trouble for myself. And so, after the Spring Festival, I settled down, and within three months, I had finished the novel *POW!* And then within another week, I had written a play.

These are the major things I've done since the last time I came to Japan. I am very lazy, and I am ashamed to accept your kindness. But I hope that after I return home this time, I can whip myself into shape and get that mysterious cow of Northeast Gaomi Township to give the readers a little pleasure.

Thank you to Professor Tomio Yoshida for translating *Sandalwood Death* into Japanese, and thank you to my Japanese readers, and I hope this book makes you think.

Thanks, all.

(Translated by Jesse Field)

15

FEAR AND HOPE

LECTURE AT
NONINO WORLD LITERATURE PRIZE CEREMONY,
PERCOTO, ITALY
AUGUST 2005

When I was a child, the experience that left the deepest impression on me, besides famine and isolation, was fear. I was born and raised in a closed-off, backward village, and I was twenty-one years old before I left. There was no electricity in that village until the 1980s. Before that we just used oil lanterns and wax candles for light. Candles were a luxury item, only ever lit on major holidays like the Spring Festival. For a long time, coal and oil could only be obtained with ration tickets, and their prices were exorbitant, so oil lanterns were seldom lit. Once I wanted to turn on a light during dinner, and I said angrily to my grandmother, "If we don't turn on a light, what's to keep me from putting food up my nose?" But sure enough, even with no lights on, we still put food into our mouths and never stuffed it up our noses.

Back then, come evening, the whole village went dark, and I mean one big patch of darkness, black as lacquer, so dark that if you stretched out your hand, you wouldn't even see your fingers. To pass the long nights, old people told the children tales of ghosts and monsters. In these tales, it seemed that all plants and animals could become people or had the power to control people's thoughts. The old people gave no hint that the stories weren't true. Anyhow, we kids sure believed them. The stories made us scared, but they also made us excited. The more we listened, the more scared we got. And the more we had to listen! Many writers first get the inspiration for literature from the tales told by their grandmothers and grandfathers, and I was no exception. Thinking back on that now, those dark nights of listening to the old people tell ghost stories were actually my first literature lessons. I think the reason Denmark produced great fairy-tale writers like Hans Christian Andersen goes back to the times before electricity, and the fact that Denmark is a country with long nights. Rooms full of light don't make for fine fairy tales, or ghost stories either. Recently I went back to my hometown, and I saw that the children there are just like the children in the city, spending their nights in lit rooms, staring at the television. That's when I realized the age of ghost stories and fairy tales is over, and the kind of fear I experienced when I was young will never be part of the experiences of today's children. They may have their own fears, but those must be very different from mine.

In the stories my grandparents told, foxes often changed into beautiful women and married poor young men. Large trees could become old people walking slowly down the street. And a big old turtle from the river could turn into a strong, hearty man who went to the town market to drink ale and eat meat. A rooster could become a handsome young man who seduced a young woman in a farmhouse. This story of the rooster who becomes a young man was one of the scariest and most riveting stories my grandparents told. My grandmother said that there once was a family with just one daughter, and she had grown very attractive by the time she'd reached the age for marriage. The parents sent for a matchmaker to arrange a good marriage, but no matter how wealthy the family or how excellent the young man, this daughter rejected them all. The mother grew suspicious as dark thoughts filled her mind. Sure enough, late one night when no one was stirring, she heard the sound of a young man and a young woman making love, and it was coming from inside her daughter's room. The mother confronted the daughter about this, leaving the daughter no choice but to tell the truth. She said that late every night, once all had gone quiet, a handsome young man would come into her room. The daughter said he wore a very odd shirt, all dazzling with different colors and shinier than silk. So the mother, together with her daughter, came up with a secret plan. The next time the handsome young man came in, the daughter hid the boy's shirt in the wardrobe. Just as the dawn began to break, the young man got up to leave, but he couldn't find his shirt, and he grew very frantic, searching and searching and pressing the girl to give it back. But she would not. And the young man had no choice but to leave, disconsolate. That night, there was a snowstorm, with a cold wind that blustered and whistled from the north. Early the next morning, they opened the chicken coop and a completely featherless rooster jumped out. Then the mother ordered her daughter to open the wardrobe. Inside, the drawer was chock-full of chicken feathers. I have always remembered this story, and I think it's truly a great story, one that certainly could be adapted into a drama about the struggle of a young woman resisting arranged marriage so that she can marry the man she has chosen freely. After hearing this story when I was young, I was afraid of the roosters in our chicken pen. And whenever I saw a handsome young man on the street, I suspected he might be a rooster. My grandmother also said there was a small animal that could talk just like a human being, and it looked a lot like a weasel. On nights when the moonlight was particularly bright, it would come out wearing a little red jacket and run about on top of the open-courtyard walls, singing songs. This made me afraid to look up at the top of any wall on a moonlit night. My grandfather said that on the stone bridge out back behind the trees, there was a "Hey, hey" ghost. If you went over that bridge late at night, you'd feel someone tap you on the shoulder from behind and then hear the sounds "Hey, hey," followed by a cold laugh. No one had ever seen what this ghost really looked like, but to me that story was the scariest of all. In the 1970s, I worked at a cotton-processing factory, and whenever I went home at night after a late shift, I had to cross over the little stone bridge. I was fine as long as there was moonlight, but if there wasn't any moonlight, I would start to sing when I approached the bridge and then run quickly over it. When I got home, I would be all out of breath, my clothes soaked through with cold sweat. That little stone bridge was about two *li* from our home. My mother would say, "We heard you before you even entered the village." That was right when my voice was changing, and it would get all hoarse and broken, so my singing probably sounded just like the sobbing of a ghost or the howling of a wolf. My mother said, "It is the middle of the night when you come back. Why do you need to howl like that?" I said I was afraid. Mother said, "Afraid of what? I said, afraid of the "Hey, hey" ghost. Mother said, "Son, in this world, the scariest things are human beings." Even though I admitted that my mother was right, every time I crossed the bridge, I couldn't help it, I had to run. And yell.

I used to be so scared of ghosts and monsters, but I have never encountered any. No ghost or monster has ever done me harm. Part of my boyhood fear of ghosts, though, was the pleasure of anticipation. For example, more than once I wished I could meet a beautiful woman fox spirit. And I did look up on the top of the courtyard walls on moonlit nights to see if that little animal was there. But in all these years, the only things that ever really caused me harm were other human beings, and now it's human beings that really strike fear in me. Before the 1980s, China was a country of class struggle; in the countryside it was the same as in the cities, and there were always some people who, for whatever ridiculous reason, had to oppress others. Some of the children were stripped of their rights to an education because their parents or grandparents had once been comparatively wealthy. And going to the city in search of a better life was not an option. Yet another group of children enjoyed both of these privileges because their parents and grandparents had been poor. And if that were all, I wouldn't have been so afraid, but what really kept me scared was that these poor people with power, and their children, kept us under surveillance—and oppressed us.

My ancestors had once been wealthy (what was considered "wealthy" back then meant no more than owning a few *mu* of land and one cow for tilling the fields), so I was forced out of school in the fifth grade. For a long time, I had to be very careful, especially of anything I said or did, out of fear that even the slightest little thing said or done imprudently could bring disaster to my parents. Many times we could hear sounds coming from the village office, harrowing cries of pain and sorrow from so-called "bad people" chained up inside, with the village cadres in there with them. That made me very, very afraid—much more than I ever feared ghosts. That was when I finally understood what my mother had said. I thought at first she meant that humans scared off the ghosts and wild animals, but now I understood: no ghost or wild animal could ever be as scary as a human devoid of reason and conscience. Tigers and wolves may have harmed humans at various points in time, and maybe monsters in the stories had too, but only human beings have caused tens of millions of their own kind to die before their time. Only human beings tortured each other, by the tens of millions. A government gone insane made this cruelty legal; a sick society endorsed and rewarded it.

Although the dark times of the Cultural Revolution ended more than twenty years ago and "class struggle" as we called it ceased, fear still lingers in the hearts of people like me who grew up during that era. Every time I return to my hometown and I see the people who used to oppress others, even though they are all smiles with me now, I still can't stop myself from bowing at the waist, head down, heart full of fear. When I pass the building where people were once shackled, I still shiver, even though the building is now condemned and crumbling to the ground, ready for the wrecking ball, and even when the day is warm—just as I still had to run and yell when I was crossing the stone bridge even when I knew there were no ghosts haunting it.

Looking back, when I was a child, I certainly grew up in the midst of famine, isolation, and fear. I have survived a lot of suffering. But in the end, I never went crazy or succumbed to despondency. And I even became a fiction writer. What was it that sustained me through those long dark years? It was hope.

In times when we didn't get enough to eat or clothes to wear, I would hope for food and clothes. During the years of "red terror," I hoped to gain friendship and love. Fear made me sing while I ran, and fear gave me the power to run away, as fast as I could, from my backward feudal home. I hope humanity will always be able to throw off fear, for hope is like a fire in the dark, lighting the way forward, helping us find the courage to defeat fear. I hope that in a future age the fear created by evil people will disappear completely—but not the fear created by ghost stories and fairy tales because these stories imbue in people the awe and the respect they should have for the world as yet unknown, as well as the impulse to live a good life. And they also hold the seeds of literature and art.

(Translated by Jesse Field)

16

My Literary Journey

Lecture on Becoming the
Grand Prize Laureate of the
17th Fukuoka Prize,
Fukuoka, Japan, September 2006

Good afternoon, ladies and gentlemen.

It's such an honor for me to lecture on this prestigious stage, and so please allow me to express my heartfelt thanks and utmost respect to the Fukuoka City Asia Culture Awards Committee and the people of Fukuoka City for this award.

I was born in 1955 in a remote and backward village in Gaomi County, in China's Shandong Province. This year I am fifty-one years old. Now, villagers view fifty as old, but I always feel like I haven't even grown up yet, that there's so much more on the long road of life, and that the literary road has just begun. This is totally ridiculous, but perhaps it's fine for a fiction writer to hold on to his childlike heart.

I once said in a lecture in the United States that hunger and isolation were the wellsprings of my creativity, and I want to reiterate that view here. And this is so even though my wife told me not to go to Japan and talk about not having enough to eat as a child, or I'd just make a laughingstock of myself. I hesitated over this, going back and forth on it, but I decided I have to talk about what really is the key to understanding my work.

In 1960, when I was five years old, China was facing some of the hardest times in all its history. My earliest memory is of my mother sitting under a pear tree in full bloom and covered with white blossoms, using a purple hammer meant for washing clothes to pound wild vegetables against a white rock. Green juice dripped down, some splashing on my mother's bosom, and the air filled up with the bitter, acerbic smell of the wild greens. The sound of the hammer on the greens, heavy and wet, imprinted on my mind. This was a portrait with sound, with color and with smell, the starting point of my life's memories, and the beginning of my literary journey. I used my ears, nose, eyes, and body to grasp life, to feel the things of this world. The memories stored in my mind are all solid memories with sound, color, smell, and shape, complex and vital forms. This manner of feeling life and remembering things to some extent determined the style and quality of my fiction.

An even more unforgettable part of this memory was that my mother, in all her sorrow, and in the middle of that hard labor, suddenly started to hum, her mouth sounding out in song. Back then, in our family with so many children, my mother's work was the worst, and she suffered the most from hunger as well. It would have made more sense for her to sob as she hammered those greens, but not only did she not sob but instead sang songs. This detail remains with me, even though to this day I don't really understand what it means. My mother never went to school, couldn't read or write, and had surely seen more troubles than she could tell. War, famine, disease—in the midst of this suffering, what force kept her alive and by what power did she sing when her stomach rumbled with hunger and her body was racked with illness? When my mother was still alive, I always wanted to ask her this question, but I felt I had no right to bring it up.

There was a stretch of time, I remember, during which a number of women, one after the other, committed suicide, which cast a huge, nameless fear in me. It was the worst period of suffering our family had ever faced, with my father falsely accused and not much grain stored up in our home. My mother's old illness had relapsed, but there was no money to seek a doctor's help. I was always afraid mother might abandon hope and seek a quick end to her troubles. Every time I came home from work, I'd call out for her the moment I got in the door, and only when she answered back would a heavy weight seem to fall away from my heart. Once it was dusk by the time I returned, and my mother didn't respond to my calls, and I looked all over in a frenzy, the cow pen, the grain mill, the toilets, but there was no sign. I felt something terrible must have happened and began to bawl right then and there. Just then, Mother came in from outside. Mother was upset with me for crying, for she thought a person, especially a man, should not cry easily. She asked me why I was crying. I hemmed and hawed, not wanting to tell her what I was really worried about. But she knew what I had been thinking, and she said, "Child, don't worry, I'm not going till King Yama calls me!"

My mother didn't yell when she said this, but still her words strangely enough gave me a sense of security and hope for the future. Many years later, when I remember Mother's words, my heart is moved all the more, for this was a solemn promise made by a mother to her son when he was afraid. Live on. No matter the suffering, we have to live on! Now, even though King Yama really has called Mother away, the courage to struggle on during suffering that Mother's words brought will stay with me forever, encouraging me.

During a break I took in writing this talk, I turned on the television and saw that Israel was bombing Beirut again. The scene was roiling with chaos; it was noisy and smoky, and then a sallow old woman came out of her house. Her body was covered in mud, and she carried a little box, and in the box were a few jade-green vegetables, some cucumbers, and a few stalks of celery. She stood on the side of the road and cried "Vegetables for sale!" When the press turned their cameras to her, she held her head up high and said in a hoarse but decisive voice, "We've lived on this land for generations, and we'll live on, even if we have to eat sand." The old lady's words shook me on a spiritual level. Huge concepts, like women, mothers, land, and life, turned over again and again in my mind, leaving me with an indestructible spiritual power. This belief in living on, even if it meant eating sand, gave a fundamental guarantee that life would go on no matter what suffering the human race faced. This love of life and respect for life are also the soul of literature.

During the famine of the early 1960s, I witnessed many situations in which respect for human character was lost; for example, to get a piece of bean cake, a group of children surrounded the village granary guards and howled like dogs. The guard said that whoever sounded the most like a dog could have a bean cake. I was one of those children barking like a dog. We all sounded just like real dogs. The guard threw the cake as far as he could, and the children swarmed after it. My father saw all this. After I got home, father scolded me harshly. Father said to me, "Your mouth is a path, and whether it's fancy delicacies or grass and tree bark, it's all the same once it's in your stomach; so how could you bark like a dog just for a bit of bean cake? A person has to have integrity!" These words could scarcely convince me because I knew fancy delicacies and grass and tree bark were certainly not the same in the stomach. But I realized that his words were about having a certain dignity, and this was human dignity, which resided in a person's bearing. Humans cannot live like dogs.

My mother taught me that humans have to suffer but live on without shame or excuses. My father and grandfather taught me that humans have to live with dignity. I couldn't completely understand what they taught me at the time, but I was able to take from them certain standards and values I could use when I faced major issues.

Months and years of famine gave me experience and observation of human nature in all its complexity and simplicity, and I was made to understand the lowest levels of human nature. I was able to see some facets of basic humanity, and many years later, when I first took up my pen to write, this experience became my most precious resource, the very reason my fiction contains depictions of our harsh reality, as well as utterly unsentimental dissections of the darkness of human nature. All this is inseparable from past life. Of course, even as I showed the darkness of society and dissected the cruelty of human nature, I didn't forget the noble and dignified side of human nature because my parents and grandparents and many others like them serve as such shining examples. The noble quality of these ordinary people is what, at the end of the day, prevents a nation from succumbing to its suffering.

I attended school until the fifth grade, when I said some stuff that I shouldn't have and found myself turned away at the school gates. I was just eleven years old then and no good for heavy labor, so I had to go out to the pasture and herd cows and sheep. Whenever I led my animals past the school, I could see through the gates the other children in the schoolyard, laughing and cutting up, and my heart was filled with a boundless, nameless sorrow. I wanted to learn so badly, but I'd been stripped of the right to learn.

Out on the pasture, I let the cows graze on their own. Without a person in sight in any direction, the blue sky was a sea overhead. There were no human sounds, only the cries of birds in the sky. I felt isolated and alone, and my heart began to wander in the wasteland. Sometimes I would just lie in the grass and look up at the white clouds swirling languorously through the sky, and many strange thoughts would flow up unbidden into my mind. In that region, we passed down many stories of foxes who became beautiful women, and I fantasized that a fox beauty would come and herd cows with me. But she never did. Sometimes I would squat down next to a cow, stare into its deep blue eyes, and look at the reflected image of myself. Sometimes the cow would push me aside because I was blocking the grass. Sometimes I'd imitate bird calls and try to talk with the birds in the sky, and sometimes I'd try to talk about my feelings with the cows eating grass, but neither the birds nor the cows ever paid me any attention. I continued to live in fantasy. Many years later, when I became a fiction writer, all those fantasies got put into my stories. Many have praised me for my rich imagination, and I've even been called the most imaginative writer in China. When readers want the secret to growing their imagination, I can only tell them this story with a wry laugh.

I have now gone over roughly the relationship between famine, isolation, and my work, and next I want to talk about the issue of why I write. I have said before that my earliest motivation for writing was neither noble nor serious, and I've also said that the reason I write is that I was thinking about how happy I'd be to eat dumplings for three meals a day. Sorry, here we get back to famine and food again. I've also said before that the reason I wrote was to get my fee so I could buy some shoes and a watch and then go back to my village to catch the eye of the young ladies. Sorry, that's still so vulgar and venal. But as time goes on, I can now have dumplings for three meals a day if I want to, and I don't want to wear leather shoes or a watch anymore, and yet my writing goes on, which makes me seriously question myself: What is my goal in writing, after all? I've looked back over the last few decades of my writing and the state of my thoughts now, and the conclusion I've reached is this: what truly motivates me to write is that there are words in my mind that I must speak—I want to use fiction to express, from the deepest part of me, my true thoughts on society and life. This is also what the Chinese writer Ba Jin, who won the first Asian Culture Award in his later years, meant when he exhorted writers to speak the truth and give their hearts to the readers. I also believe that the love for and fascination with the art of literature, along with adventurous experimentation and innovation, are powerful wellsprings that keep me writing.

Since I was a little boy, I've always had the courage to speak the truth. You could say it was my special talent. But my courage and my talent met with resistance and repression in my youth. Those were the days when a single sentence could bring disaster. My mother was always scared stiff about my gift of the gab, and she warned me more than once to talk less. This is why I later changed my name to "Mo Yan" (Don't Speak). I changed my name, but I never changed my talent, for the moment I lifted my pen, the words came flowing out like a river over a broken levee. I think all the things I didn't say when I was young got their chance later, and even more intensely, in my writing.

When I was young, I felt there were two kinds of talk in society, and even within a single family. This was the case for several decades, and even now the phenomenon hasn't disappeared completely. What people said in public was all false, a show put on for the officials, as when we found it necessary to sing praises for our happiness and good fortune when it was all too clear we lacked even basic food and clothing, to curse a person in public when what we truly felt was gratitude, or to flatter another when what we really felt was bone-deep hatred. Only at home, with our own family, did some speech start to line up with reality. For a long time, and even now, false, empty, and exaggerated talk was encouraged and rewarded, whereas speaking the truth earned only repression, attack, or serious harm. This made an entire society spread lies, even preposterous ones like a half-acre rice paddy could produce 120,000 catties of grain; it made many people lose the courage and ability to tell the truth; it made creating vicious falsehoods the fashion of the day, while accounts of true events were twisted and covered up. Literature produced in this kind of social environment could only be false and vain. And this false and vain literature, which occupied a central position for so long, only began to be corrected, bit by bit, in the 1980s when our generation of writers began coming on the scene.

I came on the scene in 1985 with the novella *The Transparent Carrot*, and this year I published the novel *Life and Death Are Wearing Me Out*. During the past twenty years, my work has caused intense controversy, with those who like my work saying I began a new era in Chinese literature, whereas my critics believe my work makes a spectacle of cruelty and ugliness and lacks beauty and ideals. I welcome criticism, but I never accept it blindly. I believe that to expose cruelty and show ugliness are signs of the conscience and the courage of a writer, for only when we look squarely at the darkness and ugliness in life and in human nature can we feature its light and beauty, making people see faint rays of ideals through the dark haze of reality.

Of course, my fiction does not provoke praise and criticism only because I bravely write the truth of society and life, but because I was bold enough to learn and apply the techniques of Western and even Japanese literature. Writers like Natsume Sōseki, Yasunari Kawabata, Junichiro Tanizaki, and Yukio Mishima had a major, even formative, influence on my work. As I've said many times before, a sentence in *Snow Country* by Yasunari Kawabata inspired me to write the story "White Dog and the Swing," which was the first time I used the name "Northeast Gaomi Township." Since then, I have been like an actor who has taken to the broadest stage ever, like a thief who has gotten hold of a key that opens all treasure chests—the stories surge like river water from the literary Northeast Gaomi Township. My innovations and those of my fellow writers caused a literary revolution in 1980s China. Many critics followed me and studied my work, with some of them including me in the "searching for roots" school, whereas others decided I was "avant-garde," and still others believed I was a "new sentimentalist" for China, or that I was a Chinese proponent of magical realism, or that I wrote the Chinese "stream of consciousness." But I kept changing, which made their categorizations all just attempts to use a part to cover the whole. I was a fish that wouldn't be caught in their nets.

After this stage of learning and borrowing broadly from Western literature, I began to consciously turn my gaze toward the traditional and folk culture of China, which was not in the least a rejection of Western literature but rather further affirmation of it. Only after gaining a broad understanding of Western history and forms could I look with new eyes at Chinese literature, discovering by comparison what it had in common with Western literature and what was distinct about it, thereby cultivating the ability to write literature with an innovative consciousness for China, for Asia, and for the world.

More than a decade ago, Kenzaburo Oe had the new idea to make Asian literature a major sphere of world literature. This would involve a literary vision with a high degree of worldliness, filled with a rich opportunity for a dialectical approach. Mr. Oe's views are, as it happens, in complete accord with the aims of the Fukuoka Asia Culture Award, for both seek to establish an Asian culture on a broad basis of exchange that preserves and passes down the uniqueness and diversity of national and regional culture, while also possessing what is universally held in common in world literature.

This is the unification of preservation and innovation, of accepting our heritage and continuing to develop it. I believe that the fundamental goal of human society is not only to preserve the old but also to create the new. Only with ample exchange and mutual learning can we create new culture and art. I believe that in the twenty-first century, Asian culture must have a greater influence, and Chinese literature, as an important part of Asian literature, must also become an important part of world literature. The glory of Chinese literature will change the patterns of world literature.

Ladies and gentlemen, in this world plagued by contradiction and chaos on all sides, literature's influence ebbs daily, which is something we can lament but cannot change. Literature will not resolve the conflict of Israel and the Arab world; literature will not stop terrorist activity; literature will not pull American troops out of Iraq; and literature will not make Iran and North Korea stop testing nuclear weapons. Faced with all these problems, literature is powerless, but literature must not cede its place; literature must not crawl into a hole to protect itself, for literature must attend radically to all that happens in this world, using literary methods to express its opinion. Literature must stand high above the whole of humanity, in consideration of the direction and fate of humanity, and bring forth its own voice. Of course, it is a soft, weak voice and may earn only scornful laughter; but without this voice, the world would grow even more monotone.

(Translated by Jesse Field)

17

Why I Write

Good evening, students and professors. I am extremely happy to be here at Shaoxing University, and many thanks to my host for those skillful and elevated opening remarks. As for me, I'm neither mountain nor sea, but rather one of the most hideous writers in China. Of course, I can use what our foreign minister, Li Zhaoxing, once said when a reporter commented that he was ugly. Minister Li said that his mother wouldn't like the reporter's comment. Of course, many people say I'm ugly, but when I go home and tell my mother, my mother says, "You don't look ugly to me." And this makes me so much more confident.

This marks my second time in Shaoxing. I came twelve years ago, and each time I come, I feel I am on sacred ground because Shaoxing was home to the great Lu Xun. Bronze busts of Lu Xun loom over Shanghai and Beijing as well, but Shaoxing is his hometown. And Shaoxing has not only Lu Xun, the great man of literature, but also Wang Xizhi, that sage of calligraphy; Cai Yuanpei, the great educator; and revolutionaries like Xu Xilin and Qiu Jin. In short, Shaoxing certainly makes the grade as a land of heroes. And there are more such dragons and tigers in store,

I am sure, here at Shaoxing University, and in good time, there will even be a figure as great as Lu Xun or an artist as amazing as Wang Xizhi. Of course, we don't hope for people like Xu Xilin or Qiu Jin anymore, for there would be no use for them. We have entered the great age of socialism, and there is no longer any need for a revolt.

In 2005, I gave a lecture at the Lu Xun Museum in Beijing, where I said that speaking on fiction in the Lu Xun Museum was like reading the *Three-Character Classic* to Confucius, like swinging a sword in front of General Guan Yu, a sure sign that one didn't know one's place in the wide world—shameful, really, to speak at all. But I'm shameless, and thick-skinned to boot, so I gathered my gumption and spoke anyhow. Tonight, no sooner do I say this than I feel a pair of eyes behind me, staring sharply at my back; this is the gaze of Master Lu Xun. But we Chinese have been under the gaze of other elders for decades, so let them look; I will still speak.

I know that at the end of last month, the Turkish writer Orhan Pamuk spoke here. The evening of May 27, I asked him to dinner, along with his girlfriend, Kiran Desai. He was so excited to tell me, "Tomorrow I'm going to speak at Shaoxing University." "What will you talk about?" I asked. And he said, "Who are we, really?" And I said, "But wait, haven't you talked about that before, in other places?" "Well," he said, "Does a writer need to switch topics every day, like a university lecturer? I can take one topic all over the world." At first, you see, I was thinking of not coming because what I'm going to say is stuff I've said before, but if Pamuk can do it, then so can I.

I've seen the text of Pamuk's lecture on whom he writes for in many different publications, and I know what it says for the most part. He ends by saying that he writes for the ideal reader. Many writers say, "I write for the peasants," or "I write for the workers," or some other people of some sort or other, and these slogans seem accurate enough—of course we do not doubt the sincerity of these writers' goals, but in actuality many such statements are problematic. I, for example, used to say, years ago, that

I wanted to write for the peasants, but later introspection revealed that these platitudes are aspirational at best.

My hometown is Gaomi, in Shandong Province, and you might say fiction by a Gaomi native ought to be read with great interest by other Gaomi natives, but in fact very few Gaomi peasants ever read my work, and even in my own village almost nobody has read it. Every time I go back, they ask, "What newspaper are you with?" I say, "I'm with the *PLA Daily*." They think journalists are the top people with unlimited power and authority. Later, when I left my work team, the reason I chose to report for the *Procuratorial Daily* was also subconsciously influenced by the elders of my village—I could go back and tell them with the pride of a fellow clansman on the rise that I was a reporter with the *Procuratorial Daily*. They said, "Wow, this kid is finally showing some promise." Even older folks would ask me, "What is your rank these days?" I told them it was about the same level as our county chief. "Well, that's pretty high up!" This is to say that a writer really doesn't have any status at all in the minds of peasants from my hometown. We can therefore hardly be so full of ourselves and should not think that writers are amazing or sacred.

And that's why I say that slogans like "Speak for the peasants, write for the peasants" sound honorable but are very false. The peasants are not our readers. Well, and we can put forth another proposition, that I make an exhortation for the peasants, that I speak out about the low social positions of the peasants and the unfair treatment they suffer, that I hope to change their fate through fiction or some other literary form, but I think this is also just empty talk. Not a single policy is the product of any writer's fiction, so for writers to think their fiction can solve social problems is naive and, frankly, a little childish.

Pamuk speaks more realistically and more honestly. He says that in his early period, he also wanted to write for the Turkish people, for the nation of Turkey, for the betterment of Turkey's common people and lower classes, but later he discovered this thinking was naive, and in the end, he concluded: I write for my ideal reader. The person who reads his books is the person Pamuk serves.

The topic of my lecture today is "why I write," but in fact, it overlaps to a large degree with Pamuk's talk on whom he writes for. Of course, "why I write" encompasses a slightly wider scope than "who I write for." In my experience, over the long course of a writer's work, the goal of writing will not be consistent and unchanging; it will not be established at the beginning, never to change later. Rather, it will change with the growth of the writer's experience, with the evolution of society, and with changes in the writer's character. From the moment you take up the pen to tackle fiction or poetry until you stop and write no more, you may go through many instances of change and development.

Of course, there are also great writers like Lu Xun, who from the beginning pursue high and noble goals. When I went to see Lu Xun's old home today, I discovered a picture of him when he was studying medicine in Japan and saw a lantern slide that showed a scene from the Russo-Japanese War, when the Japanese had arrested some Chinese who were suspected of being traitors for having committed crimes for the Russians and were being dealt with in front of a crowd. Gathering around to watch the hubbub were many Chinese, the very people Lu Xun criticizes for being "spectators." This shocked Master Lu Xun greatly, and he thought, "If I study medicine, I can cure sick bodies, but what use would such a cure be? They will still be slaughtered like pigs or dogs, and even if they aren't killed, they will turn into numbed spectators." He thought then that it would be better to cure men's souls than to cure men's flesh, so he swore off medicine for literature.

I think these extremely serious goals of Lu Xun's determined his whole life's work, and later his work progressed and moved forward centered on these goals. I think this goal was a product of its time. Today we cannot have such high and majestic writing goals as Lu Xun's, not only because we lack sufficient awareness but also because of the current prevailing conditions of society. In Lu Xun's time, literature was closely related to revolution. Many writers of Lu Xun's era were also revolutionaries and public intellectuals. Literature served as a tool for social revolution and functioned to advance this social revolution. So the fiction of Lu Xun and his ilk carried great meaning for revolution and enlightenment. Lu Xun wanted to discover the deepest, darkest flaws of the national character; he wanted to discover the serious problems deep within the souls of the Chinese people; and he hoped his work would poke and prod numb souls, jolt the Chinese awake, and in the end achieve the goal of social revolution. Such lofty goals are ones that today's authors admire greatly, but we are unlikely to achieve them.

Today, many people, from ordinary readers to critics, take a negative attitude to contemporary literature whenever the subject comes up. Many critics believe contemporary literature has no prospects to speak of; especially in comparison to modern writers like Lu Xun, our generation of writers lacks erudition, lacks vision, lacks intellectual clout, lacks talent, and of course lacks direction, for, as short-sighted as mice that see only an inch before their eyes, we seek only fame and fortune, whereas Lu Xun and his generation showed good breeding.

Not only do many Chinese critics feel this way, but Sinologists abroad have also criticized Chinese writers for the same reason. Recently in China, the famous German Sinologist Wolfgang Kubin, a good friend of mine, said he believes contemporary Chinese writers don't understand foreign languages and cannot be compared to writers of Lu Xun's generation, for Kubin doesn't believe that a writer who doesn't learn a foreign language can be a good writer.

I don't completely agree with this view because I can think of many examples of writers who produce outstanding fiction despite not knowing a foreign language. Shen Congwen had no foreign-language skills and only knew Chinese, but he is probably second only to Lu Xun among modern writers. Kubin's speech was provocative, and there is a certain logic to what he said, but it was far from complete. I think this is also one reason we writers of this generation should just grow a thicker skin and keep on writing, for even though we don't know any foreign languages, neither did Shen Congwen, so we can hold him up to shield ourselves and keep on writing, and maybe some of our work will be good.

In sum, Lu Xun's generation was certainly different from today's. What made Lu Xun—or rather his generation, which stands out so much now—able to produce that caliber of writing was as much the social environment as individual talent. It is just as Engels said: when society needs great men, it will produce them. The needs of society are perhaps more important than the talent cultivated at a hundred universities, for although universities might fail, once the social need is there, the talent will necessarily develop. So writers like Lu Xun and Shen Congwen were products of their times, and not every era can produce a Lu Xun.

Besides, do we still need writers like Lu Xun today? This is a good question for you university students to develop, discuss, and research. We must admit, this generation cannot produce a Lu Xun. It's true. But this doesn't mean we writers of today are a bunch of incompetent fools; it's because these times would not permit writings like Lu Xun's.

Writing for the Good Life of Dumplings Three Times a Day

My earliest motivation for writing actually couldn't have been more different from Lu Xun's. Master Lu Xun took the nation as his foundation, with the intention of boring a hole into the "iron house" of China, to let in a few rays of light that would help start a social revolution. But I believe we no longer need this because today there is no "iron house." The skies over the liberated areas are clear, with dazzling rays, bright and beautiful, and nary a spot to bore. Only back at the farm can we bore into the globe itself.

Back in the day, when I was a peasant, I bored quite a few holes in the earth every year myself. I had dropped out of school early, having read just very few books. I've written about my experience reading before.

There were so few books back then, you see, though every village had some; for example, the old Zhang house had a battered and incomplete copy of *Romance of the Three Kingdoms*, and Uncle Li had a two-volume *Journey to the West* at his house, and so on, such-and-such books at so-and-so's house; I felt as though I had read every single book in the world. It was only after I went into the army that I realized how short-sighted I had been, like a frog in a well who had seen too little of the sky.

My neighbor—a student in the Chinese department at Shandong University and later branded a rightist—worked right alongside me every day. During work breaks, his rightist character proved hard to reform, for he regularly told me stories about writers he had known up there at the university in the city of Jinan. One of these stories was about a famous writer who had written "Red Classics." And he said the writer's life was thoroughly corrupt, that he ate dumplings three times a day, for breakfast, lunch, and dinner. Now, in farm villages in the 1960s and 1970s, we only ever ate dumplings once a year, on Chinese New Year's Eve; they came in two colors, white ones made with refined flour, and darker ones made with coarser whole grains. I thought, "To be wealthy enough to eat dumplings three times a day! Wouldn't that be better than Chairman Mao?" We often had this fantasy. When hunger overtook our bellies, we would wonder, "What does Chairman Mao eat?" Some said he must have two oil fritters every morning, and some said it must be pork belly with cabbage. Nobody dared to think that even Chairman Mao might eat dumplings three times a day, so when my neighbor said a writer in Jinan did eat dumplings three times a day, I said, "Could I eat dumplings three times a day, too, if I were a writer?" He said, "Of course, as long as you can write a whole book, because when it's published your fee will be a lot of money, and then dumplings three times a day will be no problem."

That's when I began to dream of becoming a writer. So speaking of "why I write," the important thing is that early on, I wrote to get ahold of the good life of eating dumplings three times a day. Compared with Lu Xun wanting to save the numbed souls of the Chinese people, there's a big difference. Lu Xun could not have ever had such low and vulgar thoughts as mine, which also has to do with his background. Today when I toured his old home, I discovered that Lu Xun came from a big, powerful clan. His grandfather was a high-ranking Mandarin, and his family had many properties, so Lu Xun lived the life of the very wealthy and knew what it was like to live in affluence, and so he wouldn't have been as low and vulgar as we are.

Writing to Make Work Different from That of Others

Slowly, my thinking started to change. In the wake of China's reform policies, society began to improve slowly, and farm villages also saw reforms. The days of nonstop hunger pains, with only coarse grain half the year and just chaff and herbs for the other half, changed drastically. The problem of avoiding hunger disappeared; we were now able to get wheat flour all year long, so much so that eventually dumplings three times a day ceased to be a special luxury. At this time, my views on literary creation naturally underwent a change.

In 1982, I was promoted to officer status in the army, with a monthly salary of many tens of *yuan*. In 1984, I was admitted to the literature department of the PLA Art Academy. My writing goals during that period were not so low and vulgar.

Looking back now, the years 1984, 1985, and 1986 were a golden age for all Chinese arts, including literature, for thought was so liberal and open then not only in the literary world but also the fields of music and fine arts, where major figures, including some directors, were just starting to emerge. The mid-1980s was a great period. And back then, I thought to myself, I'm not satisfied with just publishing one or two little pieces of fiction.

The environment at the PLA Art Academy totally changed my early views on literature. In 1984 and 1985, many new works of literature were becoming popular hits. But I wasn't satisfied with them; I didn't think they were as good as everyone was saying, or at the very least, I didn't like them. So what sort of fiction did I like? I wasn't sure yet, but I always felt I should write work that was different from what was popular and accepted at the moment. That was what I was searching for in my dreams, at any rate.

And sure enough, a dream did come through eventually. I dreamed I was out in the wilderness on an autumn day, and there was a radish patch —back home we grew really huge radishes with skin as red as the lettering on the back of this lecture hall. The sun had just risen—the sun was also bright red, and beneath the sun a full-figured young woman, dressed in red, walked up with a fish spear in her hands. She came up to the radish patch and speared herself a radish, before walking off in the sunlight.

After I woke from the dream, I told my roommates in our dorm, "I had a dream, a beautiful, beautiful dream," and one of them just said, "You're such a Freudian." I said could I maybe write it into a story. Someone else said that would be great. My classmates gave me lots of encouragement. So on the basis of this dream, I wrote a story called *The Transparent Carrot,* and that's the story that launched my name. Today I have one of my old classmates with me, and now that I've come to this part, he will certainly remember the scene of us studying in that dorm, and the things he did for me before and after that story came out. To help spread the word around, they formed discussion groups to highlight my story.

The publication of *The Transparent Carrot* was certainly a turning point for me because before that, most of the stories I had written were in fact "revolutionary" and, in this sense, were all theme stories. At the time, I believed it was an honor for fiction to support our policies, or to follow a movement. That seemed like a great thing. The editor of the PLA journal took me aside and said, "We are about to publish some stories to accompany a party consolidation movement, and if your story becomes reading for the entire movement, you'll be instantly famous." And I did work really hard on this, trying my darnedest to come up with a story set during the Cultural Revolution, about how we all struggled against the "Gang of Four" and sustained the revolutionary line of Chairman Mao. This story could have been published and might even have won this or that award. But when I finished *The Transparent Carrot* and then turned back to look at the commissioned story, I felt it had a fundamental flaw: it was all false. Before the 1980s, during the Cultural Revolution era, we may have waved the flag for "revolutionary realism," but I believe this was not true realism but rather false and empty. It was clear at the time that everyone was starving, but we believed that life was good; it was clear at the time that the standards of living were much lower in China than those in other countries, but we believed that two-thirds of the world's population was worse off, that we would liberate them, save them, rescue them from their awful fates. This proves that our realism had a fundamental falsity that was its guiding principle, and so the sort of story I had written was surely false as well.

In the course of writing *The Transparent Carrot*, I realized that realism actually has a broad scope, that it's about more than just reflecting life like a mirror and more than just shoving in life events wholesale, unchanged from their original state. Realism in fact permits the boldest of fictionalizing, and it permits exaggeration. And it permits magic.

The 1980s were also the time when our generation reapproached Western literature. Before and after the Cultural Revolution, which is to say during the thirty years from the 1950s to the 1970s, one could still read Soviet literature, and of course one could read stories from Vietnam and Eastern Europe—socialist warhorses, in other words. And of course, one could read some of the classics, like the novels of Tolstoy and the critical realist stories of France. But during these decades, works of Western modernism, like the new fiction of France, or stream-of-consciousness fiction from the United States, and especially the explosive literature and magical realism from Latin America in the 1960s, were all basically unknown to us.

When thought was liberated in the 1980s, thirty years of accumulated Western works seemed to arrive in China overnight. At that time, we really were like starving cattle who'd suddenly come across a garden: the cabbage was good, but so was the radish; one hardly knew what to eat, for it felt to us that every book was unusually good. Our reading fever was a good way to cram, with the cumulative effect being our gained understanding that the techniques and skills for fiction were infinite. Many topics we used to think were not good material for fiction were in fact just fine.

Before, what worried me was finding stories to write about, and I racked my brains to create some, looked for them in the newspapers and in government files, but nothing I found was right. Only after *The Transparent Carrot* did I realize that my own life experiences held many, many topics for fiction. Like my old neighbors back in the village, like my experiences working here and there; even the fish in the river, or the cows I had once herded, could be fitted up for fiction. And in many decades of life in a farm village, the stories and tales told by my own grandmother and grandfather, as well as those from the grandmas and grandpas of the neighboring homes, could all become precious resources with which to create. Some were stories about ghosts, demons, and the strange, like one about a weasel turning into a woman, yet another featuring a fox who becomes a handsome young man, then another with a tree that becomes a sprite, still another about a place haunted by hanged man's ghost. One day they might turn to historical legends, like how on such-and-such bridge a battle was fought, and during the fight, the barrel of one gun got so hot it grew two centimeters in an instant. All these stories were very exaggerated, very much the stuff of legends; and they all just came back to me, and I could see them right before my eyes.

During my two years at the PLA Art Academy, I had to go to class, and because I was still in the army, I also had to do physical training, including running, and I had to participate in all kinds of Party activities. And even as busy as I was with all that, I still wrote seven or eight hundred thousand words of fiction. Stories like *The Transparent Carrot* had in an instant opened the floodgates of memory, and I had discovered a treasure trove. Whereas in the past, I had looked everywhere for stories, now I felt that stories were like dogs, chasing me down, nipping at my butt. Often, when I was writing one story, another would suddenly rush out, and I'd sense stories waiting in line for me to write them.

Of course, this stage didn't last very long. After two or three years of writing, suddenly there came a stage when I felt I had nothing to write. The things I'd been writing about were also now tiresome, so I sought change once again because *The Transparent Carrot* was also juvenilia, after all. Even though I was over thirty years old at the time, I wrote with the perspective of a child and the feelings of a child, the story itself featuring all the colors of a fairy tale. The child in the story could listen till his hair dropped to the ground, could endure days of freezing weather, shirtless, wearing only a pair of shorts, and yet not in the least cold; he could walk long distances, steady and calm even when he had a red-hot iron in his hands...all this was extremely exaggerated.

WRITING FOR SELF-REALIZATION

After writing *The Transparent Carrot* and the series of stories that followed it, the end of 1985 approached and I came to another turning point, which led me to write *Red Sorghum*.

The PLA Art Academy was a school managed by the General Political Department (GPD), and the Culture Department of the GPD convened an academic conference on literature. Many of the older writers at the conference were glum and cranky; in comparing Soviet military literature with Chinese military literature, they said that although the Soviet involvement in the Second World War had lasted only four years, the Soviet nevertheless had generated endless literary fiction—much of it very good—and now they had five generations of writers, one after the other, addressing the war. The Chinese revolution, in contrast, had gone on and on for a full twenty-eight years, not counting the counterstrike in self-defense against Vietnam, so why hadn't we produced military fiction in the quantity or quality of the Soviets? The conclusion was that it was because the Cultural Revolution had hindered the older generation. One reason they were so glum was that this batch of older writers who had actually been through the war, and so had all the experience and material, had been so set back by the Cultural Revolution that now they couldn't get up the gumption to write, even if they had wanted to. And we young writers, though possessed of talent and skill and some experience, had never been through war. For this reason, the prospects for Chinese military literature seemed pretty dim.

I was among those chosen to speak and, as they say, the youngest cowherd fears not the tiger. I said, many among those five generations of Soviet writers did not experience the war either. Even if we have not been through the Sino-Japanese War, or the Chinese Civil War, as you older writers have, we still know of many experiences from your work, and we've heard from your mouths many tales of the wars. These can be used as fodder to make up for our lack of war experience, and we can depend fully on our imaginations to supplement what we lack in personal experience. To give an example, even though I have never killed another person—never grappled with the enemy, blade in hand, as you all have, inflicting death with your own hands—when I was young, I slew many chickens in my home, and one could certainly extend one's experience of killing chickens to the killing of humans.

Many of the old comrades disagreed with what I said, with one person asking quietly on the side, "Who is this guy?" I left but with an idea stuck stubbornly in my mind—I would write a book about the war. And that became *Red Sorghum*.

As I said, I could use my own experience to supplement what I lacked in war experience. In *Red Sorghum*, there are many scenes in which soldiers on the march use large knives to cut off the heads of their enemies, and immediately after a head is cut off, the skin of the neck shrivels downward. Later when I was at a cholera sanatorium in Xi'an, I met an old veteran who loved to read and had read the novel. "In *Red Sorghum*," he said, "you wrote that when the Japs got their heads chopped off, the skin on their necks shriveled inward. How did you know that's what happens?" I said, "I've seen this happen when I killed chickens." He said it's just the same when you kill people. I said, "I didn't even know if it was the same or not, but I guess it is, if you say so. But, you know, it wouldn't be that important if it weren't the same because readers like you are so few. As long as it's evocative, written with a lot of lively detail that makes the scene seem to happen right before my eyes." I write detailed enough descriptions that I can get the reader to believe them, make the reader think I'm an old veteran who's lived through many battles and survived long years of war. So people began thinking I was over sixty, and they were really surprised to meet me and see that I was still in my thirties.

Another way to put it is that the goal of *Red Sorghum* was to prove to myself that someone without experience of war could write about war. There is a principle here that isn't very intuitive: there are many events one need not experience personally. We always liked to emphasize that a writer must experience life and always emphasized how life determined art and fiction, but I think such claims are a little oversold. Of course, in the most basic sense, without life there can be no literature. The richness of personal experience determines the size of a writer's creative achievement. But I think that if this claim is overemphasized, it turns out to cause the opposite. In a certain sense, scenes of war written by writers with no war experience will be even more unique because these are their own wars, their individual experiences, imaginative extensions built on the foundations of their experiences. It's like when someone who has never been in a relationship writes about love and makes it even more beautiful; this follows the same principle. Old hands at romance rarely write well on love because they already lack true feeling for it; they already know about the true nature of love between man and woman. This true nature of love is only infinitely good and beautiful in the imagination of the person who's never been in love.

After *Red Sorghum* became a big success, interpretations of the novel began to proliferate. I might not have thought of it when I wrote the novel, but when others spoke up, I just went with the flow. And so the goals for writing *Red Sorghum* became very complicated—not only did I want to prove that I could write a war story, I also wanted to fashion a memorial to my ancestors, to create a new type of narrative perspective, and to cross the boundary between history and the present.... These were things I hadn't thought of when I was writing, for when I was writing, I just wrote in whatever way I could to make it come out more fluidly, and this brought me joy.

From the very beginning of *Red Sorghum*, for example, I narrated the story using "my grandfather" and "my grandmother," which some critics would later say was my original technique. At the time, I just had to write it that way, for I thought if I used the first person to narrate my grandparents' story, it would clearly be unnatural and I wouldn't be able to keep writing because I couldn't become my grandfather or my grandmother. But if I used the third person to narrate the story of my grandparents, it would feel dated and awkward. So using "my grandfather" and "my grandmother" felt much freer. Whenever I wanted to express my own feelings, I could come right out. And yet the instant I wrote "my grandfather" or "my grandmother," I felt as if I really had become my grandfather or my grandmother, as if I had entered their inner mental worlds. And I could combine my life in the present with the historical lives I was describing, leaving no barrier between history and the present, so I could come and go between them freely—just as we commonly see with northeastern *Errenzhuan*, or comedy duets, in which the boy and girl may be playing off each other one moment, then cursing and flirting with the audience in the next, all free and easy. *Red Sorghum*'s narrative perspective is actually the same as in these duets, jumping back and forth, up on the stage and off again, mixing up history with the present.

Writing for Peasants and to Experiment with Technique

In 1987, my goals for writing shifted yet again, and this time I really did want to speak for the peasants and to write for them. The so-called "Garlic Incident" of 1987 occurred in a county of southern Shandong Province and shocked the whole country. The place produced garlic, and the peasants harvested a great deal of the stuff, but thanks to rampant bureaucracy, corruption, and government incompetence, as well as the area being a closed-off region, meaning no outside commercial interests were allowed in, tens of millions of pounds of laboriously harvested garlic were left to rot. The angry peasants carried or pushed cartfuls of garlic to the county seat and surrounded the county government offices, blocking the streets with piles of rotten garlic and demanding to see the county chief. The county chief didn't dare face the farmers and ran off to hide, so the peasants charged into the county government offices, set fire to the main administration building, and smashed the county chief's telephone. This became a major incident, for no such bold revolt by the peasants had ever occurred since the founding of the PRC in 1949.

At the time, I was on vacation in my hometown, and I read about all this in the newspaper *Masses Daily.* I felt in my heart then that the true nature of the peasants had been awakened. Even though I was working in Beijing by then and was an officer in the PLA, long out of my village, no longer an eater of rice fresh off the farm, still I remained a peasant in my bones; that was my true nature. And this event had transpired in a village just like my hometown. Many of the peasants who had incited and led the Garlic Incident were arrested and sentenced, and of course some officials lost their jobs. That was when I felt I had to speak for the peasants. I wanted to use the Garlic Incident as material for a novel about the peasants' cry for fairness. I wanted to make my own cry for the peasants.

These events had made me so excited and so overwhelmed with pent-up emotion, that I wrote in record time, completing the novel in just one month and three days. Afterwards, many readers, including some from the county where the Garlic Incident had occurred, wrote to me saying, "Did you come here in secret to hold interviews? This character Fourth Uncle in your book is definitely my uncle." Back then, Gaomi County had a vice county chief who was a friend of mine and who had served in an acting capacity in the county in question; when he came back, he took me aside and told me one of the officials involved up there had said, "If Mo Yan comes to this town, we'll break his legs." He begged me not to go there. I said, "What business do I have there? I never had any idea of going in the first place!" Besides, I hadn't written about their county but about Tiantang County—a fictional county name.

How could I write this story so quickly, and how could I have written something the real peasants had thought was exactly what they were thinking? We can see, actually, that all the trials and fates of peasants are more or less the same. I had in fact used the village I'd lived in for more than twenty years as the model: my house, the grove of scholar trees behind my house, the river behind the trees, the bridge over the river, the little temple at the edge of town, the endless fields of jute, just south of town…. I used my own village as the setting, and all the major characters came straight from my family. The protagonist was my own Fourth Uncle, and while he didn't sell garlic, he did sell beets. He filled his beet cart and happily sold his beets, hoping to earn enough to marry off his sons. But he was killed when he was struck by the car driven by the commune secretary. Not only was my uncle killed, so was the cow that pulled his cart—and this cow was pregnant, too. The cart was smashed to pieces. In the end, for the cart, the cow, the calf, and the life of my Fourth Uncle, the compensation totaled 3,300 *yuan*.

As I was grieving and feeling my lowest about Fourth Uncle's unfortunate demise, I found one of his sons over in the courtyard of the commune administration, and he was actually watching television. The family had put the body in the commune yard, you see, as if to say, if you don't figure this out for me, I will neither cremate nor bury this body. And right at that strange moment, the show *Kung Fu Master Huo*

Yuanjia was on the television, and Fourth Uncle's son had abandoned his father's body to watch that kung fu show and was pleased as could be. I found that chilling. But what were they after? Maybe they wanted to get 13,000 *yuan* instead of 3,000, but even if they'd gotten 13,000, Fourth Uncle's sons would probably just fight over it. Three thousand, three hundred, is simple to divide fairly; 13,000 would drive the young men to madness. Anyway, there was nothing we could do about it because the Party Secretary was also a distant relative, and he sought out my father to wrap up the matter, so it was settled and done with.

But I always felt the injustice of this matter pressing on my heart, so in the course of writing the Garlic Incident story, these feelings that had been in me for so long, which had become so ponderous, all got written into the story. As I said, this was to be a theme story, and moreover, one whose form came entirely from true events. The reason it wasn't just a simple didactic work, I think, has to do with writing a place I was familiar with as well as writing my own kin when I created the characters. This is also to say that to the degree to which the story manages to stand on its own is due most importantly to its creation of several characters with individual personalities that can stand on their own and are not in the least limited by their circumstances. If I had only written according to the events of the incident, forgetting fiction's basic duty to create characters, then the story would never have been successful.

I think this, too, is a case of "straightening with the crooked," which is to say that at this stage, I wanted to speak for the peasants, and this stage lasted two or three years. I wrote a great many stories about the unfairness faced by the peasants, reflecting all the injustices encountered by peasants in farm villages in those times, such as all the different taxes and fees that amounted to plain extortion, and about topics special to the farm village, like selling grain and cotton. But after I finished *The Garlic Ballads*, I realized this wasn't my path forward and that in the end that's not how fiction should be written. The idea that fiction can solve social problems is, as I've said before, naive in the extreme. At that point I was especially fascinated by the art and technique of fiction, and I thought a fiction writer should make contributions to literary form and should make a deep exploration of literary language, structure, and narration—Ma Yuan, for example, has had some great successes.

After I finished *The Garlic Ballads*, I entered a stage of experimenting with technique. This was around 1988, when I wrote a novel many of you have never heard of, *The Thirteen Steps*, set in a middle school and about some of the teachers and students there. The main thing was to conduct many experiments with narrative perspective. I experimented with all of the Chinese words of personal reference in this book—I, you, he or she, we, you all, them, shifting the personal perspective constantly. Personally, I think this is true experimental fiction. I discovered that as I rotated through all these words for personal reference, the structure of the story emerged naturally.

Of course, this also brought a huge problem, namely that the story became difficult to read. One year I went to France and ran into a reader there who said, "When I read the French translation of this book, I marked it up with five different colored pens, but I still didn't figure it all out, can you explain what is going on there, what you were saying?" I said, "Just last year I reread *The Thirteen Steps* for a collected edition of my work, and I marked it up too, with six different colors, but I couldn't figure it out either, so I guess I myself forgot how I wrote it."

This type of writing takes art and technique as its main goals. Why do I want to write this kind of story? Because I want to conduct experiments with technique. But it seems this isn't the right path forward either. Because in the end the reader has to read the story, so you still have to depend on the characters and the fates of the characters to capture the readers, to inspire a kind of common cry with the reader's sentiments—there are probably very few authors who write with technique as the main goal and very few readers who are willing to read for technique alone, which means this kind of story no doubt brings us to a dead end—who is going to buy this story, and who is going to read it? And moreover this kind of technical experimentation will quickly run out of steam, and then what? How will you, being just one person, keep coming up with new forms?

So that was when I realized that this way of writing wasn't right either. Next I wanted to write a story again, one that would combine the motivations for *The Garlic Ballads* and *The Thirteen Steps*: on the one hand, I wanted to strike out fiercely against the dark and corrupt practices of society, to boldly satirize and excoriate, even make fun of them by using a theater of farce, and on the other hand, I wanted to conduct bold experiments in fiction, playing especially with technique and story structure, to conduct games and experiments in literary form. This was my 1989 work, *The Republic of Wine*. I hear that to this day many people won't accept the book because it describes such extreme events.

The story opens in the manner of a detective story, with a special inspector from the procuratorate receiving a secret assignment to go to a coal mine to investigate a case involving cadres accused of eating infants. According to reports from ordinary citizens, the head of the coal mine and the party secretary are both very corrupt and have concocted an abominable new dish called "red-cooked baby." In the course of investigating the coal mine, the inspector unwittingly participates in a cannibal's banquet, where a femme fatale has designs on him, and the pursuer now becomes the pursued. In the beginning, he is the hunter, conducting his investigation each day, but now he is the one being hunted. This is the main plotline of the story, and it's narrated by the author; I am the one writing this story.

Another plotline involves the author of the story exchanging messages after work with a young man who loves literature. The young writer is writing a story and sends it chapter by chapter to the author, and they exchange many amusing and somewhat absurd letters. These letters are constantly going back and forth between the author and the young writer, and these too are written into *The Republic of Wine*. In the end, the story of the amateur writer and the story of the special inspector cracking the case of the red-cooked baby are combined, two into one. Then the author, Mo Yan, is invited by the amateur to this place called the Republic of Wine, where someone gets him drunk as soon as he arrives, and he never sobers up.

The motif of the red-cooked baby was taken to be a real event by Western critics with questionable motives, when in fact it is symbolic. As I explain in the story, when the inspector discovers them carrying the red-cooked baby, he is furious and shoots the dish to pieces with his gun. That's when he discovers that the dish has been prepared by a chef with truly extraordinary skills and technique: the infant's head is a carved pumpkin; the two arms, lotus roots; the eyes, grapes; ears, woodear mushrooms. The dish does bear a perfect resemblance to a human baby.

Before I wrote *The Republic of Wine*, I read an essay about someone who returned to the south and wrote a memoir about his experiences in northeast China. The person had served as vice director of the propaganda department, but his real job was being a professional drinking buddy. He didn't have a good family background, so after graduating from university with a degree in Chinese just before the Cultural Revolution, he was sent down to teach in an elementary school in some little mining town. Now, university students were so valuable then that sending one to teach elementary school was clearly a "use of the large to do the small." But because his university had marked him as a rightist, he couldn't get a break, couldn't get a wife, and started thinking of ways to kill himself. But taking poison was too painful, and the other ways he could think of were too grotesque, or just inconvenient, so he thought, screw it, just buy a little meat and wine. Dead drunk he could be happy enough. But to his surprise, he found that even after five catties of wine, he was as sober as ever, and there he had gone and spent two months' salary on wine.

News of this got around and was discovered by the local party committee, who had the guy sent to the party propaganda department just to be a drinking buddy. Someone from one of the higher agencies came down and told him to demonstrate his drinking abilities. The bibber had studied Chinese and memorized many poems and song lyrics from the Tang and Song dynasties, which he used to come up with lines of doggerel verse to toast everyone one with, and this was just right for the occasion and got everyone nice and relaxed. He ended up creating a large number of stanzas to use at the drinking table and could drink oceans without getting drunk, so in no time he became a local celebrity. Many pretty young ladies wanted to marry him, and he was promoted to vice director of the propaganda department. A person like that had to become a major character in *The Republic of Wine.*

Stories like *The Republic of Wine* actually have two goals: one is to use fiction to criticize and lay bare the dark side of society, with all its injustices, and another goal is to push forward with formal technical experimentation in fiction. I just now spoke of the main plotline, of the detective story and an amateur writer, with work by the amateur eventually getting combined with the story by the author. Moreover, every letter by the amateur writer imitates some popular writer of the times, with chapter 1 of his story in the style of Lu Xun's story "Medicine," the second letter imitating the irreverent style of Wang Shuo, and the third letter in the style of Eileen Chang. I think *The Republic of Wine* is experimental and full of complexities.

After I finished this story, I approached many periodicals, but none would carry it. Yu Hua is a good friend of mine, for we used to be classmates and even lived in the same dorm. Back then he hadn't yet moved to Beijing and was still down in Jiaxing, in Zhejiang Province, editing the journal *Rain and Mist Pavilion*, so I made a thick carbon copy and sent it down to Yu Hua to take to a major journal down there. An old editor there read it and said, "How can we publish a story like this?" It was several years later before society progressed a step, became a little more open, and works like *The Republic of Wine* could be released.

WRITING TO TELL A STORY

After *The Republic of Wine*, I once again wrote a large number of short stories and novellas. The goal of short stories and novellas is to tell a story. In 1990, I visited Malaysia, where I met the famous Taiwanese writers Zhang Dachun and Chu T'ien-hsin. We sat together at a meeting, and even though cross-strait relations were strained, with Taiwan not yet reunited with the mainland, we writers sure were united, sharing stories, telling political jokes of all kinds, and relating anecdotes of various sorts to one another. When it comes to political humor, Taiwanese writers outstrip mainland writers, but for outlandish stories of ghosts, demons, and spirits, I'm better than they are.

Later, Zhang Dachun said, "Can you write up these stories you're telling, say five thousand words apiece, and twenty pieces? I'll find a publisher for you in Taiwan and pay your fee in US dollars." So I spent one summer vacation writing one piece every day until I had more than ten. These stories were solely for the sake of telling stories—and telling a complete story, with no fancy techniques. I think this was a really great exercise.

I think the goal of these pieces was to tell a story for others to listen to. I posed as a traditional Chinese storyteller performing for his audience, as in the five great Ming collections, or like the Qing storyteller Pu Songling. This period of short story creation made me feel that if a writer takes the position of a storyteller, it should feel good. If writers imagine they are being surrounded by large audiences, then they will feel like they are using their voices to tell their stories for others to hear, except that they put it all down with pen and paper. This was likely a new principle of literary creation. Because by the 1990s, we had more or less learned about Western literature, and we had experimented with every kind of creative technique, in pretty much all the different variations, and I think we needed just then to return to the most basic goal of storytelling.

Writing to Change the Techniques of Revolutionary Historical Fiction

In 1995, I wrote the book *Big Breasts and Wide Hips*. Even just ten years ago, I would have blushed to bring up a title like that, but society is developed now, and I can talk to you all about this calmly and without anxiety. And I can see everybody here also thinks it is no big deal. But not back then, for the moment it was published, I received a lot of criticism for the title alone. Many people wrote to the military to lodge complaints, and some even wrote to the police, thinking it must be a crime—a writer using a title like that for his book. Of course the contents of the book left them even more upset, and this despite the fact that *Big Breasts and Wide Hips* was one of my most important works, which is to say it goes even further than what I had set out to do in the mid-1980s with *Red Sorghum*, writing the history of my home region and exploring the origins of my clan to dig up historical legends I could turn into fiction and to write legendary historical stories. There was a lag between *Red Sorghum* and *Big Breasts and Wide Hips* because of all the other work I've just spoken about.

By 1995, which was the year my mother passed away, I hadn't written for a long time, but I had been thinking and thinking, turning over in my mind all the incredible sufferings experienced by my mother's generation of women. They had been born in the 1920s, and even though this was the Republican era and the country had abolished foot binding, these women still bound and crippled their natural feet, in secret and illegally, and of their own accord. It was even a competition, with whoever bound her feet the smallest getting the most glory. And then their feudalist families went through war, famine, and illness, and all the while these women had to keep on bearing children. After Liberation, they faced the great famine of the 1960s, surviving by the sweat of their brows, only to face the social chaos of the Cultural Revolution. If you think about it, they rarely got more than a few days of peace and stability: first it was the 1920s, then the 1930s brought war between the Nationalists and the Communists, and then came the Anti-Japanese War, which brought invading Japanese devils, and the whole time Shandong remained a major battlefield for the Communists and the Nationalists. And then afterward, Shandong was a region that swung to the "extreme left," during the period of land reform and collectivization. Back in 1947, many of the villages had few people left. My grandfather told me that in 1947, our whole village talked like Europeans—those were his exact words, and what he meant was that they spoke quietly, not loudly like Chinese normally do, for the people had become so frightened they'd lost their voices.

I thought of my mother's generation of women. How had they been able to survive? What drove them to keep on living? It was really something to consider. Last year, when I lectured in South Korea, I spoke of my mother's experiences with this theme in mind. During the Cultural Revolution, my father was a village cadre, suffering many injuries as a result. He was so anxious that he threatened to kill himself. My mother used to console my father, "Humans have to go on. There's no mountain top we can't climb over, and no river we can't ford." As our family fell into poverty, Mother suffered through many illnesses, one after the other; one minute it was her stomach, the next her head. That's when I got it into my head that my mother might commit suicide. Every time I came home from work, I'd come into the yard yelling, "Mom! Mom! Mom!" And when my mother arrived, the relief was like a stone dropping with a thud from my heart. One day I called and called, but no one answered, and I ran frantically into every room in the house, searching, even the outhouse and the cow pens. I searched and searched, but I couldn't find her, and I thought to myself then, oh no, oh no, something must have happened to her. And just when I was about to slump down right there in the courtyard and cry, Mother came in from outside. She said, "What are you doing?" I didn't want to come right out and tell her what I had been thinking, but she guessed it later on. Mother told me, "Don't worry now. I won't go till King Yama calls me. If I did, what would happen to you? No matter how bitter it gets, humans have to go on."

I thought nothing could be simpler and more homespun than this idea, and really there was nothing particularly heroic about it. And yet, I've never forgotten it, all my life. I think this is the greatest affirmation a mother can give her son. Life held few pleasures for her, for she lived off coarse grain one half the year, chaff and wild herbs the rest, with backbreaking work to do every single day of her life, and then there were the trials of illness, of stomach ulcers and headaches, and our family background was no good, and a kid like me with no prospects but always causing trouble, so the road ahead looked pretty grim. And right then, in that moment, was when my mother said she would never commit suicide, that she would never end her life herself. I would never forget this, my whole life.

When my mother passed away in 1995, I wanted to write a story dedicated to her. At first it was just a simple idea, to write about a few of the trials and tribulations she faced in her life, but the moment the pen began to move, the bigger it all became, and I put everything into the semi-fictional Northeast Gaomi Township, until I'd written a hundred-year history of the place. I wrote how it had been a wasteland a century earlier, and how people slowly came to live there, and how it eventually grew into a small city; I wrote about a clan descended from blacksmiths, about the young mother who kept giving birth her whole life and had eight girls and one boy.

Why so many daughters? As everyone certainly knows, Chinese people prefer males over females. If a woman in a Chinese family cannot give birth, she will be discriminated against by all for she will be deemed incomplete. If she can have children but only daughters, then she will have no status and be treated with contempt, suffering beatings from her husband under the glaring, baleful watch of her elders. The mother in my story is in fact the ten million mothers in China of these times, all rolled into one.

Of course, many readers, including many critics, find this hard to accept. Because I bust open the concept of the ideal mother that we all carry in our minds—I write that this mother has nine children by seven men. Her husband, the son from a family of blacksmiths, is a weak, useless man, lacking virility, and always beats his wife. For this woman to survive in a society that demands wives bear children, she has to turn to other men in order to get pregnant. With a plot like that, the story gives us an image of motherhood that's the total opposite of the traditional ideal. Some say my character is no mother at all but a mere slattern. Yet what I write here is in fact the sharpest condemnation possible of Chinese feudalism because it is the Chinese feudal system that drives a woman to such lengths just to survive.

This mother feels great shame. One of her daughters becomes the wife of a Nationalist, one the wife of a Communist, and one the wife of a traitorous military officer who joins the Japanese. Fierce fights erupt constantly between daughters and sons-in-law, but the children they have are all sent to the old mother, who takes in the son of the Nationalist's wife one day, and the child of the daughter in the Communist army the next day; before long the daughter married to the officer who joined the Japanese also sends the old mother her child. The old mother looks after the children of Nationalists, Communists, and traitors with equal love and affection. She believes they are all good children, regardless of what class and position their fathers or mothers hold; for to a mother, all children are the same.

Of course I was most partial to the son who was created last. This boy is the child of the mother and a Swedish missionary. Some people made fun of me for this: "Mo Yan writes about a Swedish missionary in his *Big Breasts and Wide Hips*—so does that mean he wants to win the Nobel Prize?" I felt a bit embarrassed about that, but there really was a Swedish missionary in Gaomi around the year 1900, so I didn't make it up. If I had thought about it a little more, I might have made him Danish, or Norwegian, or some other nationality and been done with it.

This mother eventually marries the missionary and has his child, who is of mixed blood, grows up tall and with a large build, a head full of blond hair, blue eyes, and white skin—a very handsome lad. But because of his home environment, because of the social environment he has to grow up in, the child is perpetually infantile, unable to mature, unable to leave his mother's bosom, living off just her breast milk well into his teens. While he is at school, during physical exercise class, his mother goes to the school field to breastfeed him, making him the butt of jokes among the other students. The school principal steps in to speak with the mother, saying, "Can you please not feed your son breast milk?" But his mother says, "My son can't handle any other foods, for no sooner does he eat anything else than he throws up. Only a mother's milk can keep him alive."

This is of course a detail with symbolic significance, for although it is true enough that some boys in my hometown weren't weaned off breast milk until seven or eight years old, I wrote that he was breastfed until he was a teenager, which is an exaggeration. I think many Chinese look grown up, but in spirit they are still breast-milk drinkers. His "love of breasts" is also a symbol of how we all become obsessed with things we don't really need, how some of our passions become excessive, and how these obsessions and excesses become fetishes that can even be harmful to us.

The story continues all the way to the mid-1990s, with the second half containing many examples of satire and black humor. Why is the story called *Big Breasts and Wide Hips*? It's a title that goes with the substance of the story—the first two words are, I think, words of praise, whereas the last two words are satire, and so the title matches the story. Back in the 1990s, I think almost no one said the story was good, and in fact everyone condemned it. I think a big problem with it was that the story meddled with our views of class, which made it unacceptable to older writers and critics. When I wrote the story, I did indeed have very clear goals. Why did I write it? I wanted to change the way we wrote historical fiction and fiction about the history of the revolution.

Past fiction about the history of the revolution is, well, I can't say not good, but it has a certain quality: all of the class positions are extremely clear. When we look back today at these Red Classics, at the movies of this period, the good guys are simply good, and the bad guys are just bad, with absolute clear boundaries in between. Good guys have absolutely no flaws, or if they do, these are at most because of a daring and adventurous nature, and they certainly have no moral defects, only minor imperfections of character. And bad guys, well, they are definitely bad to the bone, both ugly in appearance and with corrupt morals, truly "ulcerous scalps to blistered soles," bad from head to toe. But in fact, in life, in history, is it really this way? I don't think so.

I lived in a farm village for many years, and some of the villagers served in the Eighth Route Army, and others really were in the Nationalist Army. Two of the guys who served in the Eighth Route Army had faces covered in pockmarks, whereas two with the Nationalists were tall and handsome, clean-cut, with thick brows and big eyes, quite the opposite of how things look in novels and movies. In other words, bad guys really don't look the way they were pictured in the old stories. And back then, whether a person was in the Eighth Route Army or the People's Liberation Army or the Nationalist Army was not always a matter of choice or will. Many sons of dirt-poor families were conscripted by the Nationalists or forced to replace others. If one family had no money, but a young man from a rich family didn't want to go, the rich family would give the poor family a little money in return for their son serving as a soldier in the rich son's place. The son from the poor family would go right into the Nationalist Army, with nothing else for it, but later the family would be labeled counterrevolutionaries. And in other families, a person with loads of money would be swept up in the spirit of the New Learning and join the Communist Party and army. There are many examples of this phenomenon.

If we use class analysis to view history, we simplify history. It's okay for writing textbooks, for these can of course be written according to the guidelines of Chairman Mao's *Analysis of the Classes of Chinese Society*, but if we use this view to guide our fiction writing to advance literary creation, I feel the resulting stories will all read just the same, a thousand songs with only one tune. So I think we should still use the method of sentiments and sensations to write fiction, turning history into feelings, into something about individuals. This is the idea guiding the good and bad characters of *Big Breasts and Wide Hips*, making officers in the Eighth Route Army, officers in the Nationalist Army, and even traitors in the Japanese army all very different from characters in the revolutionary historical fiction of the past.

Older and more traditional readers and critics find it hard to accept. They say, "Aren't you praising the Nationalists? Why do the Nationalists come off better than the Communists?" Before, Nationalists were bad, but now Nationalists and Communists have shaken hands and made up. History is unfolding. And the Chairman of the Nationalist Party, the KMT in Taiwan, and the General Secretary of the Communist Party have shaken hands and greeted each other warmly on the red carpet of the Great Hall of the People in Beijing. When Chen Shuibian's Democratic People's Progress Party was in power, we hoped that the Nationalists would get elected. Back in the day, we swore to destroy the KMT, to smash it, to sweep it from the face of the earth. But just a few decades later, Nationalists have become close friends with Communists. I think writing fiction with class views results in short-lived stories. But if we can manage to write the people we think of as bad guys and the people we think of as good guys simply as people, then our story will accord better with both life and the principles of literature, which will give it a longer life.

FORGING AHEAD ON THE PATH OPENED UP BY LU XUN

As the twenty-first century began, I wrote an important novel, *Sandalwood Death. Sandalwood Death* was storytelling fiction. This time, I really allowed myself to indulge in the feelings I had when I wrote stories during the 1990s. I felt that I should use this method and these feelings to write stories in the guise of the storyteller. I also borrowed from folk opera because in my home region there actually is a little-known drama form called "Mao-style" opera, which in my story of course becomes "Cat (*mao*) style." The story is effectively a fictionalized dramatic work, or a dramatized novel. Many characters in it are actually in full makeup, some as heroes, some as damsels, old people, or clowns, in a theatrical dramatic structure, with lines that pass back and forth with the rhythm and rhyme and beats of the theater. This kind of story, precisely because it has dramatic language, cannot be as erudite as the stories of Lu Xun. It has other priorities for its language; for example, because a storyteller's language has many repetitions and much exaggeration, these are permitted in the novel too. This was my goal in writing the novel.

Why did I write *Sandalwood Death*? I wanted to recover the writer's role as storyteller, and I also wanted to study Lu Xun. In my youth, I read Lu Xun's stories "Medicine" and *The True Story of Ah Q*, and I knew Lu Xun hated the spectator type. Lu Xun's greatest discovery was of the mindset of the spectator. But I think Lu Xun never described the mindset of the executioner.

I think, too, that all the history of China is a stage, a stage with people killing and getting killed. But still more people who neither kill nor get killed gather round and watch the gore. So in China back then, any execution ground was a scene of madcap tragicomedy for ordinary Chinese, and the audience for these killing scenes comprised well-meaning common folk. Even though they felt shocked and disturbed by what they saw, with scenes like these, they just had to have a look.

Even now, this mindset persists. During the Cultural Revolution, public trials were common, as were mass meetings, and I myself attended them. We all gathered to watch, and the goal of the officials was to make an example of one to scare straight the many, warning the common folk not to do wrong. But the common folk saw it all as theater to be watched. Lu Xun's stories have many such descriptions, but I think the writing of spectators and the punished only gets at part of the story—one of the three players is missing. So in *Sandalwood Death*, I created the executioner.

I think executioners and criminals are linked at the hip, dramatically speaking. They both perform for an audience of onlookers. The braver the criminal, the more determined he is to keep his self-respect until his death, and the more upright and dignified he is, drinking a big bowl of wine and declaring, "Twenty years from now will come another such man as I," the more pleased and satisfied is the audience. It doesn't matter what crime was committed, so long as he shows he's a real man as he's about to die. All he has to do is be fearless about death, and the audience will think he is an amazing hero, and they'll applaud him, and say "Bravo!" But if, just before he's to be strangled, he freezes and gets scared, cringes and panics, the spectators won't get satisfaction, and then they'll turn cruel and condescending. And the executioner, too, will lose interest and realize he's facing a spineless sack of shit. The executioner who meets a "real man" feels excited and brilliant himself, for the chess master needs a worthy opponent, which in his case is a true man who does not fear death. "Brother, do your work nimbly" was a scene we commonly saw in the past. In one of the *Strange Tales from a Chinese Studio*, a man about to be executed says to his executioner, "Be nimble, sir." The executioner says, "No problem! Back in the day you bought me a drink, so I owe you one, and today I have made sure the blade is good and sharp." Down it goes, the head flies off the body, exclaiming, "What a swift blade!" In other words, later on, these norms became distorted.

We have analyzed the minds of criminals, of spectators, but this killer— the executioner—what kind of mindset does he have? This type of person occupies a low place in society. There used to be a meat stall, some say, in Beijing, near Caishikou, but it closed because no one would buy meat from the stall because it was too near the execution grounds. The job of executioner is an extremely lowly and disdained one. In the 1990s, there was a French novel translated into Chinese, *Bourreaux de père en fils* (Executioners, like father like son), about a family that is more than willing to be honest about their profession. How do they manage to live? How do they come to terms with themselves over this way of making a living? I address these questions with much analysis in *Sandalwood Death*. The executioner says, "It's not I who kill people, but it is the emperor who kills people, the nation who kills people, the law who kills people. I just happen to be the one who makes it happen; I am merely doing a job for the emperor." Later he says, "I am a craftsman, perfecting my craft."

In a feudal society, a person who committed the most serious crimes, the most heinous and unforgivable crimes, earned the slowest and longest forms of torture. Making dying last a long time was thought to increase the power and intensity of the punishment. Death from one blow of the knife or one gunshot was considered merciful, and only a slow death, preventing the prisoner from dying swiftly, could produce the enormous shock and powerful impact necessary to strike fear into the common folk. But the result was that the common folk took this as the greatest of all dramas.

Sandalwood Death concerns a person who is nailed to a stake for five days, and if the executioner allows him to die before the five days are up, the executioner will lose his own head; but the longer the executioner gets the man to live, the greater the executioner's reward. The executioner must torture but at the same time sufficiently assuage the suffering so that the prisoner continues living, thereby showing the common people how the prisoner suffers from his punishment. "Were you against the emperor? Did you not oppose the court? Well, this is what happens." Such was the rationale of feudal society for administering this kind of punishment, for refusing to allow a person to have a good death. The executioner should know his work well. Does the slow torture not involve five hundred cuts of the knife? The executioner applies three thousand cuts without killing his man. There are many dark histories of cruel Chinese punishments, as *yaozhan*, the "waist breaker," or *lingchi*, slow slices, death by a thousand cuts.

Of course, while I was writing, I also thought of what is happening today. Though this story concerns events from the end of the Qing dynasty and the first period of the Republic, it still makes me think of Zhang Zhixin of the Cultural Revolution and Lin Zhao of Suzhou. Zhang Zhixin was tortured in prison—perhaps many of you young people have not heard of Zhang Zhixin, so you can look her up online—because in the most intense and heady days of the Cultural Revolution, she openly expressed her doubts about the Cultural Revolution and became a revolutionary martyr. She spoke out against many of the ways things were being done then, believing them to be wrong. This was extremely counterrevolutionary at the time, and she refused to renounce her views even under threat of death, so she suffered all kinds of torture. In the end, when she was shot, it was feared that she would cry out something rash, so they severed her windpipe. This is a true story that happened in our own socialist country, with its government of the proletariat. Of course, with the smashing of the Gang of Four, Zhang Zhixin was reinstated as a Party member and recognized posthumously as a martyr.

Not far from my hometown, there was a man from Shandong, who used to work in the northeast as an officer of the Public Security Bureau. He's now retired and has returned home. This man was involved in the Zhang Zhixin case—which is to say, when Zhang Zhixin was sentenced to death, he was one of the officers who had to carry out the sentence. Later I got to know him and I asked him, "Who was it who severed Zhang Zhixin's windpipe?" He hemmed and hawed over this question and wouldn't say. But after Zhang Zhixin had been rehabilitated, I asked him, "What was the mindset of the person who severed Zhang Zhixin's windpipe? Does he regret it? Will he think for the rest of his life that he committed a serious crime?" He said, "No, all of this was the policy instituted in the name of the revolution, and severing her windpipe was to stop her from producing counterrevolutionary speech. Maybe you wouldn't do it or I wouldn't do it, but in the end somebody had to do it."

So the mindset of the executioner is like this: whether you do it or I do it, someone will have to do it. Maybe I can do it better than you, so it is just as well that I do it. Thus, this kind of person brooks no regrets. And I think, even if he did, would others allow him to feel regret? Would we allow the police officer who cut Zhang Zhixin's throat to feel regret? Allow him to write a letter of apology? Allow him to lay bare the truth of history?

The talented young woman Lin Zhao, of Peking University, ended up getting shot; and when she was about to be shot, someone stuffed a rubber ball into her mouth. This kind of rubber ball swells up when you speak until it fills the entire cavity of your mouth. This little invention was likely the work not of scientists but our very own talented prison guards.

So, in our own lives, and I speak here of our times, not of the feudal system of the past, there were many people of great talent acting as prison guards or slaves, and their masters merely had to raise an eye or give the slightest sign of what they wanted, and the slaves worked well and would use their skills and intelligence to carry out their masters' orders to the fullest. You want to torture a certain prisoner? Or someone they know? Then these talented prison guards and talented slaves will bring their full powers to bear to come up with many cruel punishments.

Looking back on history, investigating this topic becomes harrowing, hair-raising. We think, then, if the prison guard who invented the rubber ball were still around today, would he feel regret? Would he believe that his invention was inhumane? Or would he apply for a patent? It's hard to say.

The painful episodes of the two young women martyrs of the—very recent!—Cultural Revolution helped inspire me to write *Sandalwood Death*. And they also made me think about how the culture and mindset of spectators, which Lu Xun first exposed, continue to develop in contemporary China. When I began, my goal with this novel was simple. But as I wrote, I added something more complex.

Sandalwood Death had some good reviews, and of course the voices of the critics have been strong and intense, and I think that's normal. I've defended myself before and believe these scenes of cruelty should be mulled over, which is why I couldn't delete any of them. I think that if there were no scenes of cruelty, this story would have no legs. Because this novel's main character is an executioner, if it were not written like this, I wouldn't be able to fill out the character and he would never be able to stand on his own. So even if this writing scares some readers off, I think that to create the character and for the sake of literature, it's worth it.

If I deal with these themes in the future, will I still take them to such extremes? I'll have to think carefully about that. Because in *Red Sorghum*, I also wrote a description of how a Japanese flayed the skin off a Chinese. Back then that was criticized too, but at the time we just called it naturalistic description. But in *Sandalwood Death*, the reaction was definitely more intense. I didn't realize how serious the problem was when I wrote it, but later, when I received more feedback from readers, I had to consider this problem more deeply. And I hope when I write in the future, I'll be able to come up with a different way, one that can avoid excessively graphic scenes but still allow me to create lively characters.

After I finished *Sandalwood Death*, I wrote the two novels *POW!* and *Life and Death Are Wearing Me Out*. When I wrote *POW!*, I wanted to synthesize all the writing I'd done from the perspective of a child. Many of the stories I'd written, especially novellas and short stories, take on the perspective of a child. *POW!* is an entire novel from the perspective of a child.

With *Life and Death Are Wearing Me Out*, I wanted to dig deeper into our national traditions and national culture. I used the traditional "chapter book" form to write the novel, which is of course only a minor accomplishment, like the carving of insects. Everybody can use the chapter book form. Of course, to me this is also a kind of code, for I wanted to use the chapter book form to urge us to remember and respect the role of long chapter book novels in Chinese history. Of course, some critics thought the chapter book form was too simplistic. This novel could have worked without the use of the chapter book form, and the use of this form was not some great and inventive creation—in fact I never intended to be inventive with it, but rather I meant to pay homage to the classic Chinese novel.

TO MAKE MY OWN SOUL SHINE

Since the Reform and Opening Up of the late 1970s, the past thirty years have brought immense changes to China in every area. And Chinese fiction writing has also followed a long and winding course. On this course, there have been many successful experiments, and there have been many lessons from failure—this applies to me as well, as I see it, and in fact my own personal reasons for writing have certainly changed. If you all were to ask me: If you were to write a new novel now, why would you write it? Or rather, what goals do you have for writing now, and what goals do you think you might have in the future? I'll answer this now. I think that in certain respects, the course of my writing can be summed up like this: in the early stages of the process, I take good guys as bad guys, and write bad guys as good guys. I explained the reasoning behind this just now when I talked about *Big Breasts and Wide Hips*.

"To write good guys as bad guys" in fact means to write both good and bad guys as human beings. Good guys will actually be flawed in many ways; they may exhibit many moral failures at any given moment and may have dark mindsets. Bad guys, for their part, certainly haven't lost their human nature completely, and even the vilest pirate can at some points show a heart full of charity and compassion.... Writing good guys as bad guys and writing bad guys as good guys is the basic idea I've stuck with over the last thirty years.

And now I have to square some accounts with myself. I think the next step is to write myself as a criminal, which is another lesson I learned from Master Lu Xun. Of course, today many critics and university professors in

China criticize Chinese authors for lacking self-consciousness, for lacking conscious efforts in introspection or self-analysis. In other words, we can criticize others, we can put everyone else under our lenses, finding their weaknesses and their shortcomings; we can take the moral high ground and ask questions of others, force others to experience regret. But why do we not ask this of ourselves? Do we have the courage to dissect our own souls, deeply and without the slightest shred of sentimentality?

In his day, Lu Xun served as a shining example; he dissected himself unsparingly. Can today's writers be like Lu Xun's generation, bravely facing the darkest and ugliest places deep in their souls, dissecting and criticizing unsparingly? I think they can if they try, and whether it's done thoroughly or not, it is better to try than not to be mindful at all. But now I'm at risk of sounding like a hypocrite, to put it simply, or to put it more crudely, a dog taking on a man's guise. Even though I stand here mouthing off, if I turn unsparingly back on life's long road, I find that I have certainly made mistakes, and I've even made mistakes that none can forgive, including some things that were morally problematic. My writing doesn't allow for a volume of Confessions like Rousseau's, but I can use this spirit, this sort of literary world, to shine a light on my own soul, which can, I think, give new life to my writing, allowing me to write new work, different from my old work. So in my next work, I'll take myself as a criminal.

I will end here, so I can answer questions from you all.

Thank you.

(Translated by Jesse Field)

18

READING WITH MY EARS

LECTURE AT NATIONAL TAIWAN UNIVERSITY, JULY 2008

Several years ago at a conference in Taipei, I was in a roundtable discussion with several other authors on the topic of childhood reading experiences. Except for me, every author there had been a prodigy, with some having read *Romance of the Three Kingdoms* or *Journey to the West* by age five, while others had read A *Dream of Red Mansions* at age six, which shocked and surprised me. Compared to them, I certainly was not cultured. When it was my turn to speak, I said, "While all of you were taking on all these books, I was reading too; it's just that you all were reading with your eyes, whereas I was reading with my ears."

Of course, I have to admit I also read a few books with my eyes when I was a child, but in the little village where I was from, you really couldn't find many books, and after I made the effort to get ahold of these and read them through, I got the fake impression I had read all the books in the world. It was only later, when I had a chance to go into a library, that I knew just how laughable I had been back then.

When I was ten years old, I stopped attending school and went back to the village where what I worried about most was just whether the cows and sheep I was in charge of had been fed, or whether the little birds I was taking care of on the sly had been eaten by ants. Never in my wildest dreams could I have imagined then that I'd become someone who wrote fiction for a living. To a child, such people seemed like gods. Of course, after I became a writer, I knew we were not worshipped and were not great, and sometimes writers were even lower than most people.

I spent a long, slow youth in the village and, as I said, in this period, once I had read all the books in all the surrounding villages, I didn't have much more to do with books. Most of what I knew came from listening with my ears. Just as many writers have a grandmother, many writers get their first feelings for literature from the stories their grandmothers tell, and I too had a grandmother who could tell stories, and I took in all that literary nutrition from the stories of my grandmother. But I'm even prouder to say that besides my grandmother who could tell stories, I had a grandfather who could tell stories too, and there was also "Great Grandpa"—my grandfather's older brother—who could tell stories even better than my grandfather could. In addition to the three of them, every single one of the oldest villagers carried a bellyful of stories, and because I was around them for almost twenty years, I could never count the number of stories I've heard from their lips.

Their stories were weird and scary, and they sure did get to you. In their stories, the line between the dead and the living was not clear; nor was there a clear difference between plants and animals; and even material objects, like brooms or strands of hair or lost teeth, somehow found a way to turn into spirits. In their stories, the dead were never far off but rather lived right among us, always watching us, partly to protect us but also of course to monitor our conduct. I was guilty of fewer bad deeds when I was young because I feared the punishment of the ancestors. And I also did many more good deeds because I believed they would sooner or later be rewarded. In my grandparents' stories, most animals could take on human form and interact with humans, even falling in love, marrying, and having children with them. For example, my grandmother told me the story of a rooster who had an affair with a human. She said that there was an attractive young woman from a well-to-do family who was kept cloistered in her boudoir, and many people came calling to arrange a marriage, but she stubbornly refused them all, saying she already had a groom chosen. The girl's mother kept a careful watch over her, and sure enough, late every night when no one was stirring, she'd hear the sounds of a man coming from her daughter's room. His voice was captivating. The next day the mother interrogated her daughter: Who was that man and how had he got in the house? And the daughter said the young man just appeared by her side every evening and disappeared again by dawn's first light the next day. The daughter said that every time the young man came, he wore brilliant, stunning clothes. The mother said to the daughter, next time hide the man's clothes. That evening, the man came again. The daughter hid his clothes in the wardrobe. When dawn broke, the man wanted to leave but couldn't find his clothes. Disconsolate, he pleaded with the girl to give them back, but she would not. When the roosters in the village began to crow, the man had to run off stark naked. After daybreak, the mother opened up the chicken coop, and out popped a big rooster that had no feathers at all. She had her daughter open up the wardrobe, and what clothes do you think she found? Nothing but chicken feathers. Now this is one of the stories that truly left the deepest impression on me as a boy. Later on, whenever I saw a rooster with resplendent plumage or a handsome young man, I would get the feeling the rooster had transformed from a young man, or the young man had changed from a rooster. Three hundred *li* from my hometown is the hometown of Pu Songling, the greatest of all Chinese storytellers. After I became a writer, I began reading his books, and I realized that I had heard many of these stories before, when I was a child. I don't know if Pu Songling wrote his book after hearing my ancestors tell their stories, or whether my ancestors based their stories on his book. But, of course, I now see the connection between his book and the stories I heard.[1]

Most of the stories my grandparents' generation told were about ghosts and spirits, whereas most of the stories my parents' generation told were about history, though of course the history they told was inflected with legend, quite distinct from the history in textbooks. In oral folk history, there is no class consciousness and no class struggle, but there is hero worship and a sense of fate. Only those great talents with extraordinary will and extraordinary strength get to be sung about by the people. Moreover, these characters are constantly elevated and improved as the stories are circulated. Stories of historical legend don't come with a sense of true and false. Everyone—even a crafty thief or an audacious bandit, or a courtesan of peerless beauty—has a role to play. Storytellers tell of these villains and low characters with words of praise and admiration, along with facial expressions and body language flush with enthusiasm. More than ten years ago, when I wrote *Red Sorghum*, I had already realized that the official histories laid out in books weren't trustworthy, but neither were the oral histories passed down by the common people. Distorting official history is a political necessity; filling history with legend and romance is a psycho-spiritual necessity. As a writer, I was of course willing to enter the realm of historical folk legends and be nourished by it. Because part of writing a literary work is the desire to move the human heart, a writer must tell stories that surprise and shock, and in telling surprising and shocking stories, one must fashion characters with distinct personalities, different from the norm, and these characters hardly ever exist in real life, though they appear all over in the stories my father's generation told. For example, my father told the story of a distant relative who ate half a cow and fifty large wheat cakes; his capacity for food was, of course, directly related to his physical strength. Father said this man could take the place of a horse in pulling a loaded horse cart for over ten *li*. I know there certainly was no such relative, but my father insisted that he did exist to make the story more believable, which actually is a good example of storytelling technique. Later, when I wrote *Red Sorghum*, I borrowed this technique. In the opening chapter, I wrote, "My father, a bandit's offspring who had passed his fifteenth birthday, was joining the forces of Commander Yu Zhan'ao, a man destined to become a legendary hero, to ambush a Japanese convoy on the Jiao-Ping highway." In reality my grandfather was a highly skilled carpenter, and my father was a peasant so softhearted he could hardly kill a chicken. After my novel was published, my father was very unhappy and said I had slandered him. I said writing fiction was telling stories, and hadn't he said we had a relative who could eat half a cow? When my father heard this, he understood and then declared the deepest secret of fiction in a single sentence: "So writing fiction is just coming up with a lot of lies and nonsense!"

Actually, storytelling isn't just for older people; sometimes young people and even children tell stories. When I was a teenager, a five-year-old boy who lived next door told me a story that I remember to this day. He said: "The circus bear said to the circus monkey, 'I'm going to escape.' The monkey asked: 'It's great here, why do you want to escape?' The bear said, 'It's of course great for you because the master likes you, and he feeds you apples and bananas every day, but I have to eat chaff every day, and wear chains and shackles around my neck, and the master will whip me just as soon as look at me. I've had enough of this life, so I'm going to run away.'" Well, I asked the boy, did he run away? No, said the boy. I asked why. He said, "The monkey told the master that the bear was planning to run away, and the master prevented the bear from escaping."

In my long career of reading with my ears, folk theater, especially the "Mao-style" opera of my hometown, has left a deep impression on me. "Mao-style" singing is wavering and sorrowful, and the acting gestures are unique, rendering a veritable portrait of the bitter lives led by the people of Northeast Gaomi Township. The rhythm and melodies of "Mao-style" opera followed me all through my youth, and in the slack season, when the villagers put on their costumes, I also took to the stage, and of course I always had the clown roles and performed all kind of gags and jokes, all without any makeup. For the people of Northeast Gaomi Township, "Mao style" was a day of free education and a day of pleasure, as well as an important channel to express and release pent-up feelings. Folk theater is common and easy to understand, rich with an animated, breathlessly dramatic language that can perhaps add a new quality to the language of fiction, which has become aristocratic. My recently completed novel *Sandalwood Death* is an experiment in borrowing from "Mao-style" theatrical language to refresh the language of fiction.

Of course, besides listening to the sounds from people's mouths, I listen to the voices of nature, such as the sounds of flood waters roiling, the sound of plants growing, and the cries of animals. Among the cries of animals, the most unforgettable to me is the collective cry of frogs by the thousands—it is a true chorus, a sound big and bright that deafens the ears, their green backs and cheeks, puffing in and out, completely covering the surface of the water. This scene sends shivers down the spine, and our thoughts wander outward to other things. I may not be cultured, but this type of reading with the ears was good preparation for writing later. I think my twenty years of reading with my ears have helped me cultivate a close connection with nature, as well as my historical views and moral values, and most importantly, this reading has fostered my imaginative power and helped me hold on to my childlike heart.

I believe that my imagination is the product of a life of poverty and a closed-off environment. In cities like Beijing and Shanghai, people can acquire knowledge, but they can rarely develop imagination, and it is especially hard to cultivate an imagination for literature and art. That I could become the kind of writer I am, developing my writing the way I do and producing my kind of work, is closely connected to twenty years of reading with my ears. That I have been able to sustain this writing, and always with an abundance of self-confidence, depends as well on the rich resources I gained from reading with my ears.

As for writing with my nose, this is actually the subject of another lecture, so today I'll just make a simple statement about it. Writing with the nose does not mean I put a goose feather quill up my nose, but rather when I start to write, at first unconsciously and then later consciously, I stimulate my memory and imagination for smell, which makes me feel as though I'm in the scene, and this in turn makes the readers feel that they are in the scene. Actually, as authors writes, they stimulate not only the memory and imagination of smell but all of the senses, including sight, hearing, taste, and touch, as well as the imaginative power connected to the senses. Making one's own work full of color and composition, sound and rhythm, spice and sweetness and tang, softness and hardness, cold and heat and other rich imagistic descriptions. Of course, this is all accomplished by the use of accurate and superior language. Good fiction must produce in readers the feeling that they have entered a village, a market, experience a specific familiar feeling; good fiction can make the avid reader lose himself in the characters, in their loves and enmities, their births and deaths.

This kind of fiction is not easy to write, but I try hard and never give up.

(Translated by Jesse Field)

Notes

1. This refers to *Strange Stories from a Chinese Studio*, the most enduring collection of stories in Chinese literature, written by Pu Songling at the end of the seventeenth century.

19

Six Lives in Search
of a Character

The 2009 Newman Prize Lecture
University of Oklahoma,
March 5, 2009

It seems ironic to ask someone called "Mo Yan" to speak in front of so many people. Thirty years ago, when a man with the name "Guan Moye" took a character from his given name, Mo, split it into two characters, and changed it into Mo Yan, he did not fully realize the implications of this rebellious act of changing both family and given names. Back then he was thinking that he should have a pen name because all major writers had one. As he stared at the new name that meant "don't speak," he was reminded of his mother's admonition from way back. At that time, people in China were living in an unusual political climate; political struggles came in waves, each more severe than the one before, and people in general lost their sense of security. There was no loyalty or trust among people; there was only deception and watchfulness. Under those social conditions, many people got into trouble because of things they said; a single carelessly uttered word could bring disaster to one's life and reputation as well as ruination to one's family. But at a time like this, Mo Yan, or Guan Moye, was a talkative child with a good memory, an impressive ability to articulate, and, worst of all, a strong desire to express his views in public. Whenever he felt like showing off his eloquence, his mother would remind him, "Don't talk too much." But as the saying goes, it's easier for a dynasty to rise and fall than for a man to change his nature. As soon as he was away from his mother's watchful eye, out came a torrent of words.

In *Life and Death Are Wearing Me Out*, the novel that won the Newman Prize, there is a Mo Yan who spews incessant nonsense and incurs everyone's displeasure. Though I cannot say that this Mo Yan is the real Mo Yan, he isn't far off.

Literature comes from life. This is, to be sure, an apt description, a sort of eternal truth. But life encompasses boundless experience, and all writers can use are slivers of their personal lives. If writers wish to continue to write, they must strive to expand their life experiences and fight the desire to pursue wealth and leisure. Instead, they must search for suffering, which is the salvation of an established writer, even though in the pursuit of suffering one can stumble upon happiness. Therefore, the greatest wealth of writers are the sufferings they happen upon in their search for happiness. This, of course, is purely coincidental, not something that can be planned. So I believe that, in addition to talent and hard work, fate is indispensable to one's literary success.

A writer can produce many works in a lifetime, but only one or perhaps a few will be remembered by readers. As of now, I've written ten novels and nearly a hundred novellas and short stories. I cannot say for sure which one, or ones, might pass the test of time and continue to be read. The jury, in a way, made that judgment for me when they awarded the Newman Prize to *Life and Death Are Wearing Me Out*. So if two of my novels will be read by later generations, I believe that *Life and Death Are Wearing Me Out* will be one of them, partly because it won the prize, but especially because it brings into play some of the most important experiences of my life. I have said elsewhere that the novel was written in the short span of forty-three days, but it took forty-three years to germinate and develop. In the early 1960s, Guan Moye was still in elementary school. Every morning during the calisthenics broadcast after second period, he would see an independent farmer with the surname Lan pushing a cart with wooden wheels, something that was no longer in use even then. It was pulled by a gimpy donkey accompanied by Lan's wife, a woman with bound feet. The wooden wheels grated shrilly against the dirt path by the school, leaving deep tracks. Guan Moye remembered all this. Back then, like all the other kids, Guan Moye felt nothing but disgust and disdain for this stubborn farmer who had insisted on working independently instead of joining the commune, and Guan Moye even joined them in the evil act of pelting him with stones. Lan Lian resisted the pressure until 1966, when under the cruel persecution of the Cultural Revolution he could no longer hold out and took his own life.

Many years later, after Guan Moye became Mo Yan, he wanted to turn the independent farmer's story into a novel. The commune system was abolished in the 1980s, when peasants were allotted parcels of land, essentially making them independent farmers again. Mo Yan was particularly impressed by Lan Lian, an exceptional peasant who dared to hold his own views and wage a war against society to the point of sacrificing his life to preserve his dignity. There has never been another character like him in contemporary Chinese literature. But Mo Yan delayed writing the novel because he had yet to find the right narrative structure. It was not until the summer of 2005, when he saw in a famous temple the mural of the six transmigrations of life, that he had an epiphany. He decided to let a wrongly executed landlord pass through the lives of a donkey, an ox, a pig, a dog, and a monkey before being reborn as a big-headed baby with an incurable congenital disease. The loquacious baby recounted the many strange and uncommon experiences of his different lives as various domestic animals, while examining, from the perspectives of those animals, the transformations of the Chinese countryside over the past fifty years.

Someone once asked me about the connection between the Mo Yan in the novel and the real-life Mo Yan. My response was the Mo Yan in the novel is a character created by the writer Mo Yan but is also the writer Mo Yan himself. In fact, this is the connection between novelists and all the characters in their novels.

(Translated by Silvia Li-chun Lin[1])

NOTES

1. *World Literature Today* 83, no. 4 (Jul.–Aug. 2009): 26–27

Part IV

On Beliefs

"As members of society, novelists are entitled to their own stances and viewpoints; but when they are writing they must take a humanistic stance and write accordingly. Only then can literature not just originate in events, but transcend them, not just show concern for politics, but be greater than politics.

"I am a storyteller.

Telling stories earned me the Nobel Prize for Literature.

Many interesting things have happened to me in the wake of winning the prize, and they have convinced me that truth and justice are alive and well.

So I will continue telling my stories in the days to come."
—Mo Yan, Nobel Lecture
(translated by Howard Goldblatt)

20

WRITING HAS ITS OWN ROAD

LECTURE AT KYOTO UNIVERSITY, OCTOBER 1999

My dear respected ladies and gentlemen,

That I can lecture here before you is because I have written fiction, which has been translated into Japanese by the Japanese Sinologists Mr. Tomio Yoshida and Mr. Shozo Fujii and several others. That my fiction should have been noticed by the likes of Mr. Tomio Yoshida and Mr. Shozo Fujii and others is my good fortune; that I can step onto the beautiful sovereign soil of Japan and lecture to you is my honor; and today's good fortune and honor are the kind that twenty years ago, when I began to write, I would never have dreamed of achieving.

Twenty years ago, when I took up the pen and wrote my first short story, I was still a peasant who had just emerged from the sorghum fields of my home in Northeast Gaomi Township and in the words of Chinese city dwellers about country bumpkins, "the sorghum floss still stuck to his head." My earliest motivation to write was very simple; I just wanted to take my fee and buy a shiny new pair of shoes to satisfy my vanity. Of course, after I bought the shoes, my ambitions continued to swell. Then I wanted to buy a watch made in Shanghai, put it on my wrist, and head home to show off to my family and fellow villagers. Back then I was still stationed in the military, and during the long nights I would sink into the sweetness of my imagination. I imagined parading up and down the streets of my village in those shoes with that watch, and I imagined all the coy looks I'd get from the young ladies. I would regularly excite myself to tears and even forget when our shift changes occurred. But tragically, I never did get that watch with my fee, for my first watch was paid for when my father sold off a cow and bought me one. Even more tragically, when I went up and down the road in my shoes and with my watch on, not one young lady tossed a single coy look my way; only some older married ladies saw fit to size me up, their eyes distinctly looking down.

When I first began to write, contemporary Chinese literature was just then in the latter stages of what they called the "searching for roots" movement, and nearly all these works criticized the evils of the Cultural Revolution. Chinese literature in this period was still performing a major political duty and did not yet have its own independent nature. I copied the works that were popular at the time, writing a few things that today I'd prefer to see burned. Only when I understood that literature must rid itself of the pernicious influence of having to fulfill a political duty did I write more coherent work. By then it was the mid-1980s. My realization had come from reading: it was late one winter evening fifteen years ago when I read a line in *Snow Country*, by Yasonari Kawabata: "A black Akita dog sat on the stone step, lapping long at the warm water." When I read this sentence, a vivid portrait, detailed and true to life, appeared before my eyes; I felt as if I'd been touched at last by the young lady I'd been longing for and fretted with so much excitement that I could hardly stand it. I understood what fiction was, I knew what to write, and I knew how to write it. Before this, I had struggled to figure out what to write and how to write it, and I could neither find suitable stories nor figure out how to speak in my own voice. Kawabata's sentence was like a beacon coming on in the dark, shining my way forward.

I didn't even bother to finish all of *Snow Country*; I just put the book down and picked up my own pen and wrote out this sentence: "Northeast Gaomi Township used to have a breed of large, white dogs, but after many generations of cross-breeding, it was very rare to see a pure specimen." This was the first time the words "Northeast Gaomi Township" had appeared in my fiction, and it was the first time I'd ever written about the idea of a "pure specimen." This was the story "White Dog and the Swing," which later won the UDN Grand Literary Award in Taiwan and was translated into many languages. After this, I raised my flag high for "Northeast Gaomi Township," and like a true bandit king, I began to recruit men and purchase horses, beginning the work of establishing my own kingdom.

Before I raised the great flag of Northeast Gaomi Township or, in other words, before the night I read about Mr. Kawabata's dog lapping warm water, I had not been able to find material for writing. I followed the guidance of the textbooks and experienced life in the villages and factories, but when I returned, I still felt I didn't have anything worth writing about. Mr. Kawabata's dog woke me: Who knew you could put dogs into literature? Who knew warm water could be in literature? After this, I never worried about finding material to write about again. After this, when I wrote a story, the new story would be like a hen rushing home to lay eggs, clucking and cawing behind me to take it home. Before, I was the one writing fiction, but now it was the fiction writing me; I became a slave of fiction.

Of course, every writer lives in some kind of social and political environment, and it is not possible to write works that bear no relation whatsoever to politics. But good writers are always thinking about how to give their works broader and more universal significance and always strive to make their works accepted and understood by more people. Good writers might be writing about their hometowns, about parcels of land no larger than the palm of your hand, and only about the people and events in that palm-sized plot. Before they even put pen to paper, good writers understand that their palm-sized space makes up an indispensable part of the world, so what happens there is one chapter of the history of the world, and this gives the work the potential to go out into the world and to be understood and accepted by all of humanity. This is an idea I got from the American writer Faulkner, as well as from Japanese writers like Tsutomu Minikami, Yukio Mishima, and Kenzaburo Oe. Of course, without them, I would still write this way now because I would have found the path eventually, but their writing practices gave me useful guidance and helped me avoid some twists and turns to the path.

In 1985, I wrote a batch of short fiction, including *The Transparent Carrot*, "Explosions," and "Dry River," all of which drew attention in the literary world. In 1986, I wrote *Red Sorghum*, which solidified my position in the literary world. In 1987, I wrote two novellas, *Happiness* and *Red Locust*, both of which drew intense criticism and even made many critics who had praised me before stop liking me; I knew I frightened them. During the next two years, I wrote the novels *The Garlic Ballads* and *The Thirteen Steps*. *The Garlic Ballads* was written based on true events, and the corrupt officials involved even said they wanted to break my legs. *The Thirteen Steps* was a complex work. Last year I went to speak at a university in Paris, and a French reader said she had used five different colored pens to mark up the book just to understand it. I told her that if I reread the work, I'd have to mark it up in six different colored pens. In 1989, I wrote *The Republic of Wine*, which has been translated by Mr. Tomio Yoshida into Japanese. This novel is almost unknown in China, but I believe it remains my finest work to date; I'm really proud of it. Over the next few years, I wrote a great many short stories and novellas, and while I was writing them, I never felt at peace with myself because there was a huge piece of material calling to me. This material became the novel *Big Breasts and Wide Hips*, which Professor Shozo Fujii has translated into Japanese; this book gave me a lot of trouble, but of course it also brought me new fame. Compared to *The Republic of Wine*, *Big Breasts and Wide Hips* is like a warm, stable, generous grandmother, whereas *The Republic of Wine* is like an attractive, wild lover.

Critics of Chinese literature have tried to affix many literary labels to me; at different times I've been of the "Neo-Sensationalist" school, or the "Searching for Roots" school, or even over in the avant-garde camp. I neither agree nor disagree with any of these labels. Writers care only about their own creations and do not even concern themselves with what readers think of their works. Writers care only for the fates of the characters in their fiction because these are lives that the writers have created, and these characters' lives are more important to the writers than their very own lives for they are connected to their flesh and blood. Writers can only do one thing in their lifetime: take their own flesh and blood, and even their own souls, and transfer these into their works.

A writer may write and publish just so many works in a lifetime and may create just so many characters, but even dozens of different books are all editions of a single book, and all the hundreds of characters in them are only ever the incarnations of a single character. All these books combine into the autobiography of the author, and all of the characters add up to the self of the author.

If you were to demand that I pull out an example of such a character, then I would speak first of the nameless "Heihai" ("the Dark Child") whom I wrote of in *The Transparent Carrot*. Heihai can speak but rarely does so, for he feels that talking is a heavy burden. This child's tolerance for suffering is beyond those of ordinary people; for example, in the bitter cold climate that turns drops of water into ice, he wears only a pair of shorts, with no shirt and his feet bare. And he is able to hold red-hot steel in his hands and look dispassionately at wounds on his body. He has the ability to fantasize; he can see strange and wonderful events that other people cannot see, and he can hear voices that other people can't hear. For example, he can hear the sound of a strand of hair falling to the ground; he can detect scents other people cannot smell. And of course, just like Shangguan Jintong in *Big Breasts and Wide Hips*, he loves women's breasts.... Precisely because of these unusual traits, the world he feels is much stranger and more novel than the world of ordinary people.

So he uses his eyes to throw open the wider perspective of humanity and uses his own experience to enrich the experience of humanity. And so even though he is me, he is more than me, and though he is human, he is more than human. Today, when technology is so developed that it copies life, this false but seemingly true transcendence is precisely the reason literature exists and can continue to exist.

Heihai is a spirit who grew up with me and went everywhere with me; he is my protector god. Now he is standing right behind me, and if some of you cannot see him, others perhaps can because no matter how strange a character, some of us recognize the child who is part of us, just as the character is part of the author.

(Translated by Jesse Field)

21

WRITING AS ONE OF
THE COMMON PEOPLE

LECTURE AT SOOCHOW UNIVERSITY,
OCTOBER 2001

Dear teachers and students, good afternoon!

It is such a high honor to lecture at Soochow University, which is such a beautiful place and has such a long history, but at the same time I feel that it involves some risk because most authors are not good public speakers, and I'm not even that good an author. Back when I took the pen name Mo Yan ("Don't Speak"), I warned myself not to talk, or at least to talk as little as possible, but here I am jabbering away. This is my contradiction. Coming to hang out at Soochow University, for example, sounded great; coming to Soochow University to speak, not so much. But if I hadn't come to Soochow University to speak, Mr. Wang Yao would not have reimbursed my air ticket, so if I wanted to come to Soochow and didn't want to pay for the ticket myself, I would just have to speak. This is an age of helplessness and compromise, each of us helpless to do anything other than compromise.

A few days ago, Alai, Yu Hua, and I had a day of discussion at Tsinghua University with the students of Ge Fei—one session in the morning, another that afternoon, and still another in the evening. We spoke very little and spent most of the time answering questions from the students. We thought this was a great approach, with none of the formalities of a regular class in which we'd have to serve as authorities. It was casual and intimate, even confrontational—a genuine, honest meeting of the minds, benefiting both sides. I hope today we can use the same method. As I speak, feel free to interrupt me at any time, and just pass up the slips of paper, or else just stand up and ask your question. In sum, let us come together like a chorus on the stage, so Wang Yao will reimburse my air ticket with pleasure.

The title of today's lecture—you know I hadn't thought up even as late as last night. I just didn't know what to put down. But then Wang Yao called and said there had to be a title to put on the poster, so I told him it's called "Discussing the Folk Sources of Literary Creation."

Now, "folk" is a huge topic and at present a very hot topic. I think it was Master Chen Sihe in Shanghai who first started this conversation, and all the other big names have joined the chorus since then. You say your piece, and they say theirs, and soon everyone has their own understanding of the concept of "folk." I am a writer of fiction, so I of course have my own understanding of folk culture. My understanding is certainly not as systematic as that of a theorist, or as cogent or comprehensive. It is simply derived from my experience in literature and embodied through my acts of literary creation, and so perhaps can it serve as a starting point for today. I should say in all honesty that the title of today's lecture is not my invention but comes from Alai last week at Tsinghua University when he said that he had recently written a piece for *World of Vision*, the title of which was "Folk Sources for Writing Fiction." In my haste, I just changed the wording and sent it along to Wang Yao, so if Alai comes down here to start trouble, you all can testify that I've already made an open confession.

Now, regarding the disputes still simmering in the field of folk culture, well, you all, being students of literature, must certainly know quite a bit about them. So I need not introduce them all, one by one—in fact, I couldn't do that even if I tried. I believe that what we call "folk writing" is in the end a matter of how the author feels about literary creation. One aspect of the question is why write. In the past there was revolutionary literature, as well as literature for the workers, for the peasants, and for the army, and later we spoke of "writing for the people." Writing for the people means writing for ordinary common people. This brings us to another aspect of the question, which is, do you write for the common people or as one of the common people?

Writing for the common people sounds like a humble and self-effacing slogan. It sounds like it means you'll labor for the people, as if you were their horse or cow. But if we consider it more deeply, it is an attitude that assumes a higher position to look down on a lower one. It inherently encourages the kind of wildly self-aggrandizing propositions authors make when they think they are somehow higher and more noble than others, for example, thinking they are "the engineers of human souls," or "the spokespersons of the people," or "the conscience of an age." It's like when we call officials "public servants"—it sure sounds humble, even slavish, but in real life, officials are not like that at all. If becoming an official meant becoming a person of service, a true public servant, then no one would do it. Becoming an official must mean you officiate over something!

Thus, I believe writing for the people is never a type of folk writing, but rather a quasi-official writing. When as an author you stand up and use your work to speak for the people, you have already placed yourself in a higher position than that of the common people. I believe that true folk writing means writing as one of the common people. Of course, there will be differences in the effect produced on the readership, after the writing is out there, but the person who writes as one of the common people need not think of this when writing. When one writes as one of the common people, one isn't thinking of using fiction to reveal anything or to assail something, or advocate for something, or teach something, which is why the writer can treat characters with such a calm and steady hand. Far from putting oneself above one's readers, one is not even above one's own characters.

Whether a writer of novels or poems or plays, one who writes as one of the people is not substantially different from any other folk craftsman. Experts in weaving, in pottery, in woodcarving are not in the least inferior to the writer. Anyone who writes as one of the common people agrees with this statement, but if one writes for the common people, one certainly would not agree. Folk craftsmen have lineage. They have their own schools and groups and their own brilliant and mysterious masters, and they may have egotistical conflicts with each other and look down on each other, but they never forget they are ordinary common people. They will never distance themselves from ordinary people and never take on the wild ambition to be "artists of the people." One great example comes not far from Soochow, where there once was a blind man named Abing, who now has a great reputation as a musician, one of the great old performers on the *erhu*. But way back then, when he was busking on the streets of Wuxi, bamboo cane in his hands, faded and threadbare clothes on his body, old Abing probably would not have thought of himself as a great figure. Even less so would he have thought that his erhu songs would be considered classics many decades later. He absolutely would not have believed he was anything more than a common person. He probably thought, "I, Abing, am nothing but a street beggar, a poor man who makes what little he can by selling his art. But if my songs move my listeners, maybe they'll think of giving me a couple coppers. And if my songs are no good, no one will pay any attention to me. If I play my erhu on the road, obstructing traffic, the constable may kick me to the curb." (Today's artists and performers would break the law and hand out their cards afterward, with a "Hi, I am so-and-so.") In sum, Abing's self-effacing mindset—never mistaking himself for nobility, and not even seeing himself as a particularly good common person—is the true mindset of the common person. Only when we work with this mindset can we produce something truly great because that kind of sorrow can only come from the deepest parts of the heart. Abing manages to touch the places in his heart that hurt the most. Just think of the song "The Moon Reflected in the Second Spring." Now that's the kind of thing a person who hasn't plunged to the depths of suffering could never write. So truly great works must be written as one of the common people. They are to be encountered, never sought and found, like phoenix feathers and kirin horns.

But putting this into practice is actually very difficult. The writer is human after all, and vanity cannot but entice. In real life today, writing for the common people wins more praise and reward than writing as one of the common people. The current generation need not require itself to be one way or another, but we do have to remind ourselves not to forget what is most important and not to chase after unimportant things, which is to say that you have to understand what you want to achieve through writing, and then you can decide what your attitude should be toward literary creation.

In the age when Pu Songling and Cao Xueqin wrote, there were no publishing houses, no manuscript fees or royalties, let alone prizes. This certainly made writing a lonely, even laughable, affair. In those times, the writer's motives for writing were simple. The first was that too much material had accumulated in his mind, and he needed a channel to let it out. Pu Songling devoted his life to preparing slavishly for the imperial examinations; and even knowing about all the corruption behind the curtain of the examination system, deep inside he knew he still wanted to pursue this academic endeavor. Later, when he gave up trying to pass the exams, he needed an outlet to channel his talent and so he chose fiction to express himself. With fiction, he could release some of his bitterness and pent-up resentment. Cao Xueqin's life circumstances are even more legendary; he was the scion of a truly aristocratic family, but they had gone bankrupt and left him and his generation in poverty.

To what depths must he have experienced the warmth and coolness of human affections and the heat and chill of the world's treatment of an individual! Both these writers had great skills they needed to put to use and great suffering they needed to vent, and they did both from the lower levels of society, as common people, and they employed their creativity without profiting from it in the slightest. This is why *Strange Stories from a Chinese Studio* and *Dream of Red Mansions* became such classics. Of course, they also had their own readership circles and earned praise within these circles after their books came out. This satisfied their vanity somewhat, but this sort of honor was too common and hardly counted as fame or profit. Under the system of examinations, fiction was like the muttering of a wild fox, unsuitable for the exalted halls of power, and it is likely that truly "orthodox" and "proper" people seldom wrote fiction. The same applied to poetry, for the true appreciators of poetry were the courtesans. But this was the only way for good art to emerge. If poetry had taken the place of the eight-legged essay as part of the imperial examinations, it would have been a complete disaster for the art of poetry. If fiction had been included in the examinations, then fiction would have been ruined long ago as well. Nowadays, when authors go after a writing award, it ruins them, even if they do win the award. If they never expect to win but do so anyway, that's another story. I think this is the difference between folk writing and non-folk writing. Unlike folk writing, non-folk writing is always heavily tainted by the profit motive. Of course, to make little profit is sometimes not a conscious decision of the writer but the writer's fate. Pu Songling, well into his late years, always dreamed of passing the examinations and gaining an office, but at long last he awoke to the fact that this was an impossible dream. Cao Xueqin was always nostalgic for those intensely dramatic years of past wealth and luxury, but he knew he would never get them back again, so his sorrow was inconsolable and the love of past glories shines through in his writing. Good things come to those who aren't really trying for them. The song of praise becomes a song of redemption;

the song of revenge becomes a song of love. It's not what was sought, but the work becomes a masterpiece.

I wish to emphasize that authors must absolutely not put themselves on a pedestal, and they must especially not take the role of a moral judge in their writing. Do not consider yourself higher than others, but remain in step with your characters. The painter Zheng Banqiao said we are hard pressed to find crazy foolishness in life, but it seems true that when writers write, sometimes they really must pretend to be crazy and foolish. In other words, you have to understand clearly that what you think is right may in fact not be right, and conversely, what you think is wrong is not necessarily wrong. Right and wrong are decided by time and history. Writing for the people means giving your verdict, but writing as one of the people doesn't necessarily involve a verdict.

Not long ago, a newspaper covering environmental protection asked me to write a piece about my views on sandstorms and other problems of the deteriorating environment. Now, the desertification of the North China plains has a direct relationship to the number of livestock pastured on the plain. Over-pasturing of livestock means the grass can't rejuvenate, and it leads to desertification. More than ten years ago, I went to the China-Russia border and saw that the grass on the plains on the other side was so lush and green, half the height of a man, dipping in the wind, with just a few scattered herds of sheep grazing. But on the plains over here, the grass is withered and yellow, barely an inch high, leaving the land looking like a scabby, flea-bitten head. Starving sheep meander in the muck like ghosts. That the same scheme of nature should feature such huge differences is entirely the result of human actions. The question is, Can we raise fewer sheep here? The answer of the shepherds is, "We never wanted to see the plains get like this either, but what are we supposed to eat if we do not raise sheep? If we don't raise sheep, how will you Beijingers enjoy your hot pot? We also know that our heishan sheep do terrible damage to the plains and the hills, but you would have your wool scarves and coats!" This brings us to a particularly thorny problem, which is that we want to protect the environment on the one hand, but on the other hand, the common people want to live and to prosper. Can the government hand out checks to all? No. The government doesn't have enough money, so these people just cut down trees and raise their sheep. You have to let them go on living. You can exhort people to protect precious animals, protect the pandas, protect the Manchurian tiger, but the fact is that in remote areas the lives of the common people are even more imperiled than these endangered species. Many who contract terrible diseases lie in their homes waiting to die, and who looks after them? But if a panda has an emergency, it will have the best doctors caring for it in no time, and once cured, it will appear in the newspapers and on TV. An author's essay on environmental protection looks like a very just deed, an endeavor with conscience, but in fact it only represents the good that can be done for a few. So I think that authors must learn to contemplate deeply and not stand automatically on the side they think is right, which is to say, you must not think you are higher than the common people just because you are an author. Writing for the people can also become writing for officialdom or writing for power, thanks to the limitations of the writer. But writing as one of the common people can perhaps help to avoid this bias—because you are one of the common people. In a sense, writing for the people is writing as an intellectual. This is a very old tradition. Take Lu Xun and his generation: though they wrote about the countryside, their perspectives were those of intellectuals. Lu Xun was an enlightener; and following him, more and more people played the role of enlighteners. And everyone raced to blame the backwardness of the national character and reveal its sickness, which is a classic form of condescension. Actually, there was a dark side to these enlighteners, no less than among any other people. Folk writing, as we see it, calls on you to abandon your position as an intellectual and use the mind of a common person to consider the situation. Otherwise, the folk you write of will be plastered-over folk, fake folk.

I think we can boldly say that true folk writing, writing as one of the people, really just means writing the self. Whether a writer can keep up with folk writing is not always something he can decide himself. In general, we are more folk when we've first begun to write, but when we become famous, it is hard to keep that special folk quality. When we first begin to write, if we are noticed by others, it must be because something about the writing makes people feel something new—whether it be the story we tell or the language we use, our writing should always show a clear difference from what is popular. This is to say that literary impact is always influential at the margins. But having made an impact, the margins become the center, and the side streams become the mainstream. The wild ghosts outside the temple become the orthodox gods atop the altars. Even though this process is almost unavoidable, it's still better to remain wary, for with wariness you can preserve your individual character for a longer time, preserve your mindset of the common people, preserve the position and method of the common people.

We can think of the works of Shen Congwen. In his early work, he preserved his authentic folk position and perspective. He wrote of the prostitutes in the port towns by the Yangzi River, and if he had taken the position of an intellectual, they would have been unappealing. But Shen Congwen wrote about their most endearing features because he took the same view of them as they did themselves, as well as the views of the men working on the boats. And he never wrote of them as martyrs or chaste ladies, but rather he wrote honestly about the characteristics of their trade: "Niubao, I'll wait three months for you, and if you don't come back, then I'm going to have to see other customers." He wrote about a friend who wore an otter-skin cap, and if he had used the position of an intellectual, the friend would have seemed no more than an ugly wastrel, but in Shen Congwen's writing this friend became passionate and interesting. But later, when Shen Congwen became a famous writer, it was hard for him to hold on to his position as a common person. He started to judge his characters, for he had—without ever quite being aware of it—taken up a position above them.

It's easy to say but difficult to practice, and yet we must do our best to try. "The more you know, the more reactionary you are" is a claim that does make some sense in writing.

I'll stop here and begin to take your questions. Please stand and speak, or pass up your slips of paper. Either way is fine.

(Translated by Jesse Field)

22

LITERATURE AND YOUTH

LECTURE AT READING FORUM, SHENZHEN, MAY 2004

Before I came to Shenzhen, General Editor Chen of the periodicals division of Haitian Press, which had published *Season of Flowers, Season of Rains,*[1] asked me what my topic would be, and I said, "Well, because this is a meeting of the Communist Youth League, let's talk about 'literature and youth!'" The topic of literature and youth is certainly very broad, and so many have talked about it before, that I realize I'm certainly giving myself a big challenge.

Yesterday on the streets of Shenzhen, I saw a car with a bumper sticker on the back that read, "Write the Essay of All Under Heaven, Become a Young *Junzi.*"[2] What does it mean to be a young *junzi*?

Confucius said, "Native substance over style is too wild, whereas style over substance makes one a mere scribe. Only getting both style and substance right makes for a *junzi.*"[3] There's literary ornamentation and there's substance, and only when the one lines up appropriately with the other do they produce the *junzi*. Now this was just a little jingle, a mere advertisement, but it seems to me that such jingles can only appear in places like Shenzhen. I travel to many places, and I always see the cars lined up, with ads in back selling laundry detergent, pushing hotels, and selling every other kind of good and service, but I had not previously seen a car ad that said "Write The Essay of All Under Heaven, Become a Young *Junzi.*" There was the one that read, "Enjoy the Wine of Confucius's Clan, Write the Essay of All Under Heaven"—in fact a friend of mine was pleased with himself for coming up with that one —but drinking wine isn't necessarily going to help your writing, for a drunk can only talk nonsense. The Shenzhen jingle said to first write the essay of "all under Heaven" and *then* you'd be the young *junzi.* Now this, I think, should be the motto for the Communist Youth League. Today's Reform-era Communist Youth League should not be just about organizing young people for public service, following the model set by the warmhearted soldier Lei Feng; it should also be an organization that brings together a broad spectrum of youths to work together for progress in the study of science and culture, and for making friends too. Of course, studying culture should also include the appreciation of literature, including reading and even writing literature. And now I've at last brought the topic round to literature, and even to literature and youth.

Beginning with the May Fourth Movement,[4] literature and youth have been closely linked, and literature has also been closely linked with revolution. So the slogans of literature and revolution, or rather the concepts, are linked to the names of revolutionaries like Li Dazhao, Chen Duxiu, Lu Xun, Guo Moruo, and Qu Qiubai. Back then, there was a great journal called *New Youth,* and even though it was technically a literary journal, it was also a revolutionary journal. What this crop of people, of literary youth, wanted was to end the era of classical Chinese, but more than that, they hoped to use literature as a weapon to bust things up, to end feudalism, to do away with the old China. So most of the literary figures of the time were revolutionaries. But literature and youth are not always linked with revolution, and even when the waves of revolution rocked the highest, there were those who hid away in their studios, doing research on *A Dream of Red Mansions,* on the Confucian classics, and there were still people who loved to be moved, to hurt and shed tears, over the love affairs of young men and young women. Entangled in the bonds of romantic love, some, like Yu Yongze in the novel *Song of Youth*, retreated from revolution,[5] hiding in their writing studios, digging into piles of books in pursuit of learning. Many decades later, after the revolution was won, history proved that people like Yu Yongze had made contributions to society that were of no lesser value than revolutionary characters like Lu Jiachuan, Jiang Hua, or Lin Daojing. They say that the old master on which the character of Yu Yongze was based was an essayist whose later work proved to be popular nationwide and highly sought after by younger readers, whereas revolutionary writers such as those the character Lu Jiachuan was based on, well, what happened to them? What this shows is that even in the middle of a revolution, literature should come in different forms, and so should young people.

Revolutionary literature of course functions in the great wave of revolution to unleash radical propaganda and advocacy; with slogans, bright and loud, and songs and ballads, a strong fire to set alight the hot blood of youth, urging young people not to sweat the small stuff, to turn away from comfort and toss themselves into the flood currents of revolution. Of course, some works should engage in studying the human heart and soul and portraying human sentiment; many readers are moved by such works as well. Many young people would rather stand with pure literature than participate in revolution. In the fullness of time, history proves the value of both types; revolutionary youths are worthy of study, of course, but those youths whose minds are more devoted to study are also significant in society. For if everyone went into the revolution, all learning would be lost; and if all people pursued learning, then our society would never have revolutionary change. This absolutely does not mean people should flee from revolution, but it is to say that no matter what age literature finds itself in, it must manifest itself in many forms; in revolutionary times there is revolutionary literature, but there is also romance and melodrama, what we Chinese call the styles of the winds and flowers, of the snow and moon. And there is also literature that shows the spirit and feeling of the age. Writers of revolutionary literature, like Jiang Guangchi, have value, but so do writers of romance novels, like Zhang Hengshui. They say that when Chairman Mao went to conduct negotiations in Chongqing, he saw Zhang Hengshui there and even gave him a gift of wool to make a coat.

In terms of literary significance, revolutionary literature is generally coarser in quality, but it still deserves a place in literary history. In terms of literary significance, the works that last longest are those that can take history as their setting, carve out characters with soul, and create classic characters. Master Lu Xun was best in this regard, and he established a shining example for the rest of us. Lu Xun is the main figure of the May Fourth Literary Revolution, and his judgment of old intellectuals was as unsparing as gunfire, or the torching of the fields. But when Lu Xun turned to literary creation, he immediately devoted his full attention to the human mind, to close observation of the human soul. He wrote with history and the revolution as his setting, and always with his eye on the people caught up in the waves of revolution, writing the forms and features of people in revolution, of how the souls of people in revolution undergo change, how their fates evolve and shift. Take *The True Story of Ah Q*, for example. This novella shows us the revolution; it describes the revolutionary party, how queues were cut, and how Ah Q traveled to the city to participate in the revolution, looting property in the process. But Lu Xun certainly never made these the main things he was describing; rather, by using key snatches of dialogue and making the revolution the historical setting, and through including many details, he managed to carve out the deepest parts of Ah Q's soul. Then, by revealing a soul, he gave a warning to a hundred million souls. Even today, when we bring up Ah Q, we recall that in the deepest recesses of every person's mind, there seems to be a tiny Ah Q hidden there. What we might call Ah-Q-ism is an important ingredient of our national culture. Chairman Mao Zedong later said that people need a little bit of the spirit of Ah Q, for without Ah Q's spirit, it is hard to go on living. The reason Lu Xun was able to bring all this out in his writing, to craft such a timeless and classic literary character, was that first, he had the passion and sensitivity of a revolutionary and, second, he grasped the principles of literature, unlike writers today who produce shallow works seeking to understand revolution. Therefore, true literature must focus on human life; it ought to enter deeply into the internal world of humanity and take the creation of representative characters as its highest aim.

As for literature and youth, we can expand our discussion from two different angles. The primary thing to consider with literature and youth is simply the set of young people who love literature, young people who try their hand at literature, the kind of people we may call *literary youth*. Back in the day, I was a literary youth. Make no mistake, being a literary youth is the path a writer must take, for no one is born a writer. One has to love literature first, and study it, and be crazy about it. The literary youth of each age seem to have their own fates, the places to which they return. Among those of the 1930s, for example, some turned out like Xiao Hong, and some like Eileen Chang; some turned out like Ding Ling, and some like Shen Congwen. I point out people who became writers, but of course there must have been many thousands of young people in the 1930s who loved literature but did not become writers. Perhaps they followed the call of literature, but for some other reason rushed out to Yan'an to participate in revolution, becoming professional revolutionaries. In terms of literary significance, Eileen Chang and Shen Congwen were for the longest time overlooked in the orthodox literary histories, despite their literary achievements, because they weren't "red" but "gray"; that is, they had not gone to Yan'an or joined the Communist Party, and of course they had not participated in any of the revolutionary movements organized by the Party leaders. So despite their literary accomplishments, they were always marginalized in our revolutionary literary histories. Starting in the 1980s, these forgotten writers were dug up and rediscovered, and they have won high places in the eyes of a broad swath of readers, including literary youth, to the point that these forgotten writers outshine formerly more illustrious writers celebrated in the textbooks. Eileen Chang, for example, could once hardly have been spoken of alongside Ding Ling, but since the 1980s, she has far surpassed Ding Ling. Xiao Hong's status as a writer has also gone through a tremendous change. Shen Congwen's position started to rise in the 1980s; in less recent literary histories, when writers are brought up, they are always the revolutionary writers Lu Xun, Guo Moruo, Mao Dun, Ba Jin, Lao She, and Cao Yu, but Shen Congwen is never listed. But since the 1980s, Shen has ridden high at the same height as Lu Xun. I see many writers and many literary youths, and I always ask them what contemporary writers they like, whose books they have read, and people bring up Lu Xun and Shen Congwen the most, and these days Shen Congwen gets almost more mentions than Lu Xun. Lu Xun has always been the ultimate example and role model, but he is also misunderstood, for over time there have been those who used Lu Xun as a stick to beat others over the heads, even though these are just the sort of people Lu Xun would have hated. And the literary views of Shen Congwen align well with today's society precisely because he didn't have particularly clear loves or hatreds. And even when Shen did write about traditional values that he didn't approve of or even hated, he did so with real sympathy. When we read his essays and his stories, we discover that they are filled with the heady atmosphere of the countryside and the unique flavor of the folk ways. This crop of literary youth, from the early liberation period, walked a path not so very different from ours in its general direction—for it also meant loving literature, then trying to write, then sending out the manuscripts widely, and finally publishing—step by step along the path of literature. The fates of most of these literary youth changed dramatically in the 1950s, for that was when more than half of all of the young writers were labeled rightists. For decades they didn't write, and they only started again at the end of the 1970s when they were rehabilitated. This crop then became the leaders of the China Writers' Association and the Ministry of Culture. So this crop enjoyed both good fortune and bad luck.

Yet another crop was the literary youth of the 1960s and 1970s. In those years, I went to Xinjiang, where I met a group of sent-down literary youths from Shanghai, who probably sometime around 1963 or 1964 had watched a movie and, to use their words, been so "poisoned" by the literature that they had to come out to Xinjiang from Shanghai. These people all loved literature back then, and watching movies and reading novels made them want to be part of the revolution, to stake out new ground and strike out on new enterprises, to explore difficult areas to test and forge themselves, carrying romantic ideas, leaving behind their lives in Shanghai, with its relative wealth, safety, and comforts, for Xinjiang and the sands of the Gobi Desert. Of course, this was only a half-serious way to put it because they never regretted the choice they made. In the middle of the Gobi Desert, they built an oasis, and with one glance at the fields of green they'd cultivated, the buildings they'd erected, the canals they'd built, and all the cotton and grain they'd harvested, their hearts were at peace. It's hard to say whether literature helped or harmed this crop.

Our crop of writers born in the 1950s and 1960s was quite different from the literary youth from a generation earlier, for we grew up in a time when Chinese society was far from normal, passing from the Great Leap Forward to the three years of the Great Chinese Famine and then into the Cultural Revolution. The society in which we came of age was unstable. At the beginning of the 1980s, society gradually returned to normal as it began to emerge from the chaos. Literature began to recover, and that's when we took up our pens and tried to write. I think writing at that time was driven by a strong profit-seeking mindset, with many young people like me wanting to use literature as a way to knock down barriers, to change our own fates, to change our position in society, to change our material lives, and, of course, we also loved and were fascinated by literature. Our crop of writers now serve as leaders in the China Writers' Associations and agencies. And, of course, there were some who gave up literature in the 1990s and went into business and made it big, but relatively few did so. Those who did not become leaders but still work in the literary field nevertheless find themselves at the end of their rope because crop after crop of new literary youths keep coming up; each wave in the Yangtze is pushed down the line by the wave behind, till the frontmost expires upon the bank. Of course, to expire upon the bank is also a kind of rebirth, for one becomes the water that soaks all the way down.

Our crop of literary youths had a different understanding of literature, too, from that of the group that was writing in the 1950s and 1960s. The first few years we spent starting to write, we ran up against the movement toward intellectual liberalization; in the early 1980s, many important works of Western literature that had been repressed for twenty years entered in a rush, forming a pile that reached the sky, and all in Chinese translation. Our crop, which had started school before the Cultural Revolution, could not read most of these books in their original languages, but the very moment they became available in Chinese, you can bet we read till our eyes were dry and sore. As we absorbed this literature, our views became broader and more open than those of the previous generation, which had been so deeply influenced by Russia. We were bolder in our literary methods, more avant-garde and more pioneering. The basic tone of our work was nothing like that of the 1950s writers, so proud, and gazing upward at a future so bright it dazzled them. In our work, gray tones dominated, and most of us wrote about the country villages out on the margins and the life circumstances of ordinary men or characters on the lower rungs of society. We were in agreement with the mainstream, even though in retrospect, most of the work that took the stage in the 1980s did not align with the standards of the mainstream, and only a few individual writers could be said to be mainstream at all—and even they wrote a mainstream that was very different from that of revolutionary works as *Song of Youth*, *Guarding Yan'an*, and *Tracks in the Snowy Plain*. The times had changed, and the themes had changed too, which is to say that each crop of writers comes of age in a different habitus, with different educational backgrounds, and this leads to big differences in the fundamental tone of their work. Our crop no longer believed in empty slogans, and many beliefs of the older generation left us full of questions, which is another reason our work received so much criticism. Often we wrote things that were strange, ridiculous, and warped, which is probably related to our having gone through the ten years of the Cultural Revolution, which left us with nightmare-like memories of social life then.

The most recent crop of literary youth should be categorized as writing from the 1990s until today; this group was born in the 1970s and 1980s. My daughter was born in the 1980s, and I try to tell her about the bad times and the good times, but she thinks that what we called the bad times were actually a romantic way to live, and she also believes her present happiness comes with a lot of pressure and stress, at least in her mind. I say, "You all don't need to worry about getting enough to eat or clothes to wear, and every day you pick up your bag and you go to school. Just think about when your old dad was your age, and he had to leave school before he even finished elementary school and go to work herding cows." She says, "Who wants to go to school! I want to go herd cows!" So the times have changed, and many of our ideas of pleasure and suffering, of good and bad, and of beauty and ugliness are very different now. So in every generation, the people of that generation ought to produce literature of their own. Since the appearance of the Internet, literature has become an activity for the masses, and everyone can be a writer, an author. In the past, there weren't so many journals and periodicals, not so many places to publish work, and now the Internet offers this possibility. So I think everyone can be both a writer and a reader of literature, for reading and writing seem to be complementary crafts now, with a common platform. This allows many people to approach writing as mere amateurs: today I'm interested and write a piece; tomorrow I'm not, so I don't. Literary creation ought to become an activity of the masses, so that all the king's horses and all the king's men can start producing literature, writing the essays of "all under Heaven," which presents the very distinct possibility that there will be literary elements there, that there will be youths of great talent, and in the end, there will be a great author or two. As for good and bad writing, there should be objective, not subjective, standards, and what we mean by objective standards is that each generation should have its own authors and its own spokespeople because different environments in different times call for different measures of intellectual achievement.

Our generation never writes about love because the experiences of our crop were not very good; we experienced an age with a strange warping of the human heart, when the human heart was unusually dark. So when we took up our pens, we had already lost the feeling for romance. But the new generation is different! They will go to the ends of the earth for love; give them love or give them death. Ancient and modern love have both emerged, along with those super-slick and cool figures of children and young people in animation. They exist in a semi-virtual world, with huge differences from the real world. It's really true that the new literary youth and the youth depicted in the new literature are the products of soaring imaginations, a kind of transcendence of the real world, with ideals and free wills wrapped up in this transcendence. But literature will go on in any case, with new generations of youth and children coming into it, which is the reason literature will always exist.

And let us at last turn the topic back to the jingle on that bumper sticker: "Write the Essay of All Under Heaven, Become a Young *Junzi*." What are the connotations of this term "young *junzi*," after all? Everyone can decide on their own what makes for a young *junzi* in our contemporary era, and why can't you be one just by writing the essay of all under Heaven? I really hope someday I'll be able to find that car again and ask the person who put the sticker on the back how he defines young *junzi*. In my eyes, the young *junzi* is the new person who keeps their eyes open. They represent not only the hopes and ideals of literature but also of society.

(Translated by Jesse Field)

NOTES

1. *Season of Flowers, Season of Rains* is a coming-of-age novel set in Shen-zhen, published in 1996, and written by Yu Xiu, who was born in 1974 and graduated from high school in Shenzhen in 1993.
2. *Junzi* is a term from early Chinese thought, especially the *Analects* of Confucius. In that text, Confucius expands the meaning of *junzi*, which originally referred to a ruler, or at least a man of position or of noble birth. According to Confucius, the term should be understood more broadly as connoting a man of virtue—humane, educated, and capable of leadership, regardless of his family background or social station. See Confucius, *Confucian Analects* (Beijing: People's Literature Press, 2002), 35.
3. Ibid.
4. The May Fourth Movement began in 1919. At first it consisted of a series of protests against China's unfair treatment in Europe at the Treaty of Versailles, but later it escalated into an intellectual movement calling for a reevaluation of China's culture and civilization in light of its perceived backwardness in the modern world of nation-states.
5. *Song of Youth* (1958) by Yang Mo was among the most highly celebrated novels of the early Communist era in China. The film version from 1959 remains among the classic examples of socialist realist art today.

23

A Modest Proposal on Literary Individuality

Lecture at Shenzhen Culture Forum, August 2008

Last year, I read a piece by Ye Liwen in the *China Youth Daily*, in which he said, "If you read a great many contemporary literary works, you might feel as though you had run into a karaoke bar, full of loud music and dancing, but none of it showing any individuality; the themes are all exactly alike, and the styles are also similar. Every single work closely imitates some other previous work. It really is just like karaoke, every author following an established older figure, like fans imitating rock stars, except the howling and racket of the author comes with swapped-out lyrics and the fancier name 'literary creation.'"[1]

Ye's metaphor was true to life, and it was a stark warning that really left me thinking. Certainly, in a karaoke bar, no matter how lame the performance, there will be praise and applause, and maybe even flowers for the performer, though they may be fake flowers. And of course, there will certainly also be imitations of great subtlety and nuance, lush performances of songs that can move the singer and the audience, but behind or to one side, there is always a screen displaying the message: you are not the original artist. As Ye writes in his essay, "Even if we all did karaoke, not one of us would ever become a Pavarotti."

Thunderous disputes on the topic of originality in literature have filled our ears these past few years. And of course, this is a good thing. If writers argue about originality, it means they are not willing to settle for what they have, to walk in each other's footsteps, or to parrot each other's ideas. Readers want originality and hate recycled material, for their eyes and ears long for new amusement. Theorists push for originality because they need texts worthy of their criticism. To make something original, as far as I understand it, means to *individualize* it, to make it unique. Not long ago, at the second Chinese Literature Media Awards, I gave a speech in which I said:

> In the last twenty or more years, my views on literature have changed a lot, but there is one thing I have stuck to the whole time, and that is that writing must have individuality, that one has to make the work unique. I believe that writers must maintain independence of character and a certain distance from trends and fashions; writers should pay attention to their material, to making it stand out in a crowded field, and thereby express lives rich with individual characteristics. The language writers use should be their own, making them distinct from others. The perspective with which the writer observes phenomena should be a very particular one, different from that of others. In certain ways, the perspective of a cow can be more literary than that of a human. I do not think writers can casually hold the characters and events in their works in judgment, but if they do judge them, their standards for doing so should differ from the popular and vulgar. Putting such weight on making writing unique might seem too biased to be correct. But without bias there would be no literature, and in my eyes, sticking to fairness and the golden mean are just not the kind of stances a good writer can sustain. Even in the society in which we live, fairness and the golden mean are most often the calling cards of con artists. Being in line with trends and following the crowd are humanity's weak points, especially to us writers who

have undergone collective training of an authoritarian nature, for we can never forget how great individuality is. But habit, that greatest of forces, still pushes us to the margins of the mainstream, thus rendering our voices inaudible. Though the chorus may be the dominant form of social life, the singers with their own particular values always hope their voices will not be lost in the crowd. Writers with ambition always hope their works can be distinguished from the works of others. I know that some critics have criticized my emphasis on making the work unique, but their very criticisms are yet more examples of voices hard at work at distinguishing themselves. Even now, I do not believe there is a literary work that garners praise from all readers at all times, for "a birdsong seeks its soulmate," as the saying says. In a very real sense, making the writing unique is actually the most crucial path by which the work can be made in some sense universal.

Since I said those words on making literature unique, I've given more consideration to the line of thinking I was following then. There are some things that can be felt but remain very difficult to express. I now think there are two issues to discuss when it comes to making literature unique: one is making the author a unique individual, and the other is making the work unique and individual.

As for making the author unique, we of course do not refer to the insignificant details of how to depart from the norm in a superficial way. Growing a beard and mustache and long hair, acting up in public places, causing damage, fighting, getting drunk or high on ecstasy—these are all merely the actions of a bad child and have nothing to do with art. But it is another matter altogether to be like the Seven Masters of Jian'an or the Seven Sages of the Bamboo Grove, back in the days of the Wei and the Jin dynasties. They acted crazy to save their lives, and this can of course be seen as an artistic protest against an age of corruption. I think the uniqueness of an author expresses itself mainly in independence of thought. And independence of character too. And it is precisely because of such independence in thought and character that the author must be, under most circumstances, in a state of resistance. Authors cannot and should not attach themselves to or affiliate themselves with any group or power that can bring them fame or profit, and even less so may they use their writing as a way to curry favor.

Yesterday I read issue 5 of *Writer* magazine, and there was a piece by Li Guowen called "Walking past Caishikou" in which she writes,

> A practitioner of literature had best not jump into the boat of politics, for even if it be the highest and noblest of ships, better were it to, with all due respect, keep it at a distance. Li Bai of the Tang Dynasty understood this principle with absolute clarity from the beginning. As Du Fu writes of Li Bai, "The Son of Heaven calls, yet ascends not upon the boat," in his "Drunken Songs on the Eight Immortals." But later on, perhaps in a fit of drunkenness, he came down from Lushan and boarded the flagship of Li Lin, Prince Yong, hoping to serve as an officer and advisor for a pretender he foolishly hoped would become emperor. But when Prince Yong was recalled and executed for treason, the great poet had to resign his commission and accept exile to the southwest.[2]

There is harsh satire in Ms. Li's essay, for many people have had experiences like this. But Li Bai's foolishness likely began much earlier, when he sang the praises of Yang Guifei, the imperial concubine. And from another perspective, during that age, the people able to write good compositions or good poems or songs were all men employed in politics, and indeed compositions, poems, and songs were all once means of entering public service—not like now; today if you want to become a high official, you would do best to study engineering—so Li Bai's poetic offerings were not as despicable as we imagine today. Actually, several thousand years of literary history read like the history of failed and frustrated officials, the *Classic of Poetry* and the works of Cao Cao notwithstanding. Qu Yuan, Li Bai, Du Fu, Han Yu, Liu Zongyuan, Liu Yuxi, Su Shi, and others all seem to have been exiled to the margins before they wrote works that would last through the ages, for if political employment is satisfactory, either one doesn't have time to write, or else one's writing is mostly mediocre.

If writers have no independence of thought, they can only be tools to display the thoughts of others. What we call independence of thought is actually independent consideration, a process of thinking. I think that everyone has the capacity for independent thinking, but what is key is that under the pressure of a system, people lose the courage to consider something independently. I saw an online article that analyzed the work of John Cheever, saying that the members of the American middle class in the 1950s did not want to be under tyranny, that they loved to resist the features of their social and political identity with their uniqueness as individuals, but when it came to John Cheever, the article notes that his main characters all fear being expelled from the system. And so, common values polish the horn of uniqueness, and at the same time one adapts to the system, one throws away one's independence. Their uniqueness in the end evolves into what the article describes as respect for the present system and fear of being tossed aside. Their exterior freedom then conceals the fetters on their hearts and minds, layered underneath, hiding their secret desire to have a freedom that others cannot understand, but also hating that there should be a substantial difference between themselves and others. In fact, we must admit this could just as well be a snapshot of the emotional and mental state of many Chinese writers. I think that in the half-century since liberation, Chinese writers and even the vast majority of Chinese intellectuals have become mouthpieces for others, mere yes men, because in trying to adapt to the system, what they fear most is being booted out, and so they give up their right to independent thought willingly and of their own accord. And having given it up, they eventually retreat, take a step back. Superstition and blind obedience are the result of this retreat. It's not tragic to agree that ten thousand catties of rice came off a single *mu* of land, if one does so in order to protect the resilient mind inside; the tragedy is when one really believes that ten thousand catties of rice can be produced on a single *mu* of land. Ironically, back then it was the peasants, the uneducated and the marginalized, relying only on their own direct experience, who noticed the falseness of "orthodox thought."

In my village, we held many meetings in those times, criticizing this and that, but after the meetings, those who had to work simply went to work because no grain came from a criticism meeting. And all thought it right and proper, just desserts, for the nation's grain to be given out first to the workers and the cadres and the PLA, while the peasants were left to starve. Knowing that they did not carry the grain bowl of the nation, though, actually gave the peasants a material basis from which to consider things independently. "You can't treat me like this!" one often heard during conflicts with the team leader. "You'll never strip me of my peasant identity!" Lotus blossoms might emerge from your mouth, but your team leader will always issue your work points based on your ability and attitude toward your work. When we look back at the literature of those times, there is not one work whose voice is not in harmony with the chorus of the times. The thought of writers then was empty, and this was a tragedy for writers and for literature. Of course, if I had been writing back then, I would have had to write like that too.[3]

At this point, I think of this one person who fled the country after 1989. He put out a fervent and proud set of lectures assailing the government, but then I heard that when he was expelled from the such-and-such committee, he cried like a baby. Now, this is very dubious, for it shows that the system had gotten into his bones, and his resistance to it was merely the product of his own pride. What we have here is no longer merely a matter of independence of thought, but of independence of character. Of course, I don't mean to say here that resisting the system and being a writer who opposed the system are inconsistent with being a citizen with respect for the law. All systems place some challenges on the spirit of independence, and what we call the resistance of the writer against the system refers not to open opposition to the public good but rather to the adoption of a spirit of wariness. We are independent in spirit, but we still put our trash in the correct receptacle, and we stand in line along with everyone else. The truly noble are those who face other nobles without bending at the waist or knee; the truly courageous are those who hold fast to the truth.

On the Internet, I saw something describing the three major marks of an intellectual: one, a mind that can advance scientific thinking; two, independent character; and three, having one's own ideas and the courage to devote one's life to them. Judging by these criteria, which few among the many Chinese writers can be called intellectuals? I have never thought of myself as an intellectual, and I think very few Chinese writers are deserving of being called one. Of course, there are many very knowledgeable writers, but can knowledge alone make an intellectual? Guests at the Jia mansion in *A Dream of Red Mansions* showed loads of erudition and wide knowledge, but would they count as intellectuals? They also wrote, but would their work count as good literature?

It might seem from what I have said that I have digressed too far, but actually I have not. An author who has made themselves unique in pursuing their literary work must maintain the courage to keep up independence of thought and the courage to give their life for their ideals before they can get close to the lower levels of the people, before they can understand the suffering of the people and even experience this suffering themselves, or before they can hold in contempt those with excessive wealth and power. Then they will be able to speak in their own words, speak their minds, say what they want to say; and their words will also likely be the words of the common people, the words the common people want to speak. Of course, *A Dream of Red Mansions* does not necessarily say what the common people want to say, just as the king who lost his country, Li Yu, did not speak for the common people in his poem "Oh When Will Autumn Moon and Spring Flowers End." At moments like these, Li Yu and Cao Xueqin, one the fallen scion of an aristocratic family and the other the emperor of a lost empire, were both already outside the system. Though they didn't stand with the common people per se, they hardly sang songs of praise. Rather, they elegized. Good literature rarely praises or eulogizes, but elegies frequently become classics.

The ability to make the work unique depends upon the author's independence of thought and independence of character. You can't make the work unique without making its central idea unique. I would say one's ethos as a writer must first be unique in order for one's work to be unique. As this involves both psychology and genetics, it may seem somewhat obscure, for it often seems that some things in life cannot be changed. Unique people are numerous, but having a unique personality does not mean you can become a writer.

Making the work unique also depends on making the writer's own life unique. A writer's unique circumstances, misfortunes, and experiences are what makes the work unique. Take Cao Xueqin, if you like, or Pu Songling, or Lu Xun, Shen Congwen, or Eileen Zhang; take Dostoyevsky, or Tolstoy, D. H. Lawrence, Proust, or even Kafka—all have left us lasting works. And all led lives quite different from the norm, which is perhaps we might call their fates. It's all a matter of fate, which basically means that "experiencing life" is of little use. You can of course dress up as a beggar and head out into the streets, but what you will experience is only of the flesh, only on the surface. You will see the reaction of the outside world, but the world internal to the mind, that deep interior of feeling, is not something you are going to understand because no matter how torn your clothes get, and even if a mad dog bites your leg and leaves it dripping in blood, you will not be able to forget your identity as a writer and the fact that your experience in this case is only pretend.

Making the author's personal life unique involves many elements that are of the utmost importance for literary writing. For example, the geographical environment of the place where you live, your education, and the people you grew up with all determine your outlook as a writer long before you become one. Misfortunes and hard work will of course play a role as well, but they are not the source of your basic constitution.

When we put it like this, it unavoidably pains us to say that hard work hardly seems to do any good. This is the cruel reality, and what we actually can do consists mostly of trying to preserve and show off what uniqueness we can find in the face of certain elements that just can't be changed and are brought about by external circumstances.

I think that in the earliest stages of writing, it's best to write for yourself and not for any profit motive or for any external enticements or to follow anyone else. But if you write only for yourself, it becomes easy to skate along at this level, and you will not be able to ascend the steep, icy heights. During this time, it frequently happens that once a writer more or less knows the principles of writing, has a grasp of literary technique, and is clear about the relationship between a story's plot and material from the writer's life, the pursuit of uniqueness in the writer's work turns into a technical problem, which is also the only area in which hard work matters.

First, there is language. The language of a writer, or rather the language of fiction, is the clearest indicator of a unique writer and unique work. What language the writer uses is of course determined by many factors, but working hard to be unique can cause a mature writer's language to change. These changes are externally driven, but they rouse the elements of language that are unique and internal to us. The internal and external come together to make the text. (I believe in the potential for one person to use many forms of writing.) Specifically, I think we can look for linguistic inspiration in the classics; be they modern or ancient, Chinese or foreign (for writers who don't read foreign languages, "foreign" here means the language of translators). And then we find vocabulary from the lives of common people and the vernacular of the masses. With new linguistic inspiration and new vocabulary, the forms of writing undergo a change.

Second, put unique characters into the work. In classic works, there are usually fresh, unique, and unforgettable characters, and these in fact are the archetypical personalities. The unique personality of a character must have value for it to become an archetype. What are personalities of value? I believe they are those who dare to rove around and steer their own course, to go against the current in the high and choppy seas of this vulgar, venal world; those who dare to stand up to Heaven itself, who dare to pit their individual personality against their social and political identity. And history, moreover, has proven their perseverance correct;

these are unique personalities of value—like Jia Baoyu, or the sharp-tongued Li Cuilian, or the giggling Yingning, or Pierre, who helped strap a policeman to a bear and helped throw both into a river, or Auntie Sanxian, the aging hussy in her gaudy makeup. These unique personalities of value stand as models. Forming another category of personalities of value are those who have perhaps been judged by history as tragic figures, tragic because of their own characters and not due to circumstance, like Don Quixote, like the minor civil servant who scared himself to death when he sneezed in front of his superior in the Chekhov story, like Lu Xun's Ah Q, or Camus' Stranger. These characters, regardless of whether their conduct and beliefs are right or wrong, are unique personalities that express some common characteristics of the human spirit, which makes us see ourselves in them. Thus, it is worthwhile getting to know them, and for this reason, these unique personalities are personalities of value.

In the life of a writer, one is very fortunate to encounter such a personality of value, but such resources, like rare metals, are soon used up. And we want to continue writing and writing with uniqueness, so we must discover more unique personalities in history and in real life. And when we say "discover," we mean here of course recombination and imagination; a writer can use their imagination to transform the story of another person's life to increase the power of their own life. And moreover, we must not forget that other writers, geniuses in their own way, will create unique characters from their own original ideas.

Third, the work must have a unique tone and atmosphere. But this is basically a problem that can only be addressed mentally and cannot be explained in words. This is another issue in which we can do some work; for example, we can try writing a story that is in communion with the spirit of paintings by Van Gogh, or a story similar to the world evoked in Ukiyo-e prints from Japan.

Lastly, a little on my understanding of the social nature of literature. We have emphasized uniqueness, but that doesn't mean we don't want a social dimension, for the social part of our identity is like the shadow of a person on a clear, blue-skied day; it is not possible to remove it. I think that as long as we write rich, full, and unique personalities, the social nature will be there.

And to conclude, here are a few thoughts regarding uniqueness and individuality. Giving literature the quality of uniqueness and individuality involves sticking to one's material, but there is a deeper and more important layer—the spiritual. If we pursue nothing but the novel and the new, it becomes a mere hunt for the strange and exotic. If we doggedly seek after new alternatives, we could easily end up with mere "reheated rice" from the West. It's also possible for the pursuit of the unique to tend toward the common. A person with hair dyed red who turns the story of dying his hair into fiction has certainly given the work a quality of individuality, but the tragic problem is that people who dye their hair and write about it are quite numerous, so the individual and unique thing has become a category, and that sort of uniqueness naturally has no value. So uniqueness is not about trends or fashion but rather a need to draw out from the inner mind a particular understanding of life and society.

Many things are very hard to change, but we always try anyway, and that in itself is something that makes us unique individuals. At best, this is perseverance without regret; at worst, we fool ourselves all our lives and never figure things out.

(Translated by Jesse Field)

Notes

1. Ye Liwen, "On Contemporary Literature in China," *China Youth Daily*, June 23, 2007.
2. Li Guowen, "Walking past Caishikou," *Writers* 5 (2004), 16.
3. Mo Yan did not specify his context, but he was speaking of the period of the Great Leap Forward, especially the year 1958, when government propaganda announced unbelievable production output estimates, including the assertion that a single *mu* of land could now produce 64,000 catties or more of rice, when in fact that year's crop was much less than that of the year before and the following crop was much less than that of the year before that, leading to the Great Famine of 1960–1963, when many millions of Chinese are thought to have died of policy-induced starvation.

INDEX

Lightning Source UK Ltd.
Milton Keynes UK
UKHW011829230222
399143UK00001B/37